The Emergence of Personality

Joel Aronoff is Professor of Psychology at Michigan State University. He has taught at Harvard University, Cornell University, and the Hebrew University (Israel). He is the author of *Psychological Needs and Cultural Systems* and the co-author of *Personality in the Social Process.* His primary interest is in the area of the experimental and cross-cultural study of personality and social behavior.

Albert I. Rabin is Professor Emeritus of Psychology at Michigan State University. He taught at Boston University, City University of New York, Hebrew and Bar-Ilan Universities (Israel), and the University of Aarhus (Denmark). Dr. Rabin has published more than 150 articles and reviews in different professional and scientific journals, contributed chapters to more than 30 edited books, and published 13 books in the areas of assessment, personality development, and kibbutz childrearing.

Robert A. Zucker is Professor of Psychology and Co-Director of Clinical Training at Michigan State University. He has taught at Rutgers University and at the University of Texas at Austin and has been a visiting scholar at the National Alcohol Institute. His long-term research interests are stability and change over the life course, with a particular focus on developmental psychopathology. As part of this work he also directs the Michigan State University Longitudinal Study.

THE EMERGENCE OF
PERSONALITY

Joel Aronoff
A. I. Rabin
Robert A. Zucker

Editors

SPRINGER PUBLISHING COMPANY
New York

Springer Publishing Company, Inc.
536 Broadway
New York, NY 10012

87 88 89 90 91 / 5 4 3 2 1

Library of Congress Cataloging-in-Publication Data

The Emergence of personality.

    (Michigan State University Henry A. Murray lectures in personality)
    Revised and extended versions of lectures originally delivered in Apr. 1985.
    Includes bibliographies and index.
    1. Personality. I. Aronoff, Joel. II. Rabin,
Albert I. III. Zucker, Robert A. IV. Series.
[DNLM: 1. Personality. 2. Psychological Theory.
BF 698 E53]
BF698.E58   1987   155.2   87-9640
ISBN 0-8261-6120-0

P. xi is reprinted from Robert A. Zucker, Joel Aronoff, and A. I. Rabin (Eds.), *Personality and the Prediction of Behavior,* p. xi. Copyright © 1984 by Academic Press, Inc. Reprinted by permission.

Printed in the United States of America

Contents

Contributors   *ix*
Introduction to the Series   *xi*
Preface   *xiii*

1 The Emergence of Personality   **1**
Joel Aronoff, A. I. Rabin, and Robert A. Zucker

Return to Phylogenetic Awareness   3
The Active Organism   5
Mechanisms that Support the Structuring of Personality   7

2 Personality: Primate Heritage and Human Distinctiveness   **13**
Arnold H. Buss

Primate Personality   14
Human Personality   36
Evolutionary Perspective   44

3 Personality and Experience: Individual Encounters with the World   **49**
Sandra Scarr

What's a Nice Girl Like You Doing in a Place Like This?   50
Ignoring Individuality   52
Siblings and Strangers   53
Trivializing Individuality   54
Your Parents Aren't My Parents, Brother   56

Are Some Aspects of Personality More Heritable than
    Others?   60
Theories of Development: Forgotten Individuality   62
A Model of Genotypes and Environments   64
Separation of Genetic and Environmental Effects on
    Development   66
Developmental Changes in Genotype→Environment
    Effects   68
Changing Similarities among Siblings   70
Identical Twins Reared Apart   74
Summary   74

4   Personality Psychology: Back to Basics   79
Robert Hogan

Introduction   80
What We Need   83
Personality Defined   85
Personality Development   87
Personality Assessment   93
Personality Praxis   97
Conclusion   99

5   Private Experience and Public Action: The Study of Ongoing Conscious Thought   105
Jerome L. Singer

Cognitive–Affective Perspective   107
Experimental Laboratory Studies of Ongoing Thought:
    Stimulus Independent Thought in Signal Detection
    Studies   111
Experimental Interventions and Thought Sampling   115
Thought and Experience Sampling in Daily Life   121
Psychometric Assessments   123
Ongoing Thought in the Formation and Maintenance
    of Schemas, Self-Concepts, and Action-Scripts   128
Thought and Health: Some Research Directions   135
Conscious and Unconscious Thought: Some Proposals   138

6 Script Theory 147
Silvan S. Tomkins

Overview of Script Theory 147
General Features of Scripts 153
Differential Magnification of Ratio of Positive–Negative
 Affect 158
Ideological Scripts 170
Commitment Scripts 179
Some Origins of Commitment Scripts 181
Affect Management Scripts: Sedative, Preaddictive, and
 Addictive 185
Preaddictive Scripts 189
Addictive Scripts 191
Nuclear Scripts 196
Construction of Nuclear Scripts 197
Nuclear Script Formation 199
Types of Nuclear Subscripts 204
Ways of Thinking 207

7 Personality and the Unification of Psychology and Modern Physics: A Systems Approach 217
Gary E. Schwartz

Personality and Systems Theory 219
Personality and the Unification of Psychology: Toward a
 Systems Solution 224
Personality Psychology, Modern Physics, and Health:
 Why Include Modern Physics in this Chapter? 226
Murray, Humor, and Modern Physics: On the
 Distinction between Interesting and Amusing
 Theories in Science 228
Modern Physics–Modern Psychology Connection:
 Understanding the GIST Code 231
Example 1: Heisenberg's Uncertainty Principle and the
 Self-Attention/Self-Regulation Hypothesis 235
Example 2: The Complementarity Principle, the Wave-
 Particle Theory of Emotion and Cognition, and
 Personality Styles 237

Example 3: The General Relativity/General Relaxation
  Hypothesis   240
Example 4: Health is to Wellness as Energy is the
  Matter   247
On the Changing Nature of What is Impossible in
  Science   251

Index   *255*

Contributors

Arnold Buss was trained in clinical psychology at Indiana University. Professor of Psychology at the University of Texas for almost two decades, he taught previously at the Universities of Iowa and Pittsburgh, as well as Rutgers University. His field of specialization is personality psychology, with a focus on aggression, temperament, self-consciousness, shyness, and personality style. He is married to a financial planner, and they have three children, two of whom have also entered the professional field of personality psychology.

Robert Hogan received his Ph.D. from the University of California at Berkeley and taught at Johns Hopkins University from 1967 to 1982. He is presently McFarlin Professor and Chair of the Psychology Department at the University of Tulsa. He is past editor of the Personality Processes and Individual Differences section of the *Journal of Personality and Social Psychology,* a G. Stanley Hall lecturer in personality, and the author of a number of books including, most recently, a manual for the Hogan Personality Inventory.

Sandra Scarr is Commonwealth Professor of Psychology and Chair of the Psychology Department at the University of Virginia. She is Past President of Division 7 and a fellow of Divisions 7, 9, 15, and 37 of the American Psychological Association. She was Editor of *Developmental Psychology* and Associate Editor of *American Psychologist* and has held numerous important positions in national scientific organizations. In 1985 she won the National Book Award of the American Psychological Association for *Mother Care/Other Care.* Scarr's research focuses on genetic variability in behavior; the effects that families have on their children; and interventions, including day care, educational programs, and adoption.

Gary E. Schwartz received his Ph.D. from Harvard University in clinical psychology, personality, and psychophysiology. He is Professor of Psychology at Yale University and Director of the Yale University Psychophysiology Center, Co-Director of the Yale University Behavioral Medicine Clinic, and Associate Editor of *Health Psychology* and *Biological Psychology*.

Jerome L. Singer received his doctorate in clinical psychology from the University of Pennsylvania. Professor of Psychology and Director of the Clinical Training Program at Yale University, he is Co-Director with Dorothy G. Singer of the Yale University Family Television Research and Consultation Center. He is a specialist in research on the psychology of imagination and daydreaming and is the author of 15 books and 160 technical articles on thought processes, imagery, and fantasy in adults and children. He has been President of the Eastern Psychological Association and President of the Division of Personality and Social Psychology of the American Psychological Association and has held numerous important positions in national scientific organizations. Currently he is Editor of the journal *Imagination, Cognition and Personality* and Senior Consultant to the MacArthur Foundation-supported Open Laboratory on Conscious and Unconscious Mental Processes at the University of California at San Francisco's Langley Porter Clinic.

Silvan Tomkins received his Ph.D. in philosophy from the University of Pennsylvania. Following two years of postdoctoral work in philosophy at Harvard University with Quine, Sheffer, and Perry, he became a research assistant at the Harvard Psychological Clinic. During this time he participated in the second decade of personological research at the Clinic under the direction of Murray and White. He has taught at Harvard and Princeton Universities, the Graduate Center of the City University of New York, and Livingstone College of Rutgers University. He is currently Professor, Department of Social Systems Sciences, University of Pennsylvania. His long-term project is a general theory of personality. Initially, this work focused on the centrality of affect and resulted in the book *Affect, Imagery, Consciousness*, published by Springer Publishing Company. Presently, he is engaged in completing his examination of the cognitive components of personality, under the title of script theory.

Introduction to the Series

The Henry A. Murray Lectures in Personality, presented by Michigan State University, are designed to advance our understanding of personality in depth, across situations, and over the range of the human life span. The lectures offer a spacious forum in which leading psychologists can explore the most difficult questions in personality theory and research from the perspective of their own work. It is hoped that this series will encourage the conceptual risk-taking that will lead to the imaginative, strong, and theoretically organized work that is needed to advance the science of personology.

These lectures are named in honor of Henry A. Murray in order to draw upon a spirit of inquiry that has directed much of the best contemporary work on personality. Throughout his distinguished career, Murray dealt with the most difficult theoretical and methodological questions with all the skills available to the scientist and the humanist. His wide-ranging mind took him across the gulfs that separate alternative approaches to the study of human beings. Murray argued for a science of personology that would include the physiological and the phenomenological, that would rely on the specialties of test construction as well as of literary scholarship, that saw the need for the taxonomist of personality as well as the psychotherapist of persons, that studied the isolated incident as well as entire lives, and that could encompass subjects as diverse as the study of mythology and the study of personnel selection. It is hoped that the series of Murray lectures may continue to draw upon all these sources in order to advance the science of personology and to contribute to human welfare.

Preface

In 1978, the Department of Psychology at Michigan State University decided to celebrate the fortieth anniversary of the publication of Henry Murray's book, *Explorations in Personality,* by sponsoring a conference evaluating developments in the field since the publication of this seminal book. The response to the contributions presented at the conference, and to the subsequent book, was so positive that we organized a triennial lecture series, the Henry A. Murray Lectures in Personality, to stimulate the type of theoretical exploration that is not usually encouraged in more traditional forums.

The Emergence of Personality is the third book to result from the Murray Lectures. For this volume we decided to explore the process through which personality emerges and is maintained across significant periods of life. Although the contributors to this book deal with this problem from different theoretical perspectives and different empirical bases, they all understand the human being as an active agent who emerges through an interacting process of physiological, interpersonal, and social events. Out of the many disparate mechanisms that are described in this volume emerges a new scaffold for a theory of personality development that helps to account for the similarities and differences in personality structure.

The chapters of this volume are the revised and extended versions of lectures originally delivered in East Lansing, Michigan, in April, 1985. We are grateful for the strong support that we have received from Gordon Wood, Chairperson of the Department of Psychology at Michigan State University, for helping to make the lecture series a continuing reality. For the third series we are especially proud of the fact that a large number of our doctoral alumni contributed a major share of the necessary financial support. We are most appreciative of their generous support and are delighted to acknowledge their continued participation in the work of our department. We wish to thank Ms. Marjorie Curtis for her careful attention to our communication with our doctoral alumni. The Departments of Pediatrics and Human Development, Psychiatry, and the Counseling Center, chaired by Drs. Marshall Klaus, Donald H. Williams, and Lee June, respectively, provided valuable assistance in funding and cosponsoring the lectureship. We also thank Drs. Richard Evans, of the University of Houston, Ranald Hansen, of Oakland University, Marilyn M. Kilbey, of Wayne State University, Charles G. Morris, of the University of Michigan, and Robert B. Noll and Dozier W. Thornton, of our department, for their valuable assistance in making the conference a success. Provost C. L. Winder and Dean Gwen Andrew continued to provide their valuable assistance. Within the department, many of our present graduate students were deeply involved in making the lectures possible. We are especially grateful to Christine Hall for the facility with which she managed many of the necessary conference arrangements. We also wish to thank John Curtis, Gregory Greenberg, Nicholas Ialongo, Ronald Lapporte, Eugene Maguin, Eve Reider, and Robert Weinstein for their help and enthusiasm. Finally, we are most appreciative of the professional skill of the Kellogg Conference Center staff, and especially of Marc Van Wormer, for their continued efforts in bringing each lectureship to fruition.

1

The Emergence of Personality

Joel Aronoff, A. I. Rabin, and Robert A. Zucker

In a set of introductory essays to their influential book on the cross-cultural study of personality, Henry Murray and Clyde Kluckhohn (Kluckhohn, Murray & Schneider, 1956) focused attention on an obvious proposition. Using a deceptively simple statement designed to orient researchers to many future tasks, they noted that in certain respects all people are like all other people, like some other people, and like no other people. In their words, "It is the very obviousness of this fact which makes restatements of it expedient since, like other people, we students of personality are naturally disposed to be attracted by what is unusual . . . and so overlook the common heritage and lot of man " (p. 53). It is also obvious that to understand the ways in which individuals may be similar or different, it is necessary to be explicit about the ways that these patterns arise out of our common human heritage.

In their essays, Murray and Kluckhohn (1956) attempted to view the individual as someone who developed, as the title of the book indicated, "within nature, society and culture." Their survey of the variables to be examined by the personality psychologist offered one framework to investigate how factors within the person emerge and are transformed by social experience to yield the patterns of similarity and difference that are the agenda of much current work in personality.

Regrettably, the theoretical opportunities suggested by their conceptual scheme have not yet been well utilized. There are many areas of psychology where there is much dissatisfaction expressed with the models that are available to guide work on personality development and structure (e.g., Gangestad & Snyder, 1985; Maccoby, 1980). Typically, researchers assume that an interesting aspect of personality can be accounted for by the most simple of social learning mechanisms and measured through the most

routine of mother interview–child behavior procedures. This work frequently assumes that the emergence of personality is due to the application of a set
of parenting acts, in which the prototypical parenting act is taken to be the
norm and that the aggregate of these parenting acts yields the "behavioral
system" under investigation.

As Maccoby (1980) points out, "this concept of socialization is not wrong,
but it is incomplete. It leaves out the developmental forces that determine
how children will react to the socialization experiences they have" (p. vi).
This observation directs our attention to the view that the person is an active
agent from the start of life, who emerges through the extended course of a
complex series of interacting physiological, interpersonal, and social events.
However, to carry out a successful research program following this perspective requires a substantial broadening of the model that the investigator must
bring to the research process. The central task of such a model should be not
only to describe new variables, but, more importantly, to specify ways to
connect disparate sets of events into a common framework of mechanisms
that can account for the similarities and differences in personality structure.
Out of this effort to build a new scaffold for a theory of personality development may emerge a better understanding of how human variation emerges
from a shared foundation in human life.

Within the diversity of views held generally in the field, and represented by
the contributors to this volume, there is the shared perspective that, as
personologists, we assume both consistency and variability in individual
behavior over time and across situations (cf. Block, 1981; Epstein, 1984;
Maddi, 1984). We expect that as we become more exact about the mechanisms underlying individual behavior, we will have a better understanding
of how to identify and study the behaviors that are controlled by personality
variables. Also, we need to assume that human behavior can be understood at
varying levels of complexity, ranging from the reflex, to the trait, to the
life-long schema. Thus, we take as a point of departure that hierarchies of
organizing structures underlie the human behavioral domain, which need to
be included more specifically by any investigator who attempts to construct a
general theory of behavior. Without this recognition of hierarchical differences in personality organization, we risk searching for across-level
isomorphism, when similarity or discontinuity—but not identity—may be the
most appropriate model. Finally, there is much consensus for the view that
personality processes are concomitantly biological, psychological, and social
in nature and that metatheoretical perspectives that encourage more complex
research designs are needed to grapple with the multiplicity of these very
different levels of organization.

In directing personality research to these questions, it is likely that most
progress can be made with approaches set at the middle range of theory. We
need neither a mindless listing of potential variables gleaned from the works

of all active researchers, nor an inclusive grand theory before which the researcher stands helpless. Rather, what is called for are a variety of conceptual frameworks and a variety of data bases, rather than a single organizing construct.

It is just such a task that is addressed in the current volume of the Henry Murray Lectures in Personality. This book is composed of the coordinated theoretical work of a number of distinguished psychologists, all asked to apply their expertise to the answer to a common question, "Through which set of mechanisms may we best understand the ways in which personality processes emerge and are maintained across significant periods of life?" To these experienced scholars, each working from a different vantage point in which biological, psychological, and social functions interact, we offered a forum within which they might merge their individual perspectives. From their collaboration we hoped to help clarify the process through which personality is structured. Thus, the title of this volume is carefully chosen. Rather than duplicate the substantial literature on the structures of personality and the stages through which they appear, we focus attention on an imperfectly understood issue of the processes that lead to these structures. In this volume, we wish to understand better the "emergence of personality."

The work reported in this volume is based upon a number of major metatheoretical propositions. Each of these assertions has been quite controversial throughout this century, with substantial divisions of opinion supported by separate departments, schools, and journals. Yet, enough progress has been made to permit the present generation of psychologists to synthesize ideas across areas that previously would have been regarded as unreconcilable. The first proposition argues that the course of human development is a biological as well as a psychological and a social process. The second proposition argues that the individual is an active agent seeking specific rewards from the social environment. The third proposition argues that the primary structures of personality emerge from the significant mechanisms that constitute social experience.

RETURN TO PHYLOGENETIC AWARENESS

Personality psychology has a long tradition of connections to an evolutionary perspective on behavior. In the past century, James (1890), concerned with connections between biology and behavior, saw consciousness as a display of biological energy as well as a moving and shaping force in social development. In the present century, McDougall (1921) was concerned with the transformation of biological instincts into acquired sentiments, a position that could be seen as a forerunner of more recent biosocial theorists (e.g., Maslow, 1970; Murphy, 1947; Murray, 1938). Nonetheless, theoretical and empirical work in the last 40 years has been most notable for its disregard of our phylogenetic heritage. The exploration of biological links to complex social behavior has been left to behavior geneticists, psychopathologists, and comparative psychologists, with the most interesting propositions about normal human functioning largely derived from observations of lower animals (e.g., Wilson, 1975).

The contributors to the present volume were selected for the importance of their data as well as for the diversity in their approaches to the role of biological influences on human behavior. Although they deal with this problem from markedly different theoretical perspectives and different reserves of empirical information, they all understand the human being as developing from a biological organism into an individual embedded within a larger psychosocial context. It is this interactive process, of increasing structuring and articulation over time, that results in the human personality.

Parallel treatments of this proposition in this volume underscore its usefulness in explaining different components of the structuring process. In a powerful review of the mammalian and primate behavioral literature, Buss deals intriguingly with two central questions: In what way is the course of human adaptation derived from our primate heritage? And, what is distinctly human about this course of adaptation? By asking how these similarities and differences are to be understood in an evolutionary perspective, Buss is able to clarify substantially the role these processes play in human development. Buss notes that the temperaments, such as the traits of activity (i.e., the total energy output of the individual), emotionality (i.e., the tendency to be aroused by negative situations), and sociability (i.e., the tendency to seek others), are characteristics shared not only with primates but also with other mammals. These biologically based traits, Buss argues, originated during the course of phylogenetic development in order to provide the foundation for those traits that are needed to support complex human life. Buss suggests that the temperaments lead the primate to enter into sets of social experiences that result in their transformation into more differentiated forms. For example, the temperament of sociability, emerging from the specific maternal environment provided in infancy, is seen to result in the more differentiated traits of docility or friendliness. Extending this biopsychosocial perspective, human traits, in turn, are derived either from primate traits (i.e., confidence in primates leading to self-esteem in humans) or from socialization processes that are enhanced and supported by the organism's more advanced cognitive capacities and structures (e.g., factors such as morality or self-related traits). There is a great deal in Buss' proposal that is fairly easily testable, both developmentally and comparatively. Such testing would more firmly ground the domains that we think of as simply human within a much broader evolutionary and developmental perspective. Such work needs doing.

In a chapter that parallels Buss's, Hogan notes that the socioanalytic perspective he has developed (Hogan, 1982) presumes a phylogenetic heritage in which biologically preprogrammed concerns emerge in developmental sequence, while the culture within which individuals are raised offers the opportunities through which they may be expressed. Similarly, he argues that much of the driving force of adult human activity—concerns with acceptance, status, power, and influence—are group concerns found in primates and other social mammals as well as in humans. The goals he sets for personality psychology, "to analyze the factors that account for individual differences in the manner in which people integrate themselves into their social groups," are as much goals for a general, across-species, behavior theory as they are for an understanding of human variation.

Within this context, the social interactionist model that he proposes focuses on those personality variables (such as competence) that lead to success in the evolutionary struggle. Thus, Hogan introduces a discussion of "fitness" into this analysis—a human characteristic that does not usually appear in reviews of personality theory. In his words, "fitness is the bottom line" in evolutionary theory. Yet, because of its obvious relationship to the survival of individuals, when seen in an evolutionary context fitness takes on great biological importance. Once recognized, fitness is easily linked to substantial interpersonal concerns, such as the status reached in a group, and thus links the biological argument with a significant aspect of what is usually seen as a purely sociological aspect of human life.

THE ACTIVE ORGANISM

The emerging consensus in personality theory (e.g., Maddi, 1980; McClelland, 1984) views the developing person as one who actively approaches significant life experiences. This perspective, which is often understood within an evolutionary framework, argues that from the beginning of life the individual makes claims upon the social environment; in other words, seeks specific classes of rewards. Additionally, the intensity of the desire for these rewards and the ability of the social environment to provide them help to define what might be meant by the term "significant" life event.

Scarr declares her position regarding the development of personality and individual differences quite succinctly: "I think that genes drive experience." The genes are viewed as the system that "organizes the organism to experience its world" and thus are responsible for developmental changes as well as individual differences. In her view, the origins of individuality are based on "individual differences in responsiveness to environments." She marshalls data that argue that responsiveness is not merely a passive reaction of the genotype to external stimuli, but rather that the genotype elicits those environmental circumstances to which it ultimately reacts. In other words, the individual helps to evoke and select those environments that provide just those opportunities and rewards that are most desired.

This seemingly abstract position is easily put to work in rather powerful ways. For example, it is a matter of concern that parent behavior–child personality correlations are frequently inexplicably low. While there is much consensus on the nature of "good" parenting, its empirical connection to children's characteristics are often hard to establish. It is very likely that the "brute force delivery" of good parenting acts, irrespective of the readiness of the child to receive—or make use of—such kindness, leads to neutral, or perhaps even negative, outcomes when children are not yet prepared to receive them. Scarr's position argues that we must determine the environments that are sought, whether our goal is to increase the power of our research or the effectiveness of our parenting.

Similarly, most of what we know about personality is derived from an examination of an individual's social behavior. Construct systems are frequently generated by examining the concrete claims that the organism makes upon the social environment or by examining the type of social environment to which the organism is responsive. Buss' work provides an example of this type of psychological reasoning. Drawing from observational biology, he identifies behavioral traits whose evolutionary significance, he suggests, yield sets of biological factors that determine the nature of the individual's activity. Thus, for example, for the trait of sociability (i.e., the tendency to seek others and to prefer dealing with others rather than being alone), Buss examines the interactional process and identifies social rewards (such as attention from others, sharing activities, and gaining a response from others) as the biological basis of behavioral responsiveness of the organism.

Perhaps the most straightforward delineation of the concept of the "active" individual entering into the social process is found in Hogan's chapter. Based on an analysis of the requirements of organized human society, Hogan suggests that we need to postulate three motivational assumptions about the human organism in order to account for behavior: the need for "attention and social acceptance" (and the corollary that being criticized, rejected, and ostracized is unpleasant and undesirable); the need for "structure and predictability" (and the aversiveness of the opposite state of uncertainty and randomness); and finally, the need for status, power, and influence in social groups. It is interesting to note how wide a range of complex social behavior can be derived from these elements of personality. From this point of view, there is a remarkably close correspondence between the views expressed in Hogan's chapter and those generated by Buss from a parallel examination of primate social behavior. Thus, although Hogan's major concern is to utilize a social psychological process, such as self-presentational mechanisms, as a way to better understand the structure of the self, he then is able to use these postulated motives to explain those factors that drive interactional processes.

In other words, Hogan's argument is that individuals develop complex interactional styles in order to obtain these classes of social rewards from the social environment.

Just as forces within the person are seen to be the agents that actively determine *the effects of the environment on emerging personality processes,* so, too, are these active factors understood to be involved in *the maintenance of existing personality structures.* The ability of the ongoing stream of consciousness to evoke and modify experience is the focus of Singer's discussion. The major stress in his chapter is upon the fantasies that are naturally generated in persons, independently of the stimulating environment. Singer demonstrates how the recurrence of such relatively conscious fantasies maintain a person's sense of continuity and selfhood. These competitive, often parallel, cognitive processes (the contents of the daydreams and fantasies) are shown to be related, and give rise to, a variety of personality states, as illustrated by the numerous ingenious experiments described in the chapter. Like other contributors, and most especially Tomkins, Singer stresses the centrality in fantasy of larger cognitive structures (such as scripts) to help modify conscious thought in order to create the continuing structures of personality.

MECHANISMS THAT SUPPORT THE STRUCTURING OF PERSONALITY

The contributors to this volume were asked to consider the mechanisms that might underlie or support the emergence of behavioral coherence. Clearly, in order for them to address this question, each had to have, either explicitly or implicitly, an image of the framework around which coherence emerges. It is the relatively clear articulation of these models that allowed each author to identify the ways in which the environment is able to impinge upon the developing human organism and, in turn, be utilized by the organism in the course of development. Four of the authors (Scarr, Buss, Singer, and Hogan) concern themselves with theories of the middle range, dealing with the issue of how to contruct a model to best fit a particular data arena. This level of analysis contrasts with theories of the narrow range (models required to explain single data sets) or theories of the broad range (frameworks that attempt to delimit and interrelate all the data levels with which personality psychology should deal. Two of the authors (Tomkins and Schwartz) work at the level of broad range theory, and bring to their analysis of the developing person a set of hypotheses drawn from an interdisciplinary perspective.

Scarr's special interest begins at the point of encounter of the individual with the experiential world. She seeks a model that will account for a large portion of the variance in this interaction, with a special focus on the way that personality variables contribute to the equation. Her model is especially interesting because it is both a developmental model and an individual differences one. In reviewing a variety of different individual difference data sets, she comes to the conclusion that the genome is the basic structuring unit. "Over development, different genes are turned on and off, creating maturational changes in the organization of behavior, as well as maturational changes in patterns of physical growth. Genetic differences among individuals are similarly responsible for determining what experiences people do and do not have in their environments. What is attended to and what is ignored are events that are correlated with individual differences in interests, personality, and talents" (*this volume,* p. 62). For example, Scarr uses the illustration that smiling babies receive more social stimulation than difficult babies to convey her belief that the genotype can evoke environmental responses. Thus, Scarr can argue the unusual proposition that differences in parenting treatment are caused by differences in child personality. In this way, Scarr looks to factors in the genotype to influence both the phenotype and the significant variables in the environment that can have an impact on the child. Personality structures emerge from the transactions between the phenotype and the environment, intensified (but not created) by special environmental circumstance.

Buss' treatment of mechanisms begins with the proposition that the biological temperaments are influenced by events of the infant and the juvenile periods. He notes differences between high arousal emotions, such as fear or anger, and low arousal emotions, such as love or jealousy. His analysis assumes that these two kinds of emotions have a different neurological foundation designed to fulfill different adaptive functions. At the level of the mechanisms of social influence, Buss clearly sees the social environment as central to the developing individual, since it facilitates the capacity for developing and enhancing enduring interpersonal relationships. He also sees learning processes as more central in humans than in lower organisms, since learning impinges upon a human organism that differs from its primate neighbors by way of having a longer childhood, a much more articulated socialization experience, and a complex set of cognitive structures that shape imagery and communication, and that are carried on as a group structure (or, more broadly put, as a culture). His theory differs markedly from Scarr's in suggesting that differences between human and other species should contribute to a greater overlay of learning upon constitutional factors (e.g., temperaments) as the organism reaches maturity.

This is an interactive model, where the interactions are keyed to developmental phases. Thus, during the course of childhood, Buss shows that the different social experiences of the infant and the juvenile periods interact with temperamental factors to lead to the emergence of different traits. These, in turn, when paired with the capacity for advanced cognitions and a longer socialization period are able to account for a large number of "peripheral" personality characteristics. In fact, Buss is able to derive a substantial number of the variables from Murray's original list of needs from the mechanisms described in this model of human development.

Singer's special interest is to delineate the ways that personality may be seen as the operation of a set of psychological processes. He notes the variety of different cognitive systems that are active during waking life, with at least one characterized by *symbolic, allegorical processing modes* and another involving more *rational, secondary process functioning.* At the same time, he describes *information systems,* operating largely out of awareness, which convey information that is necessary for the ongoing monitoring of bodily functioning, as well as *organizing systems* that categorize, provide meaning, and provide differential access to consciousness of these ongoing monitoring and guiding processes. Singer uses the term *"schema"* to represent such organizing structures. He notes that these schemas confront, screen and organize the complex new information that impinges on our sensory system and are, in turn, continuously strengthened by processing similar information or modifying their own structures when addressing new, slightly divergent information. Other organizing systems used in the same way include the concept of script (as described in detail by Tomkins) and prototype (which Singer sees as a cognitive structure that is a representation of an ideal type of experience).

Moreover, Singer sees the concept of conscious purposiveness as an additional dynamic mechanism that originates from the self's cognitive analysis of the ongoing stream of psychological processes. "The willingness to search for, retrieve, reexamine, and reshape our schemas in the face of new information necessitates a conscious awareness, some form of imagery replay or verbal interior monologue. It is, I believe, through such conscious processes that we enhance our decision-making abilities, deal more effectively with the unexpected, and evoke our more creative potentialities. Consciousness gives us a second chance at events, and it may be a key to control and self-correction. Of course, excessive consciousness risks awkwardness, slowness of response, social detachment. Perhaps the art of adaptive and exciting living necessitates our learning to value and to use our capacity for conscious thought, to be willing to reexamine our constructs, replay our guiding schemas or nuclear scripts, and, yet, to do so rapidly and smoothly so that we move quickly to action" (*this volume,* pp. 138–139).

In contrast, Hogan's concerns are avowedly sociocentric. Although biology provides the need structure and the developmental clock regulating the emergence of social behavior, culture is seen to offer the opportunities within which these need structures can be met. In this model, normal adult personality is presented as a distillate of social interactional processes, a negotiated structure that is at the juncture of self and group. The establishment of this intersection—an individual's social identity—is understood to be a negotiated process that recurs over time and that facilitates or impedes the activity of the larger group within which the individual is embedded.

Hogan outlines a variety of mechanisms through which the social identity is developed. Briefly stated, (1) a social group is understood to require its members to accommodate themselves to the group's requirement that a satisfactory solution be found to the twin problems of bonding and status among its members (group demands). As individuals discover solutions to these demands upon their interactional selves, (2) the attributes of the social networks provide the bases for the contents of the self-identity that forms within a culture (self-identity distillates). (3) These interactional processes are sufficiently complex and rich so as to provide the social rewards required by the core motives (interactional context as reward structure). (4) Thus, the social processes provide a basis for nature to select those individuals who can manage these social demands most successfully. From this perspective, evolutionary history selects those individuals who can make these adaptations best.

At another level entirely, Tomkins provides an intriguing expansion of script theory, one that is designed to encompass most functions of the person within the life span. In the tradition of Murray's personology, Tomkins seeks to place the person within the context of biology, the sociocultural matrix, and history. Script theory is a formal attempt to integrate that which is innately endowed with that which is experienced, recorded, processed, and then used to guide human encounters. It is a heavily phenomenological theory at the same time that it represents closely the biology of affect. It is also a distinctly teleological theory. The program suggested for exploring personality by Tomkins offers detailed prescriptions for both the definition and development of aspects of personality structure; it also contains a number of hypotheses about the mechanisms that lead to the development, change, and evolution of substructures.

The initial unit of experience is the event—which Tomkins terms the "scene." The scene is the momentary framework within which stimulus, perception, affect, drive, and response all take place. The "script" is the ordered set of rules that establishes relationships between scenes, as well as their sequence and evolution. The nature of scripts is conjointly shaped by the innate limits of the human affect mechanism and by the available frustrations and rewards that a given culture makes available. Within an individual life, the evolution of scripts is limited by the extent to which existing interpersonal relationships call into play different aspects of the complex self. In this way, script theory is an interpersonal theory as well as a process theory that attempts to account for human stability and variability over the life course.

In a similarly broad vein, Schwartz' research program for many years has been heavily concerned with relationships across systems. In his chapter, he extends considerably his earlier interest in the connections that may exist between behavioral and psychophysical systems. It has been a special feature of Schwartz' work that his approach to topics in health psychology has treated the "emergence" of illness as part of a view of the person who is embedded within a broader set of processes than those typically included within modern personality research. Therefore, it is not surprising that Schwartz turns to general systems theory in order to better understand the personality system and its linkages to other domains. This theoretical framework is one of generic mechanisms that cut across domains. A system, as a construct, is a "whole," maintained by the reciprocal interaction of its constituent parts. It is this construct that is the point of contact between personality theory and general systems theory. Schwartz suggests that the human personality *is that construct which occupies the central place in the continuum of psychological processes,* which range from those that control the input (the stimulus) to those that regulate information processing (mechanisms within the organism) to those that guide the output (the repetoire of behavioral responses).

Numerous propositions about personality structure and functioning follow from these general systems ideas and form the basis of much of Schwartz' discussion. For example, he argues that (1) an adequate theory of personality must encompass developmental time, as well as deal with the momentary processes that constitute the focus of much present work. (2) A comprehensive systems perspective suggests that the meta system—the organizing structures—may be more complex than the output and encompass a person's "potential" functioning as well as that which can be easily expressed. This implies some kind of hierarchic organizational structure that can store and organize both elements. (3) A general systems perspective implies that a change at one level "*is*" a change at other levels. From these general propositions, Schwartz suggests some imaginative conceptions that cut across systems domains and demonstrate that personality functions can influence events on levels as far apart as human health and physics.

The discussions to come, of the propositions merely outlined in this introductory chapter, offer a sizeable roster of mechanisms that are involved in the emergence of personality. Each of these mechanisms reflects an interactive process whereby social experiences are understood to transform the biological foundation of the developing person. Drawn from quite disparate perspectives, in response to the common question asked of all contributors, the chapters outline a coordinated set of ideas that allows for an expanded and more articulated view of this structuring process. Although, at present, these presentations are often couched in theoretical terms, with only partial empirical support—or occasionally using material from the laboratory or clinic more as an illustration to clarify an idea than as the test of a scientific hypothesis—taken together the discussions lay out a rich agenda of empirical work for the next generation of personality psychologists. It is our hope that such work is stimulated by these analyses and will help to continue the exploration of personality.

REFERENCES

Block, J. (1981). Some enduring and consequential structures of personality. In A. I. Rabin, J. Aronoff, A. M. Barclay, & R. A. Zucker (Eds.), *Further explorations in personality* (pp. 27–43). New York: John Wiley & Sons.

Epstein, S. (1984). The stability of behavior across time and situations. In R. A. Zucker, J. Aronoff, & A. I. Rabin (Eds.), *Personality and the prediction of behavior* (pp. 209–268). New York: Academic Press.

Gangestad, S., & Snyder, M. (1985). To carve nature at its joints: On the existence of discrete classes in personality. *Psychological Review, 92,* 317–349.

Hogan, R. (1982). A socioanalytic theory of personality. In M. Page (Ed.), *Nebraska symposium on motivation, vol. 30* (pp. 56–89). Lincoln: University of Nebraska Press.

James, W. (1890). *The principles of psychology.* 2 vols. New York: Henry Holt.

Kluckhohn, C., Murray, H. A., & Schneider, D. M. (1956). *Personality in nature, society and culture* (2nd ed.). New York: Alfred A. Knopf.

Maccoby, E. E. (1980). *Social development.* New York: Harcourt Brace Jovanovich.

Maddi, S. R. (1980). *Personality theories: A comparative analysis* (4th ed.). Homewood, IL: Dorsey Press.

Maddi, S. R. (1984). Personology for the 80s. In R. A. Zucker, J. Aronoff, & A. I. Rabin (Eds.), *Personality and the prediction of behavior* (pp. 7–41). New York: Academic Press.

Maslow, A. H. (1970). *Motivation and personality* (2nd ed.). New York: Harper & Row.

McClelland, D. C. (1981). Is personality consistent? In A. I. Rabin, J. Aronoff, A. M. Barclay, & R. A. Zucker (Eds.), *Further explorations in personality* (pp. 87–113). New York: John Wiley & Sons.

McDougall, W. (1921). *An introduction to social psychology* (14th ed.). Boston: John W. Luce.

Murphy, G. (1947). *Personality.* New York: Harper & Row.

Murray, H. A. (1938). *Explorations in personality.* New York: Oxford University Press.

Wilson, E. (1975). *Sociobiology.* Cambridge, MA: Harvard University Press.

2

Personality: Primate Heritage and Human Distinctiveness[1]

Arnold H. Buss

A dozen years ago I visited Allan and Beatrice Gardner, who live in the county of Washoe, Nevada. They hastened to say that the county was not named after Washoe and then taught me the sign for dog. When I played with one of their signing chimpanzees, it made the sign for dog, whereupon I barked a bowwow. It excitedly started signing to me, assuming that I knew the signs it did. I have rarely felt as stupid as then, for that young chimpanzee knew a language of which I was ignorant. Afterward I experienced a most peculiar dissonance when I realized that I had been responding to the chimpanzee as if it were human, an experience common to animal trainers and perhaps owners of pets.

If life were drama, that would have been the moment when I decided to theorize about personality in terms of our animal heritage and human distinctiveness, but that moment was but one in a series of events that ultimately led to this chapter. Previously I wrote an introductory psychology text that had evolution as its underlying theme. I became aware of the role of evolution in our sensory apparatus, perception, learning, motivation, and social behavior. The Gardners' research has made all of us aware of the cognitive capabilities of chimpanzees, and Harlow had demonstrated advanced learning in primates. Ethologists were documenting critical periods in development, and sociobiologists began to flourish. Most of the latter researchers were biologists, and there was an unfortunate tendency to regard

[1]This chapter has been clarified by the comments of David Buss, Stephen Finn, Hill Goldsmith, Peter Killeen, Richard Lore, and Lee Willerman.

humans as just another animal species. One does not have to be a scientist to reject this implicit assumption; just remember that we are studying them, and they are not studying us.

This chapter owes much to Murray, who theorized broadly about personality, and also to Darwin, who opened our eyes to the animal heritage of human behavior. Invoking their names in the context of this volume, however, reminds us of the need for humility.

Humans are primates, who are biologically similar to gorillas, chimpanzees, and orangutans. Though primatologists disagree about which species is closer to humans, chimpanzees or orangutans (see Wood, 1984), the important point here is that we share sense organs, most modes of perception and learning, many facial expressions, and various social behaviors. It is not much of an extrapolation to suggest that we also share some personality traits with the great apes.

To imply that we are nothing but primates would be a mistake, however. We differ from other primates anatomically and psychologically, and we possess personality traits not seen in other primates. It follows that in the attempt to understand human personality, it should be helpful to distinguish personality traits that are part of our primate heritage from personality traits that are distinctively human.

A few words on usage are necessary. The order of primates includes humans and nonhuman primates. To avoid the latter cumbersome phrase, I shall use the term primates to denote nonhuman primates and further restrict its reference to apes and old world monkeys, the so-called higher primates. Also, I shall make assumptions and draw conclusions, sometimes from scanty evidence. Repetition of the necessary qualifying words would lead to boring prose, however, and I shall generally omit them, leaving the reader to fill them in.

PRIMATE PERSONALITY

The great ape that has been most studied is the chimpanzee, and therefore the major focus of this chapter will be on chimpanzee personality traits. Though there are differences between humans and chimpanzees—and the other two great apes, for that matter—the emphasis here will be on similarities.

Some of the best descriptions of personality in chimpanzees have been written by Yerkes in the book *Chimpanzees* (1943). His account, based on many years of experience with chimpanzees, is entirely consistent with the reports of such observers as the Kelloggs (1933) and later, the Gardners (1969) and Jane Goodall (1971). The following quotations from Yerkes' book are especially apt.

The young chimpanzee is a lively extrovert, active, energetic, enthusiastic, sanguine, very sociable, ordinarily good-natured and fairly good-tempered; somewhat mercurial, timid before the unfamiliar, extremely expressive of its continuous flow of feelings and rapidly changing moods . . . It is eager to play, and its playfulness, with its mischievous and humorous turns, exhibits resourcefulness, ingenuity, and constructivity; it invents games and all sorts of activities for entertainment. (p. 27)

Long and intimate acquaintance with the animals enables one to recognize and distinguish expressions of shyness, timidity, fear, terror; of suspicion, distrust, resentment, antagonism, anger, rage; of interest, curiosity, excitement, elation, contentment, pleasure; of confidence, friendliness, familiarity, sympathy, affection; of disappointment, discouragement, loneliness, melancholy, depression. (p. 29)

Individuality expresses itself entertainingly, and also impressively, in temperament or disposition. This is well illustrated by the following contrasts. Wendy is willful, obstinate, unpredictable, courageous, rash, determined, persistent, unaffectionate . . . Bill, one of the first chimpanzees I came to know intimately, may be fairly described as her opposite. He was notably good-natured, even-tempered, buoyant, suggestible and cooperative, friendly and adaptable, dependable, cautious, and for a male, quite timid, conservative, observant, alert, gentle, and affectionate. (p. 33)

Almost four decades later, de Waal (1982), a Dutch ethologist, detailed the life of chimpanzees in a situation that allowed them some of the freedom they have in the wild. Though the focus of the book is on power and sex among apes (the subtitle), the personality traits of the chimpanzees are especially relevant here. These animals were closely observed for years, during which time their individuality became apparent to the human watchers.

Mama is an assertive female, who was once the leader of the troop. Though she no longer leads, she still tends to dominate many of the other chimpanzees by the force of her gaze, the strength of her personality, and the respect she demands of others.

Yeroen is a staid, slow-moving, crafty male, who took over leadership of the troop from Mama. Yeroen is calculating by nature. In an almost nervous way he keeps a close watch on his interests. No one else is considered when he is pursuing his goal. He is a real go-getter. . . . (p. 62)

Luit, by contrast, is seen as someone you can depend on. Playful and mischievous, he is full of youthful vigor. He is seen as open and friendly and may be the most sociable animal in the troop.

One female, though slight of physique, has such a black face and a straight back that she is named Gorilla. "In contrast to her delicate figure, she has a much fiercer character. She 'knows what she wants.' Her face has an aspect of resolution in everything she does" (p. 66). Paradoxically, she is extremely nurturant of youngsters and has served as an "aunt."

The fastest and brightest chimpanzee in the troop is Nikki: "His boundless energy and boisterous, provocative behavior has had the effect of a catalyst. Bit by bit he has disrupted the structure of the group. On cold days Nikki keeps the others warm by his constant activity and on hot days he disturbs their sleep" (p. 70).

Complementing those already described are two entirely different chimpanzees. Dandy is a clever male who delights in fooling others; tricky and guileful, he is suspected of being responsible for several escapes. Franji is a hesitant and timid female. She is the first to warn of potential danger, even when there is little or no threat. She attempts to avoid all trouble and when threatened or attacked sometimes vomits and shakes in terror.

The informal observations made on home-reared chimpanzees and those in the wild and in zoos have been supplemented by systematic observations of rhesus monkeys in laboratory colonies. In a four-year study, researchers rated monkeys for a variety of personality traits (Stevenson-Hinde, Stillwell-Barnes, & Zung, 1980). When the ratings were factor analyzed, three components emerged: (1) fearful, tense, subordinate versus aggressive, effective, confident; (2) slow, equable versus active, excitable; and (3) solitary versus sociable. These findings are consistent with earlier findings on rhesus monkeys who were deprived of their mothers but allowed to play with peers and therefore who developed more or less normally (Chamove, Eysenck, & Harlow, 1972). Again, observations were correlated and factor analyzed, and three factors emerged: fearfulness, hostility, and affiliativeness.

These personality traits do not occur in isolation but are embedded in primate psychological characteristics relevant to personality. As a way of organizing these features, I have divided them into three groups: shared with other mammals, shared with other highly social mammals, and further evolved in primates than other mammals.

Shared With Most Mammals

Activity

Dogs, lions, deer, and bears all have a daily activity cycle. Energy expenditure is lowest during the night, when the animal sleeps, whether it rests on the ground or remains standing. Animals are of course more restless during the daylight hours, especially when they are hungry and searching for food, and there are short periods of intense bursts of energy when predators are chasing their prey. The frisky young of most mammals are sprightly and energetic, their play being a rehearsal for the more serious behaviors of adulthood. Young and old, prey and predator, all have daily cycles of activity and sudden bursts of massive energy output.

Within any particular species, there are individual differences in activity level, which can be observed easily in household pets. Owners of cats have no trouble in identifying which cat is mobile and which is lethargic. Such variation is more striking among dogs, who have been bred for higher or lower levels of activity. Dogs possessed of less vigor—basset hounds, for instance—are more docile, easier to handle, and better for children and the family hearth. Vigorous dogs—terriers, for instance—are friskier, more difficult to handle, and better for the outdoors, where they can obtain the exercise they need. These extremes are merely the opposite ends of a dimension of activity level, which presumably was more normally distributed in the ancestral stock from which these breeds emerged after hundreds or thousands of generations. Even in the absence of breeding, there are individual differences in vigor and tempo, as illustrated by the chimpanzees observed by Yerkes, Goodall, de Waal, and others. Though experience may play a role in determining such individual differences, the results of breeding a variety of animals imply that activity level has a strong genetic component.

Emotionality

All mammals possess an autonomic nervous system, and it is the sympathetic division of this system that is relevant here. In the simplest terms, the sympathetic division of the autonomic nervous system programs bodily reactions to stressful or emergency situations. When a young animal is exposed to excessive novelty, temporary abandonment, or threat, the universal response is distress. In addition to the easily observed howling, shrieking, clutching, and kicking responses, there are also intense, less observable bodily reactions: increased rate of breathing, increased blood pressure and heart rate, delivery of more blood to the large skeletal muscles, and release of sugar into the blood stream. These physiological changes comprise a pattern of preparation of the body for massive action. In infancy, the action may consist of wild, uncontrolled, and diffuse responses, perhaps even temper tantrums. Later in life, the action is likely to be flight from the aversive event or attack against the noxious stimulus. It has been suggested that during human infancy, distress differentiates into fear and anger (Bridges, 1932), a supposition that may also apply to primates.

Only the negative emotions are included under the heading of emotional arousal, because only distress, fear, and anger involve activation of the sympathetic division (except for sexual arousal, which is complex). Are there individual differences in these emotions? Owners of cats and dogs will answer "yes" immediately, their pets varying considerably the extent to which they display distress, fear, or anger. Experienced observers of chimpanzees and other primates notice quickly which animals tend to be fearful, angry, and, especially in younger animals, which tend to become distressed easily. Control of animals' mating by humans is also relevant. Bulls have been bred for courage (absence of fear) in the bull ring, and dogs have been bred that vary in negative excitability (distress), ferocity (anger), and timidity (fear). Thus, at least some of the individual differences in emotionality may be attributed to heredity.

Gender Differences

As in other mammals, the major gender differences in primates involve reproduction. Females have estrous cycles, during which they vary in sexual interest and motivation. During estrous they tend to initiate sex if males do not initiate it first. The bodily changes are seen and smelled by males, who are thereby excited sexually. When not in estrous, females tend to be un-interested in sex and avoid it if males try—with an exception to be noted. Males, however, rarely try outside of periods of female estrous because the appropriate sights and smells are absent.

Females bear and rear offspring; males' contribution is insemination and little else. This gender difference has two consequences. First, females are stuck with their offspring, as both nursing mothers and caretakers who protect and nurture the youngsters. This responsibility ties down females, limiting their mobility and freedom to explore the environment. Second, they de-velop a bond of attachment to their offspring, which is intense in the years following birth. This social feeling and its behavioral concomitants (clasping, nurturance, and grooming) wane as the infant matures, but most mothers continue to be attached to their juvenile and even adult offspring. Though males are curious about newborn infants, they do not know which offspring they have sired and tend not to develop bonds of attachment with the young.

As in most mammals, primate males typically are larger and stronger than females and tend to dominate them. Males compete openly for dominance against other males. Females rarely challenge a male for dominance.

> Techniques of social control are more varied in the case of females and much more frequently employed by males. The males use such means as gestural and vocal begging; varied forms of motor suggestion, manual teasing, attempts to initiate play; vocal complaint; gestural threats, vocal gestural, and attitudinal commands; assault, by striking or pushing; active conflict, with the use of limbs, teeth, or both. As for the females, wiles, trickery, or deceitful cunning, which are conspicuous by their absence in the male list, are favorite resources. But even more so are sexual allure and varied forms of socialization, some of which might be better classified under motor suggestion; petting by means of grooming, physical contacts, and manipula-tion of body parts, bodily pressure, and crowding. (Yerkes, 1943, p. 83)

In brief, males attempt to achieve social control by dominating the others, using strength or the threat of aggression. Females attempt to achieve social control as do any of those who lack strength or ferocity: indirectly, through the use of cunning and the exploitation of weaknesses in the dominant other.

Shared With Highly Social Mammals

Sociability

Highly social mammals, by definition, prefer to associate with each other and are distressed when they are cut off from social contact. The common house cat represents a moderately social mammalian species: playful, affectionate, and occasionally even jealous, but it can take or leave the company of other cats, other animals, or humans. Cats are not sufficiently affiliative to be dominated by humans. It is not that cats are unsocial, though they are solitary hunters, but they are not *highly* social.

In contrast, dogs hunt in packs and want others' company. They easily form dominance hierarchies and can therefore be trained to defer to human owners. They crave affection and will learn difficult tricks for little more than a hug and pat on the head. Their tails can wag in greeting in a manner analogous to the human smile. They can become so strongly attached to an owner that they mourn absence or death. The tendencies to seek other animals and to crave attention and affection seem to have reached a peak in dogs, who are among the most social animals, though they are no more affiliative than most primates.

Why do animals seek proximity? One benefit is protection against attack. A group of animals can beat off even a large predator, and predators avoid attacking groups in favor of selecting single animals for prey. Except for adult orangutans, the solitary primate usually does not survive very long.

Another reason for affiliating, common to all highly social animals, is the need for stimulation from others. The essence of the social situation is responsivity (Buss, 1983). To use a human example, what I say stimulates you, what you say or do affects how I behave; when we interact, there is a back-and-forth responsiveness. All highly social animals seem to require stimulation from others, and it has been established that primates cannot tolerate social isolation (Harlow & Harlow, 1962).

What are the other rewards intrinsic to affiliation? Even in the absence of a relationship between two animals or humans, shared activities seem to be preferred. Primates like to hunt for food together and to eat together. The food is not necessarily shared (usually it is not), but the activity is carried out together. In this respect, we are no less primates than our nonhuman relations, for there are many activities we prefer to do with others rather than alone, including eating.

Primates also enjoy attention from others. Virtually all primates want to be looked at, to be listened to, and in general to be part of the awareness of others. Primates welcome attention, and the more, the better.

There are also social rewards that require a relationship. One primate can offer another affection by means of grooming, hugging, patting, or even kissing. One primate, usually a mother or dominant animal, can offer sooth-ing to a distressed animal, usually by hugging or cradling. As humans, we know that a crying infant is usually immediately pacified by being picked up and held; this is a primate characteristic.

Highly social mammals prize the presence of others and when isolated, tend to become depressed. Dogs mourn the loss of their owners, chimpan-zees the absence of their companions. After a period of social isolation, reunion elicits not just relief but elation. Social mammals are happy when they receive the social rewards they seek, depressed when denied these rewards.

Primates and other highly social mammals form strong attachments to other animals. In the sense of deep friendship, love is not limited to humans or to the mother–infant bond. Once such a deep attachment is established, it sets up the possibility of jealousy. Jealousy is most frequent among the young, who do not wish to share their mothers' affection with anyone, but jealousy also occurs in adult primates. A weak form may also be observed in cats, but among our pets, dogs are the ones likely to be jealous.

The assumption here is that elation, depression, love, and jealousy derive from bonds of attachment. These emotions occur in weaker form in mod-erately social animals such as the common cat, but are absent in less social animals such as cougars and leopards.[2] Love and jealousy obviously originate in social relationships, but what about elation and depression? I assume that joy accompanies acceptance, affection, and attention from others, and that grief occurs when social contact with an attached other is prevented. Melan-choly is the primordial response of a social mammal to being isolated from its fellows, and elation is the primordial response to being reunited or just to being accepted and loved. This formulation should apply to humans, though human emotions are so conditionable that they can subsequently be trig-gered by many stimuli.

These *relationship affects* may be distinguished from the other emotions in several ways. The more common affects of fear, anger, and sexual arousal all involve a massive reaction by the autonomic nervous system. The relationship affects (including elation) involve little or no autonomic arousal, certainly no more arousal than occurs in nonemotional states. This assertion appears to fly in the face of the experience we feel in elation, but feelings may not be the best guide here. Consider first that when we experience joy, we may leap in the air, dance around, or otherwise exercise enough muscles to elevate heart

[2]Elation and depression have been observed in highly social land mammals that roam freely, but it is not certain that these affects occur in highly social burrowers (rodents, for example). There is a problem in identifying elation and depression in many animals because we are not sure how they might be expressed, and perhaps we are anthropocentric. And there may be a problem in specifying precisely what is meant by "highly social," an issue that would take us too far afield, however.

rate, blood pressure, and breathing. Such autonomic activity is unlikely to occur if elation occurs without exercise. Consider also that we may implicitly compare autonomic arousal in elation with the absence of such arousal in a state of quiescence. A state of calmness is not the appropriate comparison condition, however. More appropriate is the autonomic arousal that occurs in such nonemotional states as solving a mathematics problem (Lacey, 1956) or in reacting to a novel stimulus with an orienting reflex (Lynn, 1966). I contend that the autonomic arousal of elation is no more than the autonomic arousal of states of active cognition and orienting response, neither of which involves an emotional reaction. Thus, when elation is divorced from the skeletal muscle activity that may accompany it and is compared with moderately aroused *non*emotional state of attention, it becomes clear that elation involves little of the autonomic arousal of rage, fear, or sex. The case is even stronger for such emotions as grief and love.

The two kinds of emotions also differ in their adaptive functions. Elation, depression, and love are all involved in cohesiveness behavior between individuals or groups. As such, they are instrinsic to social bonds (love) or consequences of the presence or absence of these social bonds (elation versus depression or jealousy). It is problematical whether any of these highly social emotions plays a crucial role in the survival of the individual or its genes. Fear and rage, on the other hand, are necessary for survival. When threatened, an animal can attempt to run away or fight off the attacker. Either way, there is an emergency, and the sympathetic division of the autonomic nervous system responds massively. Thus the autonomic components of fear (flight) and rage (fight) may be seen as emergency preparation for a maximal effort to deal with threat, which is crucial to the individual's survival. Sexual arousal does not promote individual survival but is crucial for the continuity of the genes. As Wilson (1975) and other sociobiologists have emphasized, continuing one's genes is closely linked to natural selection. These various differences between highly social and less social emotions are summarized in Table 2.1, which sharpens the distinctions in the interest of clarity.

Table 2.1 High arousal and low arousal emotions

	High arousal	Low arousal
Emotion	Fear, anger, sexual arousal	Love, jealousy, elation, grief
Occurrence	In all mammals	In social mammals
Adaptive function	Survival of the individual or species	Group cohesiveness; or perhaps a nonadaptive consequence of sociability
Kind of behavior	Preparation for massive action (motivation)	Reaction to acceptance or rejection (mood)

Dominance

Highly social animals cannot remain in groups unless there is some sort of social organization, the most prominent of which is based on dominance. In primates, as in any social animal, the strongest and most ferocious animals (the two are closely related) tend to enforce their will on weaker, smaller members of the group. In behavioral terms, such coercion means having access to food, females, or merely a place to sit or sleep. Subordinate animals pay close attention to the ascendant animal, who goes where he pleases without having to be concerned about irritating another member of the group. Dominant animals also tend to be groomed by subordinate animals.

The simplest kind of dominance hierarchy is linear: A coerces B, who threatens C, and so on. Dominance relationships, however, are often more complicated. When they are being established—childhood and adolescence, times of playfighting and occasionally real fighting—the linear sequence may be broken by the particular experiences of two maturing animals. Also, primates are capable of coalitions, clusters of three or four animals that sometimes act as a group and so can exert considerable leverage over any individual animal. Such clusters consist of either a mother and her grown male offspring or a group of male buddies who have formed a group.

The importance of coalitions has been described by de Waal (1982). In the chimpanzee colony Luit was the dominant male, Nikki was number 2, and Yeroen was number 3. Luit solidified his dominant position by being a peacemaker and often siding with the loser when there was a fight in the colony. In the course of several months, the second and third males gradually formed a partnership directed against Luit: "Both Nikki and Yeroen became less submissive towards Luit and resisted his interference more and more frequently. When the leader displayed at the two of them, they were no longer intimidated. Yeroen began to scream and furiously attacked Luit, while Nikki kept close to Luit with his hair on end, as if he were threatening Luit" (de Waal, 1982, p. 128). After several months of such confrontations, Luit's leadership was sufficiently eroded for Nikki to become the dominant male in the colony, but he was careful to maintain the coalition with Yeroen. In light of such behavior, it is understandable why de Waal entitled his book *Chimpanzee Politics.*

Closely related to strength and ferocity—in fact, determinants of these two characteristics—are age and gender. Older animals dominate juveniles, who dominate infants, and males tend to dominate females. Thus, the ladder of dominance, generally, is as follows: adult males, adult females, juvenile males, juvenile females, and infants.

Dominance is not the whole story, however; subordinate animals have some privileges and status. Females in estrous are courted by males; nursing mothers are less likely to be attacked, and they receive a great deal of attention; and infants are usually protected and nurtured not only by their mothers but by other adults as well. Status also varies with the rank of the animal's mother.

The concepts of dominance and status are necessary in describing the social organization of primates. Dominance refers to the animal's position in the group as a consequence of its own strength and ferocity or a coalition's combined strength and ferocity. Status refers to the positions or privileges of animals, especially nondominant animals, which are a consequence of age (infants), gender (females in estrous), or genealogy (the rank of the mother). Genealogy is more important for females, who tend to retain the same social position from childhood into maturity. Males can achieve a higher ranking through threats and fighting, as they progress through the juvenile period into adulthood.

These issues of social organization have implications for personality. Individual differences in dominance are important as determinants and consequences of aggressiveness, leadership, and confidence. As determinants of personality, gender and social status appear to be as important in primates as they often are in humans. Personality itself appears to play a crucial role in social behavior:

> Long-term stability of basic social relations has enabled the higher primates to develop social systems based on the membership of individuals as individuals and not just as representatives of a particular age-sex class. In other words, if you see monkey A interacting with monkey B you are not simply seeing an adult male interacting with a juvenile male. Rather you are seeing two individuals with special personalities, individual social histories, special social relations and alliances, and a history of past association with each other. (Lancaster, 1975, p. 13)

Primate Features

Curiosity and Manipulation

Dogs and cats are curious animals, sniffing and exploring the trees, grass, animals, and all the other stimuli that occupy their sensory world. Primates are even more inquisitive, and their curiosity extends beyond stimuli to problems that might be solved. There is an anecdote about an experimenter who was rewarding a chimpanzee for solving problems with slices of banana. The animal was not hungry and so merely lined up the banana slices, eventually exhausting the experimenter's store. The experimenter continued to present problems and was surprised to receive a banana slice each time he did, until all the banana slices had been returned. The chimpanzee was rewarding the experimenter for presenting puzzles.

The curiosity of most mammals takes the form of exploring the origin of smells. Primates focus attention mainly on the visual world, which is a richer source of information than the world of smells. The availability of a greater range and complexity of visual stimuli provides greater scope for the curiosity of primates. The primate hand has a capacity for manipulation far beyond the potential of most lower mammals. Chimpanzees have been taught such fine motor acts as striking a match, lighting a cigarette, threading a needle, and sewing.

In brief, primates, especially the great apes, are not only curious about stimuli but also about how to solve problems. Given their manipulative ability, this curiosity often takes the form of poking, prying, squeezing, and generally handling objects in the environment. One direct consequence is an ability to use primitive tools such as sticks to insert into termite holes and the capability of using a paint brush. Another consequence is a greater potential for innovative behavior. Primates are likely to try responses never seen before, simply because they are intelligent, curious, and manipulative. A Japanese macaque monkey discovered first that sweet potatoes tasted better when she washed them and then that grains of wheat could be separated from sand by casting the wheat on ocean water, where it floated and could easily be scooped up. This ability to originate novel solutions to the problems of everyday life, though present in some mammals, has evolved further in primates.

Communication and Imitation

Like other mammals, primates use the channels of sight, sound, smell, and touch for communication. The primate face, however, is capable of a much greater range of expressions than the face of lower mammals. To match this greater facial expressiveness, primates appear to be capable of finer discriminations of changes in facial expression. We must not equate primate expressions with human expressions, however; when chimpanzees appear to us to be grinning, for example, they are usually not happy but distressed or fearful. These negative emotions are accompanied by a wide open mouth, displaying many teeth, as well as screaming. The playface is accompanied by a less open mouth, revealing fewer teeth, and by panting or no sound at all. Such subtle differences in facial expressions are easily discerned by chimpanzees, who tend to watch others' faces more attentively than do most mammals.

As a result of their excellent visual communication and their close attention to one another, primates are exceedingly imitative. The potato-washing, mentioned above, spread throughout the monkey troop until most of the animals washed their potatoes. And we know that chimpanzees are capable of learning American Sign Language (Gardner & Gardner, 1969), which is acquired mainly through imitation.

Primates' better communication and social attention also extends their range of social behaviors. They are sensitive not only to others' momentary changes of mood but also to alterations of status from one animal to the next and from one social context to the next. Thus, they have the behavioral foundations necessary for playing a variety of social roles, though such roles exist only in the most primitive form among primates.

Single Birth and Longer Childhood

Some lower mammals give birth to single offspring; *all* primates do. A single birth means that the mother–infant bond is closer. The mother's genetic investment is, for the time, solely in the one infant, who has virtually all her attention and affection. Given the usual size of primate bands, single birth means that the primate infant will have a few agemates but many subadult playmates of varying ages.

During the evolution of primates from lower mammals, childhood stretched out in relation to life-span, so that primates have the longest childhood per years of total life. A long childhood, which offers the animal more time to learn the ways of its species and of the world, has several consequences. Childhood is typically spent near the mother, so there is a closer mother–child bond of affection. This closer bond, together with the fact of single births, makes the young primate more susceptible to jealousy when it is displaced as the youngest by a new sibling. For the mother, the longer time spent with her children also strengthens affectional ties, directing her sociability more to dyadic relationships.

Accompanying the stretching out of childhood is a corresponding diminution in the importance of innate behavioral tendencies. Built-in tendencies are crucial for animals that must mature quickly and so have little time to learn. Primates, however, care for their young for years, which diminishes the need for having many innate tendencies ready for use in adapting to everyday life. Primate offspring have much to learn and the time to learn it. More than lower mammals, their lives are shaped by their everyday experiences, which differ from one animal to the next. As a result of fewer innate tendencies, a longer childhood, curiosity and the ability to innovate, and a greater range of life experiences, one primate is likely to be different from the next in all the features that comprise individuality.

This discourse on primate psychological features has been sufficiently lengthy to require a summary. The features shared with most mammals are assumed to be cycles of activity, capacity for such intense emotional reactions as distress, fear, rage, and sexual arousal, and gender differences in behavior. Shared with highly social animals are sociability, such social affects as elation, grief, love, and jealousy, and the social control of aggression through dominance relationships. Primate features that appear to be even further evolved are intense curiosity and dexterous manipulation, expressive communication and imitation, and single birth, longer childhood, and a diminution in the potency of innate tendencies.

Presumably, these psychological features are major determiners of which personality traits arise. The origins of these traits would seem to be the same as the origins of human personality traits: inheritance and the events of development.

Temperament

The term "temperament" refers to the minority of personality traits that have an inherited basis. Inheritance is assumed to establish a potential for the development of particular traits, which are also shaped by life experiences. Inherited personality dispositions are not immutable as is eye color. Rather, they are like body build, which can be modified by diet and exercise but not pushed beyond the limits set by inheritance.

There is evidence from twin studies for human temperaments. The three that have been unequivocally and consistently found are emotionality, activity, and sociability[3] (Buss & Plomin, 1984). We do not know if these traits are inherited in primates, because there has been so little behavioral genetic research in primates. One possibility is that these temperaments are limited to humans, which implies that selective pressure that occurred only during the period of human evolution. It is anyone's guess what such selective pressure would be, and therefore I prefer the simpler and less speculative assumption that the three temperaments are shared by humans and primates (Buss & Plomin, 1975). If this assumption is correct, when behavioral genetic research is carried out with primates, evidence for these three temperaments will emerge. For now, their presence in nonhuman primates is assumed by extrapolation from research on humans.

Emotionality

Emotionality is defined as the tendency to become aroused and upset in the face of frustrating, annoying, or threatening situations. The situations are unpleasant, and the reaction is negative. The positive emotions of elation and

---

[3]There is evidence for the inheritance of other personality traits, but there is disagreement about precisely which traits belong on a list of inherited traits. Also, there are twin data showing an inherited component in shyness, but shyness can be derived from the inherited traits of emotionality and sociability; the point here is that some of the traits known to be inherited may be derivable from the three temperaments used in this chapter. Furthermore, of all the inherited traits, only emotionality, activity, and sociability appear early in life, which makes it easier to regard them as determinants rather than consequences. For these various reasons, this discussion is limited to the three temperaments.

friendliness are specifically excluded here, though they may be linked to sociability. Emotionality includes only three of our conventional emotions, all negative: distress, fear, and anger.

All three involve high levels of arousal of the autonomic nervous system, part of the bodily preparation for massive action in the face of threat or noxious stimuli. What is inherited appears to be how the sympathetic division of the autonomic nervous system reacts in the face of stressful life situations. Greater emotionality is reflected in a more intense physiological reaction to stress, usually accompanied by more intense facial expressions of distress, fear, or anger. The emotional individual is more sensitive to disturbing situations and reacts emotionally to situations that would be too mild to elicit such a reaction from a less emotional individual. In brief, emotionality consists of the twin tendencies to be easily aroused and to react intensely.

The occurrence of distress, fear, and anger follows a developmental sequence. Distress, the primordial negative emotion, appears on the first day of life. Infants kick, whimper, and struggle, all signs of being upset. Whatever the discomfort, it can usually be relieved by cradling the infant. In fact, a major task of mothers is to ensure that their infants do not suffer discomfort for very long, and being able to soothe an infant is reinforcing for the mother.

Distress may be overlooked, because it is often confused with fear or anger, especially during infancy, when emotional reactions are diffuse and facial expressions of emotion are undeveloped. When an infant is screaming, what does the howling signify: fear, anger, or merely the more generalized distress? In the absence of any differentiating features, the answer that stays closest to observations and therefore requires the least inference is distress.

Distress presumably continues throughout life, for juveniles and adults become upset and fretful in the absence of fear or anger. The response appears to be roughly synonymous with the reaction of frustration: when food is out of reach, when there is a barrier to an observable reward, when there is a prolonged wait, or when sexual advances are rebuffed. In these various situations, the problem usually cannot be resolved by running away (fear) or by attack (anger), and this lack of instrumentality parallels that of an infant who can respond to aversiveness only with undifferentiated distress.

Fear is similar to distress not only in diffuseness but in relative lack of instrumentality. Less coordination and motor skill are required to shrink back and recoil than to attack or at least push away the aversive stimulus. The most direct developmental path, then, is for the distress to differentiate into fear rather than into anger, unless other personality traits or life events push emotional development in the direction of anger.

Activity

Activity is defined as the total energy output of the organism. It refers not to mental work but to actions, and it is easier to describe in those who are extremely active. They are quick, sprightly, and animated. When young, they like to bounce, hop, jump, and run. Often in motion, they are brisk, busy, and apparently without fatigue. When others are ready to rest, the active ones want to keep on playing. The fast tempo is usually accompanied by considerable vigor. Those who are active tend to vocalize louder, gesticulate more broadly, and in general prefer energy-intensive activities. They may annoy others with their bustle and movement, and their dynamic character can intensify any conflicts that are latent within a group.

At the opposite end of the dimension are those whose pace is slow, whose supply of energy seems to dissipate quickly, and in general, whose ambition seems to be a life of indolence. No normal, healthy primate is devoid of energy, but there are large variations among individuals in both tempo and vigor. These variations, observed in many primate species, are assumed to be largely inherited.

Sociability

Sociability refers to the tendency to seek others and to prefer being with them rather than being alone. The basic primate pattern involves existence in groups, and most primates are sociable. Even the orangutan, an animal that in adulthood may spend much time alone in the forest, plays with and clings to other members of its own species and humans as well. But there are marked individual differences in sociability. Some individuals are strongly motivated to seek others and tend to remain in their presence even when there is conflict, punishment, or other kinds of aversiveness. Their need for companionship is so strong that they are willing to tolerate discomfort that might easily be terminated merely by leaving. At the opposite end of the sociability dimension are those whose need for others is mild. They tend not to go looking for others but do not actively avoid contact. They easily become bored in social contexts, and when such contexts start becoming aversive, they quickly leave. Purely social incentives appear weak for these low-sociable individuals, who tend to seek reinforcement elsewhere.

The relevant social incentives are the social rewards mentioned earlier: attention from others, sharing activities, and responsivity. Sociable individuals strongly desire these rewards and suffer from their absence. And they want the most arousing reward, responsivity, but may settle for the weaker rewards of attention and sharing activities. Unsociable individuals need these rewards less and suffer little from their absence. Consequently, they will put up with little of the aversiveness of social situations and are just as likely to stay away from others as to seek their company. Presumably, a major determinant of these individual differences in sociability is inheritance.

Attachment

Like all mammals, newborn primates need the mother to feed, nurture, protect, and love them. Infants respond to these maternal offerings, and a close mother-infant bond develops. The bond and this initial social relationship are called attachment.

Mother's Behavior

The period of attachment has been divided into three phases (Harlow, Harlow, & Hansen, 1963). In the earliest phase, the mother is loving, nurturing, and protective. Next, the mother is less frequently attentive and loving, still protective, and she begins to push away the infant or leave it. In the last phase, the mother has less time and affection to lavish on the youngster, often because of the arrival or imminent birth of her next offspring; now the first offspring is displaced and receives less nurturance and protection.

The mother serves as a base of security, a haven of safety and nurturance. If she is sufficiently attentive and protective, the infant will be secure and will busily explore novel environments. If she does not soothe the infant and reassure it sufficiently when it is upset and unable to cope with stress, the infant will be cautious, fearful, and clinging; it will explore less and tend to react to strangers with wariness or anxiety. Presumably, how good a base of security is furnished by the mother determines whether the infant is exploratory or clinging, secure or afraid, and independent or dependent. This formulation rests on the assumption, suggested by Mason (1970), that security and curiosity are related to arousal in opposite ways and that there is an optimal level of arousal. Above this optimal level of arousal, the infant seeks security; below this level, it seeks arousal. Mason tested this idea with infant chimpanzees, who were exposed regularly to two trainers, each with a distinctive costume. One wore gray coveralls and a black hood over his face, and he always soothed the animals and let them cling to him. The other was dressed entirely in white and never held the infants but always played roughly with them. (For the other half of the chimpanzees, the costumes on the trainers were reversed.) At first there was no preference for either trainer, but gradually the infant chimpanzees came to prefer the playful, arousing figure. Whenever the infants were aroused, however, this preference was reversed. They tended to choose clinging and being soothed when separated from fellow animals, when placed in an unfamiliar room, or when administered the arousing drug amphetamine. Evidently, arousal-seeking occurs only when young primates are sufficiently secure for their arousal level to be below an optimal range.

The second phase is marked by inconsistent punishment and withdrawal of affection or attention. Likely reactions to this chaotic set of contingencies are withdrawal, negativism, or resistance. Primate young are not fragile, however, and early negativism and tantrums are often the first signs of independence and self-assertion.

In the third phase, the mother gradually (or suddenly, if there is a new birth) turns her attention elsewhere and is less loving toward her infant, who is expected to become more self-sufficient and less clinging. If this shift is too abrupt or too early, it is likely to react with resentment. The presence of the new baby is likely to evoke inordinate jealousy toward it and aggression toward the mother. If the transition is gradual and not too early, the older offspring is likely to display no more than mild jealousy and perhaps even affection toward the younger sibling and no particular aggression toward the mother.

Infant's Temperaments

The mother's behavior during the three phases of the period of attachment is one determinant of the infant's reactions. These reactions and any associated traits, however, are also determined by the infant's temperaments, the most important being emotionality. The emotional infant becomes distressed easily (by definition), requires inordinate maternal security, and is likely to cling to the mother and display stranger anxiety. Later, when faced with punishment or withdrawal of affection, the emotional youngster is likely to react in one of two ways, depending on how the primordial distress has differentiated. If the tilt is toward fear, the youngster withdraws and is sullen. If the tilt is toward anger, open jealousy and aggressiveness are likely.

Sociability is important for its relevance to social rewards. The mother's attention and stimulation are crucial for a sociable infant. Such an infant is likely to be more pliable and conforming in the face of being denied sharing activities, attention, or responsivity, because these social rewards are so powerful. In addition, a sociable youngster should be more friendly and react to strangers more positively. An unsociable infant tends to be less friendly, needs social rewards less (by definition), and therefore tends to be less docile. The other temperament, activity, is not especially relevant to the personality traits that arise in the context of mother–infant relationships.

For completeness, the mother's temperament should be mentioned. An emotional mother, for instance, tends to become distressed easily and so offers the infant a less secure base and perhaps an inconsistent regime of social rewards and punishments. The infant's reaction to the mother's emotionality depends on its own emotionality. Thus, the match (or mismatch) between the mother's and infant's temperaments is perhaps even more important than each one's temperament considered alone.

Juvenile Period

The juvenile era starts immediately after the period of attachment and ends with adulthood. If we were dealing with humans, there might be four stages (the addition of adolescence) or even more. For generalized primates, however, a long juvenile period suffices. The development of personality traits is affected by two major issues, both involving play: social bonds and aggression.

Social Bonds

Play is intrinsically pleasurable. Juveniles who especially like the rough-and-tumble of tag, follow-the-leader, and primitive games may be expected to remain frisky and playful. The ones who find lively play rewarding tend to be high in the temperaments of activity and sociability.

Juveniles tend to develop friendships and alliances, both of which offer security, stimulation, and a sense of belonging. The minority who lack friends and stay out of alliances are likely to be insecure and may well try to continue being dependent on their mothers. The basic personality dichotomy to emerge from such social relationships is friendly versus withdrawn. Youngsters enter the juvenile period already tilted toward either extreme because of the outcome of the mother–infant relationship (amiable versus hostile) and the temperament of sociability (sociable versus unsociable).

Gender affects the kinds of social bonds that develop. Females, who tend to remain closer to their mothers, are very interested in infants. Long before adulthood, they participate vicariously by acting as "aunts." After becoming mothers, they form the nucleus of a group consisting of their own children. They typically develop closer and more enduring social bonds in primarily dyadic relationships, and therefore any inherited tendency to be sociable is enhanced among females.

Male juveniles are more likely than females to wander away from the mother. Though interested in infants, as are primates at all ages, they are not pulled as strongly as are juvenile females. Males usually form social bonds with their male playmates, their play being practice for adulthood. These relationships are ambivalent, however, for friendship is accompanied by competition and eventually by differences in status. The relevant trait dimension is the dichotomy of cooperation–competition.

Power Relationships

Social behavior includes not only affectional bonds, individuals sharing or exchanging various social rewards, but also power relationships, one individual being ascendant over others. Dominance is ordinarily achieved by means of successful aggression, and fighting starts when there is sufficient mobility and muscular control. By then, males tend to be stronger than females and dominate them. Females tend not to fight with each other, perhaps because social bonds are more important for them and because they are developing the affectional tendencies that will be needed when they become mothers.

In the framework of a primate heritage, the focus must be on physical aggression. Developmentally, the earliest form of aggression is mock fighting, mainly by young males. They wrestle, pounce, and chase one another, and though occasionally the bouts may escalate into the real thing, most of it is merely playful. By early adulthood, mock fighting becomes real, though threats replace most actual aggression. By this time, there are clear individual differences.

Who becomes aggressive? Observational learning plays a role, but inherited anatomy and physiology would seem to be more important. Size and strength are crucial. Larger, stronger juveniles tend to win fights, which builds up a strong habit of fighting through instrumental conditioning. The same process leads to the opposite trait for small, weak juveniles. The regular punishment of being whipped in mock fighting tends to render them nonaggressive. Less important but still of some consequence are two temperaments. Active youngsters are more likely to enjoy the vigor of fighting, and their restless push for tempo and vigor is likely to involve them in more fights. When distress differentiates mainly toward anger, temper outbursts lead to more fighting. In brief, the trait of aggressiveness may be explained in terms of the physical characteristics of size and strength, the temperaments of activity and emotionality (anger), and the processes of observational learning and instrumental conditioning.

During the juvenile period, aggression gradually becomes less playful and more serious. Fighting disrupts group activities and weakens social bonds, so it needs to be controlled. The major basis of control is the development of a dominance hierarchy. Reduced to simplest terms, years of threats, fighting, and attempts to get one's way result in each individual's knowing his or her place in the group. As this hierarchy is established, fighting diminishes and occurs mainly when maturing males assert themselves. Thus, considerable conflict occurs in the establishment of dominance, which helps organize the group and thereby diminishes conflict. There are intrinsic rewards for dominance: the sheer pleasure of winning and the ability to control others. The extrinsic rewards are being the center of attention and better access to such things as food and mates.

In addition to aggressiveness, dominance is associated with several other personality traits. Dominant individuals tend to be confident and secure in the knowledge of their high status in relation to others. Having been aggressively competitive in achieving dominance, they remain competitive and aggressive. Nondominant individuals tend to lack confidence, because they must regularly defer to those higher in the hierarchy. In brief, the juvenile period and early adulthood may produce variations in the trait dimensions of aggressiveness, dominance, competitiveness, and confidence.

Dominant individuals enjoy higher status: Others frequently look at them, back off when confronted, retreat when threatened, and assume deferential postures. Though successful aggression is the major path to such status, it may also be attained by association. The female who attaches herself to a dominant male achieves status through this association. Similarly, the offspring of such a high status female is also accorded high status. And occasionally the friends of a high status male also share his status. Such vicarious status confers a modicum of self-confidence on the associates of dominant individuals. They have not earned their high position through successful aggression, however, and therefore are not high in the trait of aggressiveness.

Primate Traits

In brief, personality traits are assumed to originate from three sources: temperaments, the events of infancy, and the events of the juvenile period. These personality traits are summarized in Table 2.2. Emotionality, activity, and sociability are expected to continue throughout development, though the level of each may fluctuate (again, in a manner comparable to body

Table 2.2 Primate personality traits

Temperaments
    Emotionality: distress, fear, anger
    Activity: tempo and vigor
    Sociability
From the period of attachment
    Exploratory–cautious
    Autonomous–dependent
    Affectionate–jealous
    Friendly–withdrawn
From the juvenile period
    Playful–serious
    Competitive–cooperative
    Aggressive–nonaggressive
    Dominant–submissive
    Confident–insecure

build). These temperaments can also affect the development of wholly acquired personality traits. Thus, an active infant is likely to become exploratory rather than cautious, and a sociable infant has a head start on being friendly rather than withdrawn.

What about the stability of the personality traits acquired during development? This is a fundamental question in personality, and there is no simple answer. If we extrapolate from the little that is known about the stability of human traits, primate traits should be at least moderately stable during development. Traits acquired in infancy may be less stable. As youngsters mature, they are less frightened by novelty and better able to depend on their own resources. As a result, cautious infants might become more exploratory juveniles, and dependent infants might become more autonomous juveniles. Similarly, as juveniles develop relationships among peers, residuals of infantile jealousy may wane. The traits at the other end of these three trait dimensions may be stable, however, and infants who are exploratory, autonomous, and affectionate should remain so as juveniles. Both ends of the friendly–withdrawn trait dimension are expected to be stable because this dimension is linked to the temperament of sociability.

The personality traits that develop during the juvenile era should persist over time. They develop over a longer period of time and in the context of enduring social relationships. Thus, by adulthood, virtually every primate knows its place in the group. It is true that there are occasional shifts in dominance as adolescents become stronger, old males become weaker, and some adults form coalitions, but these changes affect only a minority of the group. Most individuals remain stable in their niche along the dominance–submission dimension, as well as the traits associated with this dichotomy.

When the temperaments are excluded, Table 2.2 reveals that most of the acquired traits are interpersonal. Primates live out their lives in a moderately small social group, and there is virtually no privacy. Almost all their behavior is social, so we are not surprised that the majority of acquired personality traits are interpersonal.

If these personality traits seem familiar, it is probably because they are also seen in humans. In recent years, psychologists have been classifying human interpersonal traits in a circumplex. The best known of these is that of Wiggins (1979), whose terms have distinctly human connotations— "arrogant" instead of "confident," and "aloof" instead of "withdrawn," for example. The interpersonal circle of Kiesler (1983) contains terms that allow comparison between human and primate traits (see Table 2.3). Kiesler's traits have been listed for the purpose of comparison and are not in the same order as in his circumplex. Also, his human traits and the primate traits derive from widely different perspectives, so we cannot expect a precise match.

Table 2.3 Human and primate interpersonal traits

Human (Kiesler, 1983)	Primate (acquired only)
Dominant–submissive	Dominant–submissive
Competitive–cooperative	Competitive–cooperative
Friendly–hostile	Affectionate–jealous (cooperative–competitive)
Sociable–aloof	Friendly–withdrawn
Warm–cold	Affectionate and friendly vs. jealous and withdrawn
Assured–unassured	Confident–insecure (autonomous–dependent)
Trusting–suspicious	
Exhibitionist–inhibited	
	Playful–serious
	Exploratory–cautious

Nevertheless, the first two human traits, dominant–submissive and competitive–cooperative, are the same as the primate traits. There is reasonable agreement between the human friendly–hostile and the primate affectionate–jealous (and cooperative–competitive). The human sociable–aloof[4] is synonymous with the primate friendly–withdrawn. The human warm–cold has no precise parallel in primate traits, but the combination of affectionate and friendly versus jealous and withdrawn yields a dichotomy similar to warm–cold. The human assured–unassured has as a primate counterpart confident–insecure, though Kiesler also seems to mean autonomous–dependent.

Though the human interpersonal traits do not always precisely match the primate traits, the fit is close. We must bear in mind that the primate dichotomies could have just as easily been chosen as human interpersonal traits, for the primate traits seem entirely apt in describing human personality. Furthermore, the two primate traits below the line in Table 2.3, though not especially interpersonal, could easily be applied to humans. The opposite is not necessarily true of both human traits below the line in Table 2.3. The trusting–suspicious and exhibitionistic–inhibited traits may apply only to humans, though there is room for argument on this issue. The main point,

[4]Kiesler (1983) uses the term "sociable," as do many psychologists, to mean something like friendliness, hence the equivalence between the two. Kiesler's usage is necessary for this comparison, but elsewhere in this chapter "sociability" refers to the motive or tendency (largely inherited) to be with others.

however, is that the majority of human interpersonal trait dimensions seem to be present in primates. This generality appears to be true even if their developmental origins, outlined earlier, are not accepted.

Given the occasion of this symposium, it is relevant to examine Murray's (1938) list of personality traits, the 20 needs. His definitions of the traits are couched in terms that apply mainly to human behavior, which has caused me to take certain liberties in assuming that certain of the traits are also seen in primates. Some of his traits have already appeared in Table 2.2 as part of our primate heritage: affiliation (sociability), aggression, autonomy, deference (submissiveness), dominance, play, and succorance (dependence). To these may be added Murray's exhibition, harm avoidance (fear?), nurturance, and sex, which I have not suggested as primate traits but may be.

The remainder of Murray's list would seem to be distinctly human personality traits: abasement (low self-esteem?), achievement, counteraction (reactance?), defendance, infavoidance (avoiding humiliation), order, rejection, sentience (sensation-seeking?), and understanding. With the benefit of hindsight, we can suggest that some of Murray's needs were not entirely appropriate as personality traits, but this is a minor issue. Of more interest in the present context is the appearance of 11 of Murray's traits on my list of primate personality traits.

HUMAN PERSONALITY

Distinctive Features

The evolution of our species involved the continuation of trends already occurring during primate evolution. The proportion of the lifespan occupied by childhood increased in primate evolution and continued to increase in human evolution. The ratio of brain size to body size, already large in primates, became larger in humans. And the freeing of the hands for manipulation, already begun in primates, was completed in our species. Though these features have implications for human personality, it is evolutionary changes in cognition and social behavior (the individual in relation to the group) that are crucial for the distinctively human aspects of personality. These evolutionary changes are best regarded as quantitative, not qualitative or unique (Mason, 1976). Thus, we know that chimpanzees are capable of rudimentary language (Gardner & Gardner, 1969), but our language capability is quantitatively greater. Of course, some quantitative differences are so large as to warrant being considered qualitative in impact. It would be tedious, however, to repeat quantitative comparisons with other primates, and for ease of exposition the more advanced human cognitions and social behavior will be discussed as though they were unique.

We are capable of complex and abstract concepts of the kind seen in religion and science. We make rules that govern how to speak and how to act in social situations; and we are good at following rules, knowing that it is less important whether one drives on the left or right side of the street, for example, than whether everyone abides by the rule.

Beyond curiousity about stimuli, we seek understanding of the world, a tendency that leads to religion and science. The search for understanding inevitably causes us to make attributions, generate hypotheses, and seek causes. We tend to construct ways of interpreting the world and are capable of operational intelligence and formal operations. We possess advanced imagery, which enables us to envision worlds that do not exist; animals have no ghosts, no heaven, no hell. When this imagery is harnessed to operational intelligence, we can plan far into the future. When dexterity is added, we can produce tools of great inventiveness.

We can leave behind the egocentricity of young children and animals to view the world from nonegocentric perspectives. Thus, an adult may adopt the perspective of a child, hunters the perspective of their prey, and a teacher the perspective of the learner. Animals can serve as models for their young, but we are the only species capable of teaching because of our perspective-taking. When the teaching is connected to language, we can pass on to future generations our knowledge and traditions. The cumulativeness of human knowledge and technology is one key to our continuing advances in mastering the environment, for the present generation may be as different technologically from primitive humans as they were from primates.

The evolution of social behavior has produced changes in the way individuals behave in a group. Blood relationships are known in a community, and relatives are expected to play roles dictated by tradition. A child knows its own family and clan; a father knows his own children. The incest taboo is universal. True social roles occur, determined mainly by age and gender but also by status and ability. Roles are linked to a division of labor, and cooperation is the rule, not the exception. Individuals are not limited to a single role, and their relationships are marked by flexible role-taking.

Goods are accumulated and owned by individuals, families, or clans. Goods are bartered, and individuals tend to develop a keen eye for value and potential value. Solitude is possible, so that individuals can escape from social interaction and focus attention inward.

All these social behaviors are linked with true socialization, which teaches the young the ways of their society. They learn about kinship, roles, status, and social rules. They learn the skills that allow them to escape from dependence on adults. They acquire a code of morality that is related to instrumental self-control. They are taught myths and heritage of the group, which enhance patriotism and group solidarity. And they may be encouraged to engage in empathy and altruism, especially in relation to kin.

Impact on Personality

These specifically human features have consequences for personality. A longer childhood, more socialization, true social roles, and the possibility of solitude and reflection combine to produce greater individuality. We vary along dimensions of ability that are distinctively human. These include individual differences in imagery, imagination, speaking and writing skills, music, art, and mathematics. Such abilities are not usually considered under the heading of personality, however, and I shall deal only with traditional personality traits.

Differentiation of Primate Traits

Primate traits are also present in humans, but several of them have differentiated into more specific dispositions that are present only in humans. The primate trait of jealousy, when combined with advanced cognitions, elaborates into the human traits of resentment and suspicion (Buss & Durkee, 1957). Sample items for resentment are "I don't seem to get what's coming to me" and "Almost every week I see someone I dislike," and for suspicion, "I know that people tend to talk about me behind my back" and "My motto is never trust strangers." The two sets of items load on a hostility factor.

Human language and a capacity for subtlety also open up the trait of aggressiveness (Buss, 1961). In addition to the physical aggressiveness seen in primates, there is also human verbal aggressiveness. In addition to primate active aggressiveness, there is the human passive aggressiveness called negativism. Sample items of verbal aggressiveness are "I often find myself disagreeing with people" and "When arguing, I tend to raise my voice;" examples of negativism are "When someone makes a rule I don't like, I am tempted to break it" and "When someone is bossy, I do the opposite of what he or she asks" (Buss & Durkee, 1957).

Successful aggression in primates leads to dominance over other animals. Given the economic and political nature of our species, dominance differentiates into power, which has been assessed by the Thematic Apperception Test (TAT) (Winter, 1973). TAT stories are scored for power if they deal with impact, control, or influence over others, a concern for reputation or status, or actions that ordinarily lead to power. Add planning and strategy, and another aspect of dominance in humans is Machiavellianism, one facet of which is attaining control and leadership even when one must resort to underhanded means (Christie & Geis, 1970).

The primate trait of submissiveness, which is shared by humans, involves knuckling under in personal confrontations. There is also a human derivative of submissiveness, derived from socialization, that welcomes control by a strong leader or those in a position of power. It is authoritarianism (Adorno,

Frenkel-Brunswik, Levinson, & Sanford, 1950), a sample item of which is "Obedience and respect for authority are the most important virtues children should learn."

Socialization training and expanded environmental opportunities also open up primate traits. Thus, the primate trait of competitiveness differentiates into the human trait of need achievement (McClelland, Atkinson, Clark, & Lowell, 1953). McClelland and colleagues have insisted that the trait could be assessed only by means of the TAT, but achievement has also been measured by self-report questionnaires. One such questionnaire (Jackson, Ahmed, & Heapy, 1976) yields three second-order achievement factors, each of which may be considered a trait: competitiveness (doing better than others), prestige-seeking (which is little different from power-seeking), and competence (striving for excellence).

There are variations among individual primates in confidence, dominant animals moving about as if they owned the world and submissive animals backing off as if they were unsure of themselves. When humans are confident, whether because they are dominant, achievers, or just sure of themselves, they are also high in self-esteem. Self-esteem, regarded in this light, is the cognitive-evaluative component of confidence in the only species capable of self-evaluation. Thus, primate confidence differentiates into human self-esteem. It is not clear how such differentiation evolved, but an anthropologist offers this speculation:

> I am now going to argue that natural selection has transformed our ancestors' general primate tendency to strive for high social rank into a need to maintain self-esteem.
> With the development of a sense of self, our ancestors' primate tendency would have been transformed. Having a self means that self-evaluation is possible. The social dominance imperative would have taken the form of an imperative to evaluate the self as higher in rank than others: *To evaluate the self as higher than others is to maintain self-esteem.* (Barkow, 1975, p. 554)

Socialization

Children are trained to assume social roles, follow social rules, and fit in with others in the group. These various aspects of socialization are taught more to some children than others and learned better by some children than others. One outcome is a set of personality traits related to socialization.

The concepts of masculine and feminine, as distinct from male and female gender, are exclusively human. There is variation from one society to the next in the clusters of personality traits labeled masculine and feminine. The most commonly used questionnaire of masculine and feminine traits is that of Spence and Helmreich (1978).

Children are taught a code of morality, especially a code of punishment for wrongdoing. Learning an adult code requires advanced cognitions; some people lack the intelligence, others are poorly taught, and others refuse to learn. These variations lead to individual differences in the maturity of one's knowledge and use of moral rules (Kohlberg & Kramer, 1969). Another aspect of morality involves altruism, which has three components or subtraits (Davis, 1983): perspective taking, being able to feel another's experiences via fantasy, and empathic concern for another's distress.

The rules of social behavior must also be learned, but people vary in manners, propriety, and the importance they attach to status. The personality trait is formality (L. Buss, 1984), and two sample items are "Conforming to established social conventions is the mark of a civilized person" and "I have a strong sense of what is proper behavior."

Cognition

The presence of advanced cognitive capabilities provides a fertile arena for individual differences that appear only in humans. There are numerous cognitive styles (see Goldstein & Blackman, 1978), too many to review here, so only two will be mentioned. The two best known cognitive styles are field dependence–independence or psychological differentiation (Witkin, Dyk, Faterson, Goodenough, & Karp, 1962) and the impulsive–reflective approach to solving matching-to-sample tasks (Kagan, Rosman, Day, & Phillips, 1964).

There are also individual differences in attribution, and the most prominent trait involves attribution of causality. The trait is locus of control (Rotter, 1960), which is treated as dichotomous: The events that occur are generated by internal, self-generated actions or by external, uncontrollable forces. The original simplicity of this disposition has been dissipated by the discovery that it comprises several factors (Collins, 1974; Mirels, 1970).

Locus of control represents a cognitive approach to individual differences in motivation. This approach has been expanded in the General Causality Orientation Scale (Deci & Ryan, 1985), which assesses the way people characterize the initiation and degree of self-determination of their behavior. Autonomy-oriented people assume that their behavior is self-determined, and they seek information that would allow them to make choices. Control-oriented people seek to relieve needs or to attain specific incentives and therefore are at the mercy of their motivational states. Impersonally-oriented people believe that they have no control over what happens and are therefore susceptible to learned helplessness. These three novel traits represent a promising way to deal with individual differences in personal causality and cognitions involving choice.

Recent developments in personality research have yielded two other cognitive traits. Openness to experience involves being interested in novelty, the arts, and one's own fantasies and feelings (McCrae & Costa, 1983). Intrinsic intellectuality means being motivated to discover knowledge for its own sake, in contrast to wanting to learn only "if it will be on the exam" (Lloyd & Barenblatt, 1984).

Self

Are primates or any other animals self-aware? It has been demonstrated that the great apes can recognize themselves in a mirror. When a chimpanzee has a red dot placed on its head and looks in the mirror, it tries to touch the marked area on its head (Gallup, 1970). Orangutans respond the same way. Gallup (1977) concludes, "To the extent that self-recognition implies a rudimentary concept of self, these data show that contrary to popular opinion and preconceived ideas, man may not have a monopoly on the self-concept. Man may not be evolution's only experiment in self-awareness" (p. 333). In attempting to explain why the great apes have mirror-image recognition but monkeys do not, Gallup (1977) suggests, "The monkey's inability to recognize himself may be due to the absence of a sufficiently well-integrated self-concept" (p. 334).

Humans, of course, are capable of mirror-image self-recognition, which develops during the second year of life, and by age of two years the majority of infants possess this capacity (Amsterdam, 1972; Schulman & Kaplowitz, 1977). Do infants have a self-concept, and are they capable of the same kind of self-awareness as older children and adults? These questions can be answered by considering attributes of older children and adults that are absent in infants.

The first is the presence of self-esteem. There is no evidence that before two years of age, infants have the capacity for self-evaluation, though no one doubts that the bases for later self-esteem are being established. Nor are infants clearly aware of the difference between private feelings and public behavior. They are still in the process of developing a sense of covertness that is seen in silent speech and an awareness that their private thoughts and feelings cannot be observed. Infants are still egocentric in perspective; they do not yet know that others perceive the world in different ways, and they cannot solve even the simple Piagetian perspective tasks.

Thus, there are three aspects of the self that develop after infancy: self-esteem, a sense of covertness, and perspective-taking. They constitute an advanced sense of self that must be distinguished from a primitive sense of self. The distinction can be maintained by labeling the advanced kind a "cognitive" self and the primitive kind a "sensory" self (Buss, 1980). Clearly, the great apes and human infants possess a sensory self, but I have seen no evidence of a cognitive self. The advanced, cognitive self is distinctively human, as are traits related to the cognitive self.

The trait of self-esteem is well known and apparently so generalized that all measures of it intercorrelate. A decade ago, two self-awareness traits were introduced (Fenigstein, Scheier, & Buss, 1975). Private self-consciousness refers to self-introspection, sample items being "I'm always trying to figure myself out" and "I'm generally attentive to my inner feelings." Public self-consciousness refers to oneself as a social object: "I'm concerned about what other people think of me" and "I'm self-conscious about the way I look." A recent addition was private body consciousness, which is related to private self-consciousness but different from it; sample items are "I can often feel my heart beating" and "I am sensitive to inner bodily tensions" (Miller, Murphy, & Buss, 1981).

There is a well-known questionnaire that assesses self-monitoring (Synder, 1974); sample items are, "when I am uncertain how to act in social situations, I look to the behavior of others for cues" and "I would probably make a good actor." The questionnaire is not unitary, however, and three factors have been extracted (Briggs, Cheek, & Buss, 1980): acting, extroversion, and other-directedness.

Erikson (1963) has popularized the concept of identity, an important aspect of the self. Individual differences have been measured in a structured interview designed to elicit the stages of identity status: diffusion, foreclosure, moratorium, and identity achievement (Marcia, 1966).

Social anxiety is a related trait involving intense consciousness of oneself as a social object. It has been assessed as a global trait (Fenigstein, Scheier, & Buss, 1974; Watson & Friend, 1969), and its two main components have been isolated. Thus, one social anxiety trait is speech anxiety; sample items of a recent questionnaire are "I always avoid speaking in public if possible" and "I feel extremely self-conscious while I am speaking in front of a group" (Slivken & Buss, 1984).

The other specific trait is shyness, which consists of tension, concern, and feelings of awkwardness and discomfort when with strangers or casual acquaintances, in contrast to sociability, which is the tendency to prefer being with others (Cheek & Buss, 1981). Shyness appears to consist of two subtraits, one involving self-consciousness and the other, anxiety (Buss, 1986). Self-conscious shyness cannot occur unless there is an advanced, cognitive self, that is, unless there is something to be self-conscious about. A reasonable developmental marker is the presence of embarrassment, which begins for most children in the fourth or fifth year of life (Buss, Iscoe, & Buss, 1979). Anxious shyness develops during the first year of life and tends to be labeled stranger anxiety. It is not limited to humans and may be seen in a variety of animals in the form of wariness and caution in approaching strange animals or humans. Thus, anxious shyness is part of our evolutionary heritage, but self-conscious shyness is distinctively human.

Summary of Human Personality Traits

Distinctively human traits are listed in Table 2.4.[5] Not all human traits are included. Nor is the list intended as a formal taxonomy, if indeed such a classification were possible or useful at present. Rather, the list simply summarizes the traits that derive from two crucial human features: advanced cognitions and socialization. The four categories are not exclusive. Thus, self-esteem is listed as a differentiated primate trait, but it is also a self trait (though not listed to avoid redundancy). Some of the differentiated primate traits are products of socialization—need achievement and authoritarianism, for example. And all the self traits involve cognitions. The value of the table resides in its demonstrating the constrast between human and primate traits.

Primate traits, it will be recalled, consist of temperaments and acquired traits, the latter being mainly social traits. As Table 2.4 shows, social traits comprise a minority of distinctively human dispositions. Primate social traits also occur in humans, but when cognitions and socialization are added, the primate social traits differentiate into distinctively human traits. Thus, human aggressiveness can be verbal or passive; dominance may take the form of seeking power or trying to gain the upper hand by being Machiavellian; submissiveness may be seen as seeking strong leadership and demanding comformity to it (authoritarianism), and competitiveness may show up in modified form as need achievement.

Primates have a rudimentary socialization, but human socialization is necessarily more complete and complex to prepare children for the diverse roles and relationships of human societies. The social roles of humans are reflected in the masculine and feminine traits that are stereotyped in each culture. Social behavior is dominated by rules, and there are individual differences in the extent to which these rules affect behavior, as reflected in the traits of morality, altruism, and formality. Children are also encouraged to have tender feelings for others, which yields the trait of empathy.

Human cognitive abilities allow for variations in cognitive styles (field dependence–independence and reflection–impulsivity), attributions of causality (locus of control), approach to potentially controlling events (auton-omous-, control-, and impersonally-oriented), and intellectual curiosity (openness to experience and intrinsic intellectuality). Cognitive abilities also

---

[5]It might be argued that some of the traits listed as distinctively human are so regarded merely because they cannot be reliably observed in primates or perhaps because observers have not thought to look for them. These are possibilities, of course, and to the extent that they are true, some of the traits now listed as distinctively human would become primate personality traits. Such a revision of the current formulation would be entirely in keeping with the evolutionary approach that underlies it. On the other hand, we need to be aware of the dangers of anthropomorphizing and also that we are different from other primates in important ways, including personality traits.

Table 2.4 Distinctively human personality traits

Differentiated primate traits
    Jealousy → resentment, suspicion
    Aggression → physical vs. verbal, active vs. passive aggressive
    Dominance → power, Machiavellianism
    Submissiveness → authoritarianism
    Competitiveness → need achievement
    Confidence → self-esteem
Products of socialization
    Masculinity, femininity
    Morality
    Altruism, empathy
    Formality
Cognitive traits
    Field dependence–independence
    Reflective–impulsive
    Locus of control
    Autonomous-, control-, impersonally-oriented
    Openness to experience
    Intrinsic intellectuality
Self
    Private, public self-consciousness
    Body consciousness
    Self-monitoring
    Identity
    Social anxiety
    Speech anxiety
    (self-conscious) shyness

establish the necessary condition for an advanced self, which provides the basis for the traits of self-esteem, two kinds of self-consciousness, self-monitoring, identity, and the social anxieties.

EVOLUTIONARY PERSPECTIVE

The present framework suggests that we examine the animal heritage of human personality. The first step is to identify primate personality traits and personality-relevant features that primates share with other mammals—individual differences in activity and emotionality, for example. As highly social mammals, primates possess low arousal, social emotions (love, elation, sadness), which are barely evident or absent in nonsocial mammals. And compared to other mammals, primates tend to be more curious, manipulative, imitative, and cognitively advanced, and they tend to have single births and a relatively long childhood.

This focus on our animal heritage culminates in an examination of the personality determinants that occur during infancy and the juvenile era among primates, the outcome being a set of primate traits that overlap many human interpersonal traits (see Table 2.1). Such commonality immediately extends the domain of personality to include other species. Are the developmental origins of these traits the same in humans as in primates? The answer would seem to be "yes" for many of the traits, for we share with primates the developmental events of mother–infant attachment, social bonds with peers, and struggles for power. If the developmental origins of the shared traits are common to humans and other species, there are two consequences: (1) our explanations apply to more than our own species, and (2) explanations that involve peculiarly human features—advanced cognitions and human culture, for example—would have to be discarded for this set of traits. Any theorist who insisted on a separate explanation for the human traits that are shared with primates would require new evidence to make the case.

Comparing primate and human personality traits is a two-way street. Emotionality, activity, and sociability have been shown to have an inherited basis in humans, but are these temperaments also inherited in primates? There is only tentative evidence for the inheritance of emotionality in rhesus monkeys (Suomi, 1982) and no evidence for activity or sociability. If these three traits turn out to be inherited in primates, it would suggest a continuity in the evolution of humans from a primate ancestor. If not, there would be a discontinuity, and our species would suddenly have evolved three inherited traits that are present but not inherited in closely related species.

When primate and human features and traits are compared, we can distinguish between two kinds of distinctively human traits: those that have differentiated from traits already present in primates and those that are absent in primates. We can discern traits deriving from advanced cognitions, traits involving the self, and traits emerging from specific kinds of socialization.

For personality, the crucial features that mark humans as different appear to be advanced cognitions and being socialized to live in a society that is also distinctively human. Neither feature is present in infants, who have not yet developed advanced cognitions or been exposed to significant socialization. It follows that human infants may be regarded as possessing only primate personality traits and no distinctively human traits.

Finally, the evolutionary perspective offers a crude but meaningful classification of extant personality traits. There are two kinds of traits shared by primates and humans. One set is inherited: temperaments. The other set originates in the social conditions common to most primates: the mother–infant attachment and peer relationships during the juvenile period. And there are two kinds of distinctively human traits. One set is differentiated or elaborated from traits already present in primates so that their similarities are obvious—primate confidence and human self-esteem, for example. The second, larger set consists of cognitive traits, self-related traits, and traits that originate in socialization practices. Thus, the classification is a preliminary attempt to cluster personality traits on the basis of their evolutionary or developmental origin, which also implies a rationale for the existence of these traits.

REFERENCES

Adorno, T. W., Frenkel-Brunswik, E., Levinson, D. J., & Sanford, R. N. (1950). *The authoritarian personality.* New York: Harper & Row.

Amsterdam, B. (1972). Mirror self-image reactions before the age of two. *Developmental Psychology, 5,* 297–305.

Barkow, J. H. (1975). Prestige and culture: A biosocial interpretation. *Current Anthropology, 16,* 553–572.

Bridges, K. (1932). Emotional development in early infancy. *Child Development, 2,* 324–341.

Briggs, S. R., Cheek, J. M., & Buss, A. H. (1980). An analysis of the self-monitoring scale. *Journal of Personality and Social Psychology, 38,* 679–686.

Buss, A. H. (1961). *The psychology of aggression.* New York: Wiley.

Buss, A. H. (1980). *Self-consciousness and social anxiety.* San Francisco: Freman.

Buss, A. H. (1983). Social rewards and personality. *Journal of Personality and Social Psychology, 44,* 553–563.

Buss, L. (1984). A personality measure of formality. Unpublished research, University of California, Berkeley.

Buss, A. H. (1986). Two kinds of shyness. In R. Schwarzer (Ed.), *Anxiety and self-related cognitions* (pp. 65–75). Hillsdale, NJ: Erlbaum Associates.

Buss, A. H., & Durkee, A. (1957). An inventory for assessing different kinds of hostility. *Journal of Consulting Psychology, 21,* 343–349.

Buss, A. H., Iscoe, I., & Buss, E. H. (1979). The development of embarrassment. *Journal of Psychology, 103,* 227–230.

Buss, A. H., & Plomin, R. (1975). *A temperament theory of personality development.* New York: Wiley-Interscience.

Buss, A. H., & Plomin, R. (1984). *Temperament: Early developing personality traits.* Hillsdale, NJ: Erlbaum Associates.

Chamove, A. S., Eysenck, H. J., & Harlow, H. (1972). Personality in monkeys: Factor analysis of rhesus social behavior. *Quarterly Journal of Experimental Psychology, 24,* 496–504.

Cheek, J., & Buss, A. H. (1981). Shyness and sociability. *Journal of Personality and Social Psychology, 41,* 330–339.

Christie, R., & Geis, F. L. (Eds.). (1970). *Studies in Machiavellianism.* New York: Academic Press.

Collins, B. E. (1974). Four components of the Rotter Internal-External scale: Belief in a difficult world, a just world, a predictable world, and a politically responsive world. *Journal of Personality and Social Psychology, 29,* 381–391.

Davis, H. (1983). Measuring individual differences in empathy: Evidence for a multidimensional approach. *Journal of Personality and Social Psychology, 44*, 113–126.

de Waal, F. (1982). *Chimpanzee politics.* New York: Harper & Row.

Deci, E. L., & Ryan, R. M. (1985). *Intrinsic motivation and self-determination in human behavior.* New York: Plenum.

Erikson, E. H. (1963). *Childhood and society* (2nd ed.). New York: Norton.

Fenigstein, A., Scheier, M. F., & Buss, A. H. (1975). Public and private self-consciousness: Assessment and theory. *Journal of Consulting and Clincal Psychology, 43*, 522–527.

Gallup, G. G., Jr. (1970). Chimpanzees: Self-recognition. *Science, 167*, 86–87.

Gallup, G. G., Jr. (1977). Self-recognition in primates: A comparative approach to the bidirectional properties of consciousness. *American Psychologist, 32*, 329–338.

Gardner, R. A., & Gardner, B. T. (1969). Teaching sign language to a chimpanzee. *Science, 165*, 664–672.

Goldstein, K. M., & Blackman, S. (1978). *Cognitive style.* New York: Wiley-interscience.

Goodall, J. (1971). *In the shadow of man.* Boston: Houghton Mifflin.

Harlow, H. F., & Harlow, M. K. (1962). Social deprivation in monkeys. *Scientific American, 207*, 136–146.

Harlow, H. F., Harlow, M. K., & Hansen, E. W. (1963). The maternal affectional system of monkeys. In H. L. Rheingold (Ed.), *Maternal behavior in mammals* (pp. 254–281). New York: Wiley.

Jackson, D. N., Ahmed, S. A., & Heapy, N. A. (1976). Is achievement a unitary construct? *Journal of Research in Personality, 10*, 1–21.

Kagan, J., Rosman, B. D., Day, J. A., & Phillips, W. (1964). Information processing in the child: Significance of analytic and reflective attitudes. *Psychological Monographs, 78*.

Kellogg, W. N., & Kellogg, L. A. (1933). *The ape and the child.* New York: McGraw-Hill.

Kiesler, D. J. (1983). The 1982 interpersonal circle: A taxonomy for complementarity in human transactions. *Psychological Review, 90*, 185–214.

Kohlerg, L., & Kramer, R. (1969). Continuities and discontinuities in childhood and adult moral development. *Human Development, 12*, 93–120.

Lacey, J. I. (1956). The evaluation of autonomic responses: Toward a general solution. *Annals of the New York Academy of Science, 67*, 123–163.

Lancaster, J. B. (1975). *Primate behavior and the emergence of human culture.* New York: Holt, Rinehart, & Winston.

Lloyd, J., & Barenblatt, L. (1984). Intrinsic intellectuality: Its relation to social class, intelligence, and achievement. *Journal of Personality and Social Psychology, 46*, 646–654.

Lynn, R. (1966). *Attention, arousal, and the orientation reaction.* Oxford: Pergamon Press.

Marcia, J. E. (1966). Development and validation of ego identity status. *Journal of Personality and Social Psychology, 3*, 551–558.

Mason, W. A. (1970). Motivational factors in psychosocial development. In U. J. Arnold & N. M. Page (Eds.), *Nebraska symposium on motivation.* Lincoln, NE: University of Nebraska Press.

Mason, W. A. (1976). Environmental models and mental modes: Representational processes in the great apes and man. *American Psychologist, 31*, 284–294.

McClelland, D. C., Atkinson, J. W., Clark, R. A., & Lowell, E. L. (1953). *The achievement motive*. Englewood Cliffs, NJ: Prentice-Hall.

McCrae, R. R., & Costa, P. T., Jr. (1983). Joint factors in self-reports and ratings: Neuroticism, extraversion, and openness to experience. *Personality and Individual Differences, 4*, 245–255.

Miller, L. C., Murphy, R., & Buss, A. H. (1981). Consciousness of body: Private and public. *Journal of Personality and Social Psychology, 41*, 397–406.

Mirels, H. L. (1970). Dimensions of internal versus external control. *Journal of Consulting and Clinical Psychology, 34*, 226–228.

Murray, H. A. (1938). *Explorations in personality*. New York: Oxford.

Rotter, J. B. (1960). Generalized expectancies for internal versus external control of reinforcement. *Psychological Monographs, 80*.

Schulman, A. H., & Kaplowitz, L. (1977). Mirror-image response during the first two years of life. *Developmental Psychology, 10*, 133–142.

Slivken, K. E., & Buss, A. H. (1984). Misattributions and speech anxiety. *Journal of Personality and Social Psychology, 47*, 396–402.

Snyder, M. (1974). The self-monitoring of expressive behavior. *Journal of Personality and Social Psychology, 30*, 526–537.

Spence, J. T., & Helmreich, R. L. (1978). *Masculinity and femininity: Their psychological dimensions, correlates and antecedents*. Austin, TX: University of Texas Press.

Stevenson-Hinde, J., Stillwell-Barnes, R., & Zung, M. (1980). Subjective assessment of rhesus monkeys over four successive years. *Primates, 21*, 66–82.

Suomi, S. J. (1982, October). *Consequences of differences in reactivity to stress*. Paper presented at Temperament Conference, Salem, MA.

Watson, D., & Friend, R. (1969). Measurement of social-evaluative anxiety. *Journal of Consulting and Clinical Psychology, 33*, 448–457.

Wiggins, J. S. (1979). A psychological taxonomy of trait-descriptive terms: The interpersonal domain. *Journal of Personality and Social Psychology, 37*, 395–412.

Wilson, E. O. (1975). *Sociobiology*. Cambridge, MA: Harvard University Press.

Winter, D. G. (1973). *The power motive*. New York: Free Press.

Witkin, H. A., Dyk, R. B., Faterson, H. F., Goodenough, D. R., & Karp, S. A. (1962). *Psychological differentiation*. New York: Wiley.

Wood, J. H. (1984). The evolutionary relationships of man and orangutans. *Nature, 308*, 501–505.

Yerkes, R. M. (1943). *Chimpanzees*. New Haven, CT: Yale University Press.

3

Personality and Experience: Individual Encounters with the World

Sandra Scarr

Two metaphors for personality can be found in "the bad seed" and "the blank slate." The themes of emergent but preestablished personality versus the tabula rasa have infected debates over the ages about how personality differences come to be. In a version of the nature/nurture debate, personality theory has not been spared the crazy Cartesian dualism that pits mind against body, environments against genes, human against animal, and generally makes a mess of our thinking. In this chapter, I address issues of theory and research on the genetic bases of personality and the role of experience in its development. The theory avoids, I pray, the pitfalls of our Cartesian heritage.

There are many legitimate questions that can be asked about personality; fortunately for the reader I do not intend to address them all. One can ask questions at several levels of analysis (see Scarr, 1985) from proximal to distal, from mechanistic (efficient) to evolutionary (final) causes. This chapter will address the questions, "Why do people differ in personality?" and "How do differences in personality arise?" These questions are best addressed by research on the sources of variation in personality (an evolutionary focus) and the developmental events that shape life courses (distal as well as proximal causes). In my opinion, research on personality in recent years has focused too often on immediate situational variation, which has little to say about individual personality as coherent ways of being and doing that develop across the lifespan.

Thus, I will not describe relationships among personality variables, nor relationships of personality to other variables, such as intelligence, interests, or success in occupations. I will not deal with the structure of personality, as several other contributions to this volume do, nor with a comparative perspective on primate personality. Rather, I will focus on how people come to develop individuality in their personal ways of being and doing, across time and space. This chapter will explore what is known about sources of individuality in personality and propose a theory to account for the individuality of persons as responders, evokers, and selectors of their own experiences.

Murray puzzled and thought for many years about the unique ways human beings deal with their lives, about the enduring stories they tell themselves and others to account for their behaviors. Above all, Murray was concerned with individuality—that unique configuration of needs each of us has and presses to which each responds. Each of us is unique in the patterning of our needs and presses, creating a complexity that only a few investigators have been able to comprehend. Surely, Murray was not only able to comprehend such complexity but relished it. He was challenged by personal myths and by myths grown large, as in *Moby Dick*. I like to think that the year I spent working with him has influenced my thinking ever since. He taught me to respect scientific methods of investigation but to be dubious of personality theories and research that do not focus on individuality. In my field, developmental psychology, I have never found reason to doubt his wisdom.

WHAT'S A NICE GIRL LIKE YOU DOING IN A PLACE LIKE THIS?

My own interest in personality began naturally in adolescence when, like most teenagers, I pondered my own becoming. Intent on studying psychology, and especially personality, I entered Vassar, only to find that psychology consisted of conditioned eyeblinks, rats running mazes, and memory drums. Even then I was appalled. Clark Hull and Yale were unfortunately only 75 miles from Vassar, and it showed in the curriculum. Undaunted, I postponed my interest in psychology and majored in sociology and anthropology. At least the traditions of Emil Durkheim, Talcott Parsons, Ruth Benedict, and Margaret Mead spoke to the human condition. The late 1950s were intellectually rich for the social sciences, which had emerged from the Depression and the Second World War with confidence in their enterprise.

I was fascinated by ideas of cultural and social variation in human behavior, but the explanations of individual differences were never satisfying. How could it be that individuals varied so much on every dimension of behavior (I merely observed this as a youth), yet sociological and anthropological concepts dealt only with group differences? There must be something more to the determinants of human behavior than social class, cultural mores, and linguistic customs.

My father, being a medical researcher, believed in biology and in biological differences. I am not sure that he knew much about genetics—at least I do not recall discussing genetics with him—but he knew that social conditions did not determine everything about individuality. After all, he had two children who were quite different. From this radical (or reactionary, if you wish) background, I challenged my professors with ideas about individual differences. I was told in no uncertain terms that genetics had nothing to do with individual differences. The social science cant of the day prohibited any thought that people could be biologically different.

After graduating with distress and honors, I decided to work for a couple of years before contemplating further education. It was hard to imagine that further training in the social sciences or in psychology as I knew it was going to address my interests. For the first postbaccalaureate year, I worked in a Family Service agency that kindly sent me part-time to graduate school in social work. That experience convinced me forever that I did not want to deliver services to people. The next year I worked as a research assistant to a social psychologist, Carmi Schooler, at the National Institute of Mental Health. Research on the social behaviors of chronic schizophrenics gave me the first opportunity to explore what being a human psychologist could be. More importantly, Carmi gave me the courage to seek a more suitable place in psychology.

I applied to Stanford, Yale, and Harvard. At the moment, I am not sure why. After interviews at Yale Psychology and Harvard Social Relations Departments, it was obvious that I had found a home at Harvard. Despite blatant sexism, the faculty represented my ideal mixture of human psychology, sociology, and anthropology. Life in Social Relations was heady. The personality program, where I was enrolled, had its headquarters at 5 and 7 Divinity Avenue, the homes of David McClelland and Henry A. Murray, respectively. I worked in both places, and with the Whitings at Palfrey House. I switched to developmental psychology and did a dissertation with Irving Gottesman in clinical psychology and behavior genetics. Ever the eager multidisciplinarian (perhaps more accurately, the dilettante), I *loved* the experience of multiple perspectives from population genetics to cultural anthropology—passionately.

Before earning a Ph.D., I committed the then sin of marrying and having a baby in my third year of graduate school (a well-planned but notorious event that signaled the end of professors' support for my career). Although I got the Ph.D. in 4.2 years, I was written off as a Mother. To make a 20-year story short, I have overcome.

My four children have taught me most of what I know about individuality. Rearing four children is an intense and intimate experience with genetically different people, who evoke different parenting. Their environments are different because they are different, yet as a parent one can see that all of these variations in disciplinary techniques, rewards, and relationship are within one's parental repertory. Parenthood is a truly fascinating human psychology in action. Parenting more than one child raises issues that psychology has largely ignored. Murray did not ignore such issues; he cherished them.

IGNORING INDIVIDUALITY

We have to admit that the study of personality, and particularly Murray's brand of personology, has been a sideline activity in psychology. In fact, concern with individual differences in general has been relegated to the more applied fields, such as clinical and school psychology, where individual cases actually matter. The historical roots of this neglect of individual and species variability are not hard to find: They resulted from the rejection of evolutionary theory by the founders of experimental psychology, who came to be more influential in the English-speaking world than the followers of an evolutionary view.

In the nineteenth century, there was a fight between advocates of models of mind drawn from evolutionary theory and those drawn from physics. Unfortunately for personality research, the experimental physicalists won on the principle of parsimony: If the animal mind could be explained on the basis of simpler rather than more complex processes, the simpler explanation was to be preferred (Boakes, 1984). Parsimony is the greatest reductionist scam of all time. The legacies of parsimony are the general, now discredited, laws of learning and a research tradition that considers only those processes so general to mammalian species that even a rat can learn it under deprived rearing conditions. Whatever the religiously motivated metaphysics of that tradition, it is clearly inappropriate to our understanding of animal behavior today and inapplicable to the study of individual variation in human personality.

We still suffer a nostalgia for simplicity, even if such simplicity masks and distorts species and individual variation in patterns of being and doing, which are the heart of personality. The contemporary residue of the physical tradition in the study of human behavior is a preference for the simplest models that toss individual differences into the trashbin of error terms and fail to account for more than a trivial portion of personality variation. Most often group differences are the focus of investigations; for example, sex differences in aggression, age differences in identity, and all sorts of family and other so-called environmental classifications crossed with average differences between groups.

If the developmental psychology literature on personality were to be read literally, one would think that investigators have theories with only main effects. That is, environmental agents or events hypothesized to influence personality development are supposed to act on everyone in the same way. Children who have been through divorce, had unemployed parents, were abused, or reared by authoritarian methods are said to have unfavorable personality outcomes from those experiences. Children from intact homes, with employed parents, not abused, and reared by authoritative methods develop more adaptive personalities, *because* of their more favorable rearing experiences.

Actually, most intelligent investigators do not believe that such theores of main effects answer all questions about personality development. They recognize that their results apply to groups who differ *on average* and that within every group there is more individual variation than there is mean variation between groups. Developmentalists may even acknowledge informally that they try to predict average differences between groups, variously defined, because that is the only variance that their theories *can* predict. They may not recognize, however, how very small a portion of the total personality variance is actually addressed by theories with main effects.

SIBLINGS AND STRANGERS

Let me illustrate the problem of accounting for individuality with data from family studies of personality. Studies of sibling similarities and differences reveal that siblings, reared together all of their lives and sharing about half of their genes, are barely more similar on personality inventories than randomly paired members of the same population. Adopted children are slightly less similar than biological siblings and little more similar than randomly paired members of the population.

The typical sibling correlation for self-report personality measures is about 0.20 (Ahern, Johnson, Wilson, McClearn, & Vandenberg, 1982; Carey & Rice, 1983; Grotevant, 1978; Grotevant, Scarr, & Weinberg, 1977; Loehlin, Horn, & Willerman, 1981; Rowe & Plomin, 1981; Scarr, Webber, Weinberg, & Wittig, 1981). If the personality correlation between biological siblings is 0.20 and the standard deviation of the personality measure is 4.5, which is typical of the measures used in these studies, then the average absolute difference between siblings is 4.54 points on the scales, a difference of one standard deviation. This value is calculated by a general formula that assumes a normal distribution, an assumption that is met by IQ and personality scales (Jensen, 1980, p. 459).

$$/\bar{d}/ = (2\sigma\sqrt{1-r}/\sqrt{\pi})$$

where $/\bar{d}/$ is the average absolute difference between siblings' scores, σ is the standard deviation of the scores, r is the correlation between the siblings, and π is 3.1416.

Given that randomly paired people in the population have scores that are not correlated, their average difference is 5.08 points, compared to the sibling difference of 4.54 points—hardly a *jnd* on a personality scale.

Adopted adolescent siblings, reared together since infancy, have negligible correlations (median = 0.07) on the same personality scales, so that their average difference of 4.90 points is close to that of the general population.

To quote myself from an earlier discussion of these surprising findings:

> Lest the reader slip over these results, let us make explicit the implications of these findings: Upper middle class brothers who attend the same schools and whose parents take them to the same plays, sporting events, music lessons, and therapists, and who use similar child rearing practices on them are little more similar in personality measures than they are to working class or farm boys, whose lives are totally different. (Scarr & Grajek, 1982, p. 361)

Brothers and sisters who have had objectively similar experiences with divorce, parental unemployment, abuse, and authoritarian childrearing practices (or lack of same) do not turn out to have similar personalities. If the siblings are unrelated but reared together, there is a 3.6% reduction in their average difference over randomly paired people. If the siblings are genetically related, there is an 11% reduction in their differences—statistically significant in most studies but not very impressive. Somehow, there is a mismatch between the nature of personality theories and the data about individuality.

TRIVIALIZING INDIVIDUALITY

Most standard psychological and sociological concepts about families represent environments that siblings share and that therefore *cannot* account for the vast differences among them. Parental occupations, parental beliefs about childrearing, parental education and intelligence, family size, rural/ urban residence, income, and so forth are measures of characteristics that are common to all children in the family. If the goal of the research is to explain individual differences in personality, the theories do not even contain concepts that can address the majority of the variance to be explained.

Unfortunately, investigators do not always make clear what variance they are attempting to explain. A prime example of this confusion between group and individual variances is found in the birth-order literature. Ironically, theories about the effects of sibling constellations (birth order, age spacing, age, and sex of siblings) are the only well-developed theories of individual differences between siblings (Scarr & Grajek, 1982). The confluence model (Zajonc & Markus, 1975; Zajonc, Markus, & Markus, 1979) is the only operational model that has attempted prediction of sibling IQ scores by a set of constellation variables, most notably birth order. The spectacular model fits in regression models of IQ on birth order are achieved with *average* IQ scores for thousands of young men at each birth order. Thus, the model eliminates individuality by averaging out all other sources of individual differences.

In models of family constellation variables fit to *individual* IQ values, birth order accounts for 2% to 4% of the total IQ variation (Brackbill & Nichols, 1983; Galbraith, 1982; Grotevant, Scarr, & Weinberg, 1977). Thus, the confluence model can account for 90+% of 2% to 4% of the individual IQ variation. Whoopee! In personality variation, even the confluence model cannot make claims, as the world's literature shows no association between birth order or any other sibling constellation variables and personality variation (Ernst & Angst, 1983).

One crafty strategy to produce seemingly impressive results is the universal practice in developmental psychology of studying only one member per family and attributing the results to differences in parenting practices or other parental characteristics. On the face of it, attributing causality to environments that are shared by siblings but that differ among families would seem to require a test of within- versus between-family models. So far, investigators have largely escaped the logical consequences of this non sequitur. Of course, investigators of personality variation in college sophomores and police recruits are also guilty of sampling one child per family, but they less often attribute personality variation back to the parental environment. The variance they seem to want to account for is a small portion of the total variance, anyway. Again, these studies account for only tiny fractions of the total personality variation.

A Morality Tale: An old tale about the drunk and the lost coin has him looking for the coin on the pavement in the light cast by a street lamp, even though he knows the coin is lost somewhere in the dark alley. When asked why he is looking on the pavement if he knows the coin is in the alley, he replies that's where he can see.

And so it is, I fear, with research on individual differences in personality; we explore those places where our theories illuminate the terrain, and not the dark areas where the important data lie but where there are no ideas to light the search. If you are now persuaded that most of the variance in personality can be found *within* families (that is, among siblings), why then do we study variation *between* families? The problem is that we have no adequate theories about the causes of individuality among members of the same family. There is no light to guide the search, even if we know the coin is there. At this time, however, some investigators are trying to find a light for the sources of individuality.

YOUR PARENTS AREN'T MY PARENTS, BROTHER

Although most investigators would agree that siblings experience somewhat different environments when growing up in the same family, there is little theory to guide research on the critical features of those environmental differences. Rowe and Plomin (1981) reviewed the causes of environmental variation among siblings and classified them into five types: accidental factors of each sibling's experiences, like Bandura's (1982) random experiences; sibling interaction in which each affects the other; family compositions; differential parental treatment; and extrafamiliar sources, such as teachers, peers, and TV. The correlation between any one of these potential sources of sibling differences and any behavioral difference is very small, however. Even more discouraging is their finding that no common environmental factor can be extracted to account for more than a tiny fraction of the vast behavioral differences that siblings display on all behavioral measures.

Rather than despair, Rowe and Plomin (1981) and Scarr and McCartney (1983) advise that understanding how family environments affect individual members will require behavior genetic designs with more than one sibling per family and more than one degree of genetic relatedness. Recent research on siblings perceptions of family relations and parental treatment (Daniels & Plomin, in press) shows that children in the same families perceive different parental treatment, especially in affection and to a lesser extent in control. There are "his" and "her" parents, just as there are "his" and "her" marriages.

Of course, research on children's perceptions of family treatment and relations is just one way to examine within-family effects. We have not yet begun to explore how differences in family environments, measured by an observer, relate to personality differences. Nor have we considered seriously the possibility (in my mind, the probability) that differences in parental treatment are instead largely caused by differences in children's personalities or by the match or mismatch between parental and child characteristics (Buss & Plomin, 1984; Scarr, 1985; Thomas & Chess, 1977).

Parents may be differentially responsive to their children, depending on the children's characteristics and depending on the flexibility of parents in dealing with children of different temperaments (Bugenthal & Shennum,

1984). Some "difficult" children may be hard for most parents to foster to normal personality development, while other "easy" children in the same families may escape parental irrascibility and despair (Plomin & Daniels, 1984), but corroborating data are hard to find (Daniels, Plomin, & Greenhalgh, 1984).

Children are also likely to differ in the degree of their vulnerability (Garmezy, 1983) to environmental pressures, making parental treatment more of an issue for some children than others. For all of these reasons, family environments need to be conceptualized in finer grain than is now the mode (Wachs, 1983; Wachs & Gruen, 1982). And, more importantly, children need to be conceptualized as providing different events for parental treatment and as being differentially responsive to those treatments.

Behavior Genetic Challenges to Personality Theory

Seemingly unbeknownst to most personality researchers, behavior geneticists who study personality have arrived at a startling concensus about two major points:

1. The heritable portion of personality variation is a modest but demonstrable 25% to 40% of the total variance.
2. Most of the nonerror variance in personality is due to *individual experiences*—those not shared by members of the same family, neighborhood, or social class—and therefore unaccounted for by any contemporary theory of personality.

The basis for estimations of heritable variation in personality is twin and family studies of parents and children (genetic $r = 0.50$), brothers and sisters who are related as identical twins (genetic $r = 1.00$), as fraternal twins and ordinary siblings (genetic $r = 0.50$), and as adopted siblings (genetic $r = 0.00$). Assuming that all of the members of families have been reared together and that there is little assortative mating between parents for personality traits, the formula for calculating the heritability of personality measures in the population is straightforward:

$$h^2 = 2 (r_{ia} - r_{ib})$$

where h is the estimate of heritability based on the comparison of r_{ia} for pairs of persons genetically related by 1.00 and r_{ib} for pairs related by 0.5 , or r_{ia} for pairs genetically related by 0.5 and r_{ia} for pairs genetically unrelated, 0.0.

Each comparison controls for environmental similarity (for twins, see Scarr & Carter-Saltzman, 1980; for adoptees, see Scarr, Scarf, & Weinberg, 1980) and estimates half of the genetic variance; hence, the multiplier. If there is significant assortative mating for personality (as in Buss, 1985), adjustments can be made in the multiplier to reflect the lower genetic variance within the family and the greater genetic variance between families.

Comparisons of family resemblances can also take differences in rearing environments into account, as when identical twins (MZs) reared apart are compared to MZs reared together. From comparisons of family resemblances by genetic and environmental relatedness, models can be fit to estimate the degree of genetic and environmental variability in personality measurements. Furthermore, the genetic and environmental components of variance can be divided into within- and between-family components to reflect the degree to which assortative mating and common rearing environments affect the sources of personality variation in the population.

Twins and Siblings, Together and Apart

In a previous paper (Scarr & McCartney, 1983), we reviewed evidence about how monozygotic (MZ) twins come to be more similar than dizygotic (DZ) twins, and biological siblings more similar than adopted siblings on nearly all measurable characteristics, at least by the end of adolescence (Scarr & Weinberg, 1978). We also reviewed the evidence on the unexpected similarities of MZ twins reared in different homes. All of these data can be fit nicely to our theory of declining family influences and increasing individuality.

Representative findings from twin and family studies of personality are presented in Table 3.1. Twin and sibling resemblances on typical personality scales show a pattern that parallels their genetic resemblance. Minor var-

TABLE 3.1 Correlations of twins and siblings for personality test scores in late adolescence

	Twins			Siblings	
	MZ together	MZ apart	DZ	Biological	Adopted
Genetic correlation	1.00	1.00	0.50	0.50	0.00
Personality scale					
Introversion–extraversion	0.52	0.61	0.25	0.20	0.07
Neuroticism	0.52	0.55	0.22	0.28	0.05
Impulsivity	0.48	—	0.29	0.20	0.05
Median	0.52[a]	0.65[b]	0.25[a]	0.20[c]	0.07[c]

[a]27 CPI scales from Nichols (1978).
[b]11 DPQ scales from Bouchard (1984) and EPI scales from Shields (1962).
[c]EPI, DPQ, and APQ scales from Scarr, Webber, Weinberg, and Wittig (1981).

iations on the genetic pattern are apparent in the slightly higher correlations of DZ twins than ordinary siblings (but then twins are the same ages when tested) and the slightly higher correlations of MZ twins raised in different homes than those reared in the same home. What, you ask? Twins reared *apart* have more similar personality scores than twins reared *together?*

For laypeople, the most fascinating results are the unexpectedly great similarities between identical twins reared in different homes. Bouchard (1981, 1984) and colleagues have reported on the personality resemblance of their sample of 30 pairs of adult identical twins reared apart for most or all of their lives. They find, as did Shields (1962) before them, that identical twins reared largely apart are *at least as similar* in personality as identical twins reared together. The correlations on multiple personality scales, including the MMPI, the CPI, and the DPQ average 0.65. In fact, twins reared apart in both studies have slightly greater correlations on personality tests than those reared together. The reason for this seems to be an environmental press on MZs to develop individuality when reared together (Hopper & Culross, 1983). When reared apart, of course, there is no press for contrast or differentiation to deter them from their genotypic similarity in responsiveness to their environments.

In contrast to the considerable similarity of identical twins reared apart or together, fraternal or DZ twins are little more similar than ordinary siblings. The average personality correlation of DZ twins is 0.25 and for siblings 0.20. For adopted siblings, rearing from the early months after birth to adolescence results in a median correlation of 0.07 on personality scales.

There is a range of values for heritabilities calculated from the twin and family data. If the MZs reared in different homes are compared to the genetically unrelated adopted siblings reared in the same home, the comparison is between individuals with all of their genes but none of their rearing environment in common and individuals with none of their genes but all of their rearing environment in common. The difference in their correlations is an estimate of heritability (0.60 − 0.07 = 0.53).

The comparison of identical (MZ) and fraternal (DZ) median correlations of 0.52 and 0.25, respectively, yields a heritability coefficient of 0.54. So far so good. By contrast, the comparison of the biological with adopted siblings' median correlations yields an estimated heritability of only 0.26. How can this be? Others in addition to myself (Carey & Rice, 1983) have pondered the discrepancy between the twin and family data. We wondered about the possibly reduced within-family environmental variance that MZ twins may experience, being the same sex, same age, and looking and acting much alike. DZ twins and siblings, on the other hand, are not so similar in appearance or behaviors, nor are their correlations markedly different. Adopted siblings, as predicted, bear little resemblance to each other in personality. None of this speculation about sibling versus twin results really addresses the unusual similarity of MZs reared in different homes or the lack of similarity of adopted children reared together. A theory of declining family effects and increasing individuality will address these observations.

Similar to heritability estimates, one can calculate the effects of being reared in the same home, neighborhood, and social class by holding genetic resemblance constant and varying degree of shared environment. A comparison of identical twins reared together with others reared apart yields a negative effect for common rearing environments ($0.52 - 0.60 = -0.08$). A comparison of fraternal twins' resemblance with that of ordinary siblings gives an estimate of the effects of "twinness" or unusually similar environments ($0.25 - 0.20 = 0.05$), a slightly positive effect. The small effect of "twinness" is about the same as that created for adopted children reared together (0.07), compared to genetically unrelated members of the population reared apart (0.00). In all cases, environmentability has a small effect on personality.

An environmental theory of main effects cannot account for the stunning findings from personality research on adoptees, siblings, and identical twins. A theory of genetic determinism does not speak to the less than perfect resemblance of identical twins or the slight resemblance of adopted siblings. But it is certainly more correct than an environmental theory of main effects that relies on proximal family influences. An environmental theory cannot possibly account for the impressive resemblances of identical twins reared apart or the lack of resemblance of adopted adolescents reared in the same homes since infancy. Our theory of genotype → environment effects *can* account for these data by predicting the degree of environmental similarity that is experienced by the co-twins and sibs, whether they live together or not.

ARE SOME ASPECTS OF PERSONALITY MORE HERITABLE THAN OTHERS?

One of the most intriguing and troublesome research questions for investigators of genetic variability in personality is whether or not all measured aspects of personality are equally heritable or whether some traits are more fundamentally under genetic influence. In addition, one would like to know whether the same genes influence all personality traits or whether different traits are influenced by different parts of the genome. The second question cannot be answered at present, as even an approach to it would require an answer to the first.

Some have argued that variations in the heritabilities found from study to study and from personality scale to scale are only sampling errors (Carey, Goldsmith, Tellegen, & Gottesman, 1978). Given that each study samples a finite and fallible group of twin and family members, it may be that inconsistent heritability estimates from study to study result from the vagaries of sampling. This possibility applies to all studies in all areas of science.

Others have not found differential heritabilities for "true" personality scales, such as introversion-extraversion and neuroticism, but lower heritabilities for scales sampling social and political attitudes, such as masculinity–femininity and intolerance of ambiguity (Loehlin, 1982; Loehlin & Nichols, 1976; Zonderman, 1982). On the other hand, attitude scales that sample intellectual differences, such as the California F-Scale turn out to have high heritabilities (0.4 to 0.6), because of their saturation with intelligence, which is, after all, highly heritable (Scarr, 1981). On the question of differential heritabilities for various personality scales, I agree with Loehlin (1982):

> Yes, personality scales are differently heritable, but it is not easy to show this with typical personality measures. Such measures tend to be heavily saturated with Extraversion and Neuroticism, two traits which are substantially heritable . . . and nearly equally so. However, if one extends the study to scales orthogonal to these two, one can indeed expect to demonstrate differential heritability with sufficiently large samples. (p. 427)

Another interesting issue is sex differences in heritabilities. Most studies report sex differences in the heritability estimates for whatever scales are used in the study. Structural equation models of environmental and genetic variances usually require a sex-difference parameter to achieve a model fit. I have not seen, however, or been able myself to decipher consistent trends in the results across studies. Perhaps, true sex differences exist for genetic variance in personality scale, but so far we have no theory about sex differences or consistent data.

I am not satisfied with the variance approach to personality and individuality. Putting together variance components and announcing that personality is moderately heritable does not speak to the important questions of "Why do people differ in personality?" and "How do differences in personality arise?" To say that on scales of introversion–extraversion, for example, individuals vary because 25% to 50% of the variation is genetic and 50% to 60% is within-family or individual experiential variation, is not an adequate answer to the major questions in this chapter. To find that adopted siblings do not resemble each other in personality, regardless of being reared together since infancy, still does not answer questions about how individuality is expressed and how it develops.

Individual Differences in Experience

Each of us encounters the world in different ways. We are individually different in the ways we process information from the environment, which makes our experiences individually tailored to our interests, personality, and talents. Human beings are also developmentally different in their ability to process information from the environment. Preschool children do not glean the same information from a football game as older children or adults. Preschoolers may wonder why grown men are mauling each other, while adults accept the rules of the competition and forget to ask why players are rewarded for being so aggressive toward one another. Each of us at every developmental stage gains different information from the same environments, because we attend to some aspects of our environments and ignore other opportunities for experience. Each individual also processes information against a background of previously different experiences—not different environments but different experiences gleaned from those environments.

I propose that these differences in experience—both developmental changes and individual differences—are caused by genetic differences. Over development, different genes are turned on and off, creating maturational changes in the organization of behavior, as well as maturational changes in patterns of physical growth. Genetic differences among individuals are similarly responsible for determining what experiences people do and do not have in their environments. What is attended to and what is ignored are events that are correlated with individual differences in interests, personality, and talents. Thus, I argue that individual and developmental differences in behavior are more a function of genetic differences in individuals' patterns of development than of differences in the *opportunities* available in most environments.

In an earlier paper (Scarr & McCartney, 1983), I proposed a theory of environmental effects on human development that emphasized the role of the genotype in determining not only which environments are experienced by individuals, but also which environments individuals seek for themselves. To show how this theory addresses the process of becoming an individual, the theory was used to account for seemingly anomalous findings from deprivation, adoption, twin, and intervention studies. I will here review the theory and in the last section apply it more specifically to personality development.

THEORIES OF DEVELOPMENT: FORGOTTEN INDIVIDUALITY

Theories of behavioral development have ranged from genetic determinism to naive environmentalism. Neither of these radical views has adequately explained the process of development, the nature of individuality, or the role of experience in development. For the species, human experience and its effects on development depend primarily on the evolved nature of the human genome. In evolutionary theory, the two essential concepts are selection and variation. Through selection the human genome has evolved to program human development. Phenotypic variation is the raw material on which selection works. Genetic variation must be associated with phenotypic variation, or there could be no evolution. It follows from evolutionary theory that individual differences depend in part upon genotypic differences.

I argue that genetic differences prompt differences in which environments are experienced and what effects they may have. In this view, the genotype, in both its species specificity and its individual variability, largely determines environmental effects on development, because the genotype determines the organism's responsiveness to environmental opportunities.

A theory of personality development must explain the origin of new psychological structures. Because there is no evidence that new adaptations can arise out of the environment without maturational changes in the organism, genotypes must be the source of new structures. Maturational sequence is controlled primarily by the genetic program for development. As Gottlieb (1976) said, there is evidence for a role of environment in (1) maintaining existing structures and in (2) elaborating existing structures; however, there is no evidence that the environment has a role in (3) inducing new structures. In development, new adaptations or structures cannot arise out of experience per se.

The most widely accepted theories of development are vague about how new structures arise; for example, Piaget (1980) fails to make the connection between organism and environment clear in his references to interaction. Nor is development well described by maturation alone (see Connolly & Prechtl, 1981). Neither Gesell and Ilg (1943) nor contemporary nativists (e.g., Chomsky, 1980) appreciate the inextricable links of nature and nurture in a hierarchically organized system of development.

I believe that the problem of new structures in development has been extraordinarily difficult, because of a false parallel between genotype and environment, which are not usefully seen as constructs at the same level of analysis. The dichotomy of nature and nurture has always been a bad one for two reasons. First, both a genotype *and* environment are required for development. This is so obvious as to require no additional comment. Second, I think that a false parallel arises between the two concepts when they are juxtaposed. Development is indeed the result of nature *and* nurture, but I think that genes drive experience. Genes are components in a system that organizes the organism to experience its world. The organism's abilities to experience the world change with development and are individually variable. A good theory of the environment can only be one in which experience is guided by gentoypes that both push and restrain experiences.

Personality *development* depends on both a genetic program and a suitable environment for the expression of the human, species-typical program for development. But personality *differences* among people can arise from both genetic and environmental differences. The process by which differences arise is better described as genotype → environment effects. The genotype determines the *responsiveness* of the person to those environmental opportunities.

I distinguish here between environments to which a person is exposed and environments that are actively experienced or "grasped" by the person. Individuals simply do not learn the same material, given equal exposure. In addition, individuals *prefer* to spend time in different settings. Given leisure time, some people gravitate to the sports field or the television set, others to libraries, still others to concerts, films, self-help groups, gardening, horse races, butterfly collecting, and so forth. The environments they choose from the vast array of possibilities are determined in part by their individual personalities, interests, and talents. The development of the Strong–Campbell Interest Inventory (Campbell, 1974) is based on the idea that different personalities are more and less satisfied with different occupations. The Holland Scales (Holland, 1966) are even more explicit about the connection between personality and the nature of the work environment. Any theory of individuality must take into account the selective nature of experience and the compatibilities and incompatibilities of persons and environments.

A MODEL OF GENOTYPES AND ENVIRONMENTS

Figure 3.1 presents the model of behavioral development. In this model, the child's phenotype P_c, or observable characteristics, is a function of both the child's genotype G_c and her rearing environment E_c. There will be little disagreement on this. The parents' genotypes G_p^- determine the child's genotype which in turn influences the child's phenotype. Again, there should be little controversy over this point. As in most developmental theories, transactions occur between the organism and the environment; here they are described by the correlation between phenotype and rearing environment. In most models, however, the source of this correlation is ambiguous. In this model, both the child's phenotype and rearing environment are influenced by the child's genotype. Because the child's genotype influences both the phenotype and the rearing environment, their correlation is a function of the genotype. The genotype is *conceptually prior* to both the phenotype and the rearing environment.

I argue that developmental changes in the genetic program prompt new experiences through maturation. Before the full phenotype is developed, the person becomes attentive to and responsive to aspects of the environment that previously were ignored or had other meanings. Just before puberty, many children become attentive to the attractiveness of the opposite sex. Little do they know what is to come, but they are responding to a preliminary, changing relationship with peers that will change their biological and social

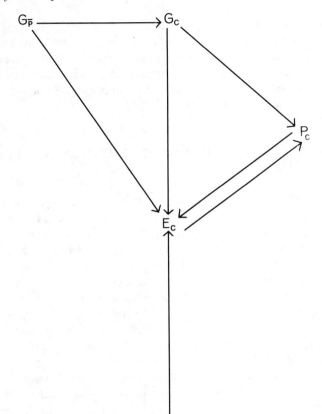

FIGURE 3.1 A model of behavioral development.

lives for many years to come. What is "turned on" in the genotype affects an emerging phenotype both directly through maturation and through prompting new experiences.

It follows from the preceding argument that the transactions we observe between phenotypes and environments are merely correlations, determined by developmental changes in the genotype. The correlation of phenotype and environment is represented by the double arrows from P_c to E_c. The theory states that developmental changes in phenotypes are prompted both by changes in the effective genotype and by changes in the salience of environments, which are then correlated. I recognize that this is not a popular position, but it accounts for data discussed in the final sections of this chapter far better than any other theory.

The path from the G_c to P_c represents maturation, which is controlled primarily by the genetic program. New structures arise out of maturation, from genotype to phenotype. Behavioral development is elaborated and maintained, in Gottlieb's sense, by the transactions of phenotype and environment, but it cannot arise *de novo* from this interaction. Thus, in this model, the course of development is a function of genetically-controlled, maturational sequences, although the rate of maturation can be affected by some environmental circumstances, such as the effects of nutrition on sexual development (Watson & Lowry, 1967).

SEPARATION OF GENETIC AND ENVIRONMENTAL EFFECTS ON DEVELOPMENT

At any one point in time, personality differences may be analyzed into variances that can be attributed more or less to genetic and environmental sources (see Plomin, DeFries, & Loehlin, 1977; Scarr & Kidd, 1983). Depending on how much genetic variation and how much environmental variation there are for the characteristic of interest in the population studied, sources of individual differences can be estimated. But such an account does not describe how development of those differences occurred.

The theory that we proposed does not attempt to allocate variance but to describe how individuals evoke and select their own environments to a great extent. There may appear to be arbitrary events of fate, such as one's spouse running off with another mate (how friendly and rewarding are you?) or falling ill (a personal lifestyle that lowers resistance to disease?), but even these may not be entirely divorced from personal characteristics that have some genetic variability. Please understand that I do not mean that one's environmental fate is *entirely* determined by one's genotype—only that some genotypes are more likely to receive and select certain environments than others. The theory is not deterministic but probabilistic.

An Evolving Theory of Behavioral Development

Plomin et al. (1977) described three kinds of genotype–environment correlations that I believe form the basis for a developmental theory. The theory of genotype → environment effects we proposed has three propositions:

1. The process by which children develop is best described by three kinds of genotype → environment effects: a *passive* kind whereby the genetically related parents provide a rearing environment that is correlated with the genotype of the child (sometimes positively and sometimes negatively); an *evocative* kind whereby the child receives responses from others that are influenced by his genotype; and an *active* kind that represents the child's selective attention to and learning from aspects of his environment that are

influenced by his genotype, and indirectly correlated with those of his biological relatives.

2. The relative importance of the three kinds of genotype → environment effects changes with development. The influence of the passive kind declines from infancy to adolescence, and the importance of the active kind increases over the same period.

3. The degree to which experience is influenced by individual genotypes increases with development and the shift from passive to active genotype → environment effects, as individuals select their own experiences.

The first, passive genotype → environment effects, arise in biologically-related families and renders all of the research literature on parent–child socialization uninterpretable. Because parents provide both genes and environments for their biological offspring, the child's environment is necessarily correlated with her genes, because her genes are correlated with her parents' genes, and the parents' genes are correlated with the rearing environment they provide. It is impossible to know *what* about the parents' rearing environment for the child determines *what* about the child's behavior, because of the confounding effect of genetic transmission of the same characteristics from parent to child. Not only can we *not* interpret the direction of effects in parent–child interaction, as Bell (1968) argued, we also cannot interpret the *cause* of those effects in biologically related families.

An example of a positive passive kind of genotype–environment correlation can be found in social skills. Parents who are very sociable, who enjoy and need social activity, will expose their child to more social situations than parents who are socially inept and isolated. The child of sociable parents is likely to become more socially skilled, for both genetic and environmental reasons. The children's rearing environment is positively correlated with the parents' genotypes and therefore related to the children's genotypes as well.

An example of a negative passive genotype–environment correlation can also be found in sociability. Parents who are socially skilled, faced with a child who is a social isolate, may exert more pressure and do more training than they would with a socially more adept offspring. The more enriched environment for the less able child represents a negative genotype → environment effect (see also Plomin et al., 1977). There is, thus, an unreliable, but not random, connection between genotypes and environments when parents provide the opportunities for experience.

The second kind of genotype → environment effect is called evocative, because it represents the different responses that different genotypes evoke from the social and physical environments. Responses to the person further shape development in ways that correlate with the genotype. Examples of such evocative effects can be found in the research of Lytton (1980) and the

review of Maccoby (1980). Smiley, active babies receive more social stimulation than fussy, difficult infants (Wachs & Gandour, 1983). Cooperative,
attentive preschoolers receive more pleasant and instructional interactions
from the adults around them than uncooperative, distractible children. Individual differences in responses evoked can also be found in the physical
attractivess; people who are considered attractive by others receive more
positive attention, are thought to be more pleasant, desirable companions,
and so forth (Bersheid & Walster, 1974).

The third kind of genotype → environment effect is the active, niche-
picking or niche-building sort. People seek out environments they find
compatible and stimulating. We all select from the surrounding environment
some aspects to which to respond, learn about, or ignore. Our selections are
correlated with motivational, personality, and intellectual aspects of our
genotypes. The active genotype → environment effect, we argue, is the most
powerful connection between people and their environments and the most
direct expression of the genotype in experience.

Examples of active genotype → environment effects can be found in the
selective efforts of individuals in sports, scholarship, relationships—in life.
Once experiences occur, they naturally lead to further experiences. Buss
(1984) argues that mate selection is a niche-selection process by which
personal similarities make for compatibility and lead to further environmental shaping of personal characteristics. I agree that phenotypes are elaborated
and maintained by environments, but the impetus for the experience comes,
I think, from the genotype.

DEVELOPMENTAL CHANGES IN GENOTYPE → ENVIRONMENT EFFECTS

The second proposition is that the relative importance of the three kinds of
genotype → environment effects changes over development from infancy to
adolescence. In infancy, much of the environment that reaches the child is
provided by adults. When those adults are genetically related to the child, the
environment they provide in general is positively related to their own characteristics and their own genotypes. Although infants are active in structuring
their experiences by selectively attending to what is offered, they cannot do as
much seeking out and niche-building as older children; thus, passive genotype → environment effects are more important for infants and young children than they are for older children, who can extend their experiences
beyond the family's influences and create their own environments to a much
greater extent. Thus, the effects of passive genotype → environment effects
wane when the child has many extrafamilial opportunities.

In addition, parents can provide environments that are negatively related to the child's genotype, as illustrated earlier in social opportunities. Although parents' genotypes usually affect the environment they provide for their biological offspring, it is sometimes positive and sometimes negative and therefore, not as direct a product of the young child's genotype as later environments will be. Thus, as stated in proposition 3, genotype → environment effects increase with development, as active replace passive forms. Genotype → environment effects of the evocative sort persist throughout life, as we elicit responses from others based on many personal, genotype-related characteristics from appearance to personality and intellect. Those responses from others reinforce and extend the directions our development has taken. High intelligence and adaptive skills in children from very disadvantaged backgrounds, for example, evoke approval and support from school personnel who might otherwise despair of the child's chances in life (Garmezy, 1983). In adulthood, personality and intellectual differences evoke different responses in others. Similarities in personal characteristics evoke similar responses from others, as shown in the case of identical twins reared apart (Bouchard, 1981). These findings are also consistent with the third proposition.

Genetic Resemblance Determines Environmental Similarity

The expected degree of environmental similarity for a pair of relatives can be thought of as the product of a person's own genotype → environment path and the genetic correlation of the pair. Figure 3.2 presents a model of the relationship between genotypes and environments for pairs of relatives who vary in genetic relatedness. G_1 and G_2 symbolize the two genotypes, F_1 and F_2, and their respective environments. The similarity in the two environments (path a) is the product of the coefficient of each genotype with its own environment (path x) and the genetic correlation of the pair (path b). On the assumption that individuals' genotypes are equally influenced by their own

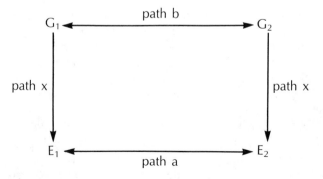

FIGURE 3.2. A model of environmental similarity based on genetic resemblance.

genotypes, the similarity in the environments of two individuals becomes a function of their genetic correlation.

This model can be used to describe the process by which MZ twins come to be more similar than DZ twins, and biological siblings more similar than adopted siblings. For identical twins, for whom $b = 1.00$, the relationship of one twin's environment with the other's genotype is the same as the correlation of the twin's environment with her own genotype. Thus, one would certainly predict what is often observed: that the hobbies, food preferences, choices of friends, academic achievements, and so forth of the MZ twins are very similar (Scarr & Carter-Saltzman, 1980). Kamin (1974) proposed that all of this environmental similarity is imposed on MZ co-twins, because they look so much alike, a proposal that fails utterly to account for the personality findings on identical twins reared apart. Theories of genetic resemblance do not speak to how close resemblances arise. We propose that the responses that the co-twins evoke from others and the active choices they make in their environments lead to striking similarities through genotypically determined correlations in their learning histories.

The same explanation applies, of course, to the greater resemblance of biological than adopted siblings. The environment of one biological sibling is correlated to the genotype of the other as one-half the coefficient of the sibling's environment to her own genotype, because $b = 0.50$, as described in Figure 3.2. The same is true for DZ twins. There is virtually no correlation in personality characteristics between parents of unrelated children adopted into the same household, so that their genetic correlation is effectively zero. And thus their resemblances in behavioral characteristics are also predicted to be low, because they will not evoke from others similar responses nor choose similar aspects of their environments to which to respond.

CHANGING SIMILARITIES AMONG SIBLINGS

The second discrepant set of observations from previous research concerned the declining similarities of dizygotic twins and adopted siblings from infancy to adolescence on tests of intelligence. Unfortunately, the data on personality are only suggestive on this point, as there are no comparable tests for young children, adolescents, and adults. I will illustrate this part of the model briefly with the intelligence data and then discuss what might be expected for personality.

It is clear from Matheny, Wilson, Dolan, and Krantz's (1981) longitudinal study of MZ and DZ twins that the DZ correlations for intelligence of 0.60 to 0.75 are higher than genetic theory would predict in infancy and early childhood. For school age and older twins, DZ correlations were the usual 0.55. Similarly, the intelligence correlations of a sample of late adolescent adopted siblings were zero compared to the 0.25 to 0.39 correlations of the samples of adopted children in early to middle childhood (Scarr & Weinberg, 1978).

Neither environmental nor genetic theories can effectively address the intelligence data, however. How can it be that the longer you live with someone, the less like them you become? One could evoke some ad hoc environmental theory about adopted sibling relationships becoming more competitive and deidentified, but that would not account for the continued, moderate resemblance of biological siblings. Genetic theory has, of course, nothing to say about decreasing twin resemblance or any resemblance among young adoptees.

The theory put forward here predicts that the relative importance of passive versus active genotype–environment correlations changes with age. Recall that passive genotype–environment correlations are created by parents who provide children with both genes and environments, which are then correlated. Certainly in the case of DZ twins, whose prenatal environment was shared and whose earliest years are spent being treated in most of the same ways at the same time by the same parents, the positive, passive genotype → environment effect is greater than that for ordinary sibs. Biological and adopted siblings do not, of course, share the same developmental environments at the same time because they differ in age. The passive genotype–environment correlation still operates for siblings, because they have the same parents, but to a lesser extent than for twins. Table 3.2 shows the predictions of the model for intelligence.

MZ twin correlations for intellectual competence do not decline when active genotype–environment correlations outweigh the importance of the passive ones, because MZ co-twins typically select highly correlated environ-

Table 3.2 The similarity of co-twins and sibling's genotypes and environments for intelligence

		Correlations in the environments of related pairs	
	Genetic correlation	Positive passive genotype → environment effects in early development	Active genotype → environment effects in later development
MZ twins	1.00	High	High
DZ twins	0.50	High	Moderate
Biological siblings	0.50	Moderate	Moderate
Adopted siblings	0.00	Moderate	Low

ments anyway. DZ pairs, on the other hand, are no more genetically related than siblings, so that as the intense similarity of their early home environments gives way to their own choices, they select environments that are less similar than their previous environments and about as similar as those of ordinary siblings.

Adopted siblings, on the other hand, move from an early environment, in which parents may have produced similarity, through positive, passive effects or through compensatory, negative ones, to environments of their own choosing. Because their genotypes are hardly correlated at all, neither are their chosen environmental niches. Thus, by late adolescence, adopted siblings do not resemble each other in intelligence, personality, interests, or other phenotypic characteristics (Grotevant, Scarr, & Weinberg, 1977; Scarr, Webber, Weinberg, & Wittig, 1981; Scarr & Weinberg, 1978).

Biological siblings' early environments, like those of adopted children, can lead to trait similarity as a result of positive, passive genotype → environmental effects. As biological siblings move into the larger world and begin to make active choices, their niches remain moderately correlated, because their genotypes remain moderately correlated. There is no marked shift in the intellectual resemblance of biological siblings as the process of active genotype → environment influence replaces the passive one.

Whether the same model that explains intellectual data will also work for personality remains to be seen. Based on the data so far, I doubt it for several reasons. First, living with the same family seems to increase intellectual similarity and decrease resemblance in personality. There is a small *positive* effect of common family environments in nearly all studies of intelligence; that is, siblings are more similar when reared in the same family than when reared in different families. This is also true for the comparison of identical twins reared together and apart; the IQ correlation of MZs together is about 0.82 and for MZs reared apart about 0.76. But for personality scales, estimates of the small effects of common family environment are frequently *negative;* that is, living in the same family makes siblings and twins slightly less similar than they are when living apart (Bouchard, 1981; Hopper & Culross, 1983; Loehlin, 1982).

Second, there are good theoretical reasons for predicting different effects of common family environment on intellectual talents and personality traits. There is only one desirable end to the IQ scale, and presumably everyone knows that to be smarter is better than to be dumber. On personality scales, being extreme at either end is undesirable, and there is lots of room in the middle for normal but variant personality scores. Thus, there is also room for siblings and twins to differentiate themselves and for parents to create negative passive genotype → environment effects.

It is commonly observed by twin researchers that parent of MZs stress how different their twins are. They tell the investigator that Twin A is the dominant one or the outgoing one, whereas Twin B is more submissive or retiring. Parents of twins have no difficulty differentiating their children by contrasting them. On the other hand, when asked to rate each child independently on behaviorally anchored, personality scales, parents of MZs usually rate them as quite similar. In the range of personality variation that exists in a population, small differences between MZ co-twins are magnified as important within-family differences—significant within the family but small in relation to the total variation.

Parents of DZ twins also have no difficulty differentiating their twins' personalities. On objective, behavioral measures, however, DZ co-twins are usually rated as far less similar than MZs.

Third, the data on personality resemblance among siblings in childhood and between parents and their children, measurement problems aside, show negligible correlations, regardless of the genetic relatedness of the family members (Loehlin, Horn, & Willerman, 1981; Scarr, Webber, Weinberg, & Wittig, 1981). Some evidence for increasing sibling resemblance in personality during middle childhood is found in a large twin study in Sweden (Fischbein, 1984). Behavioral adjustment ratings by teachers and by the twins themselves showed greater MZ than DZ correlations in both grades, but the sixth-grade twins were more similar in personality than fourth-graders. By the end of adolescence, data on family members show the patterns of correlation reported in Table 3.1. Thus, there are data to support the hypothesis that personality resemblance between genetic relatives increases as the influence of the family decreases and as the active genotype → environment effect increases.

Table 3.3 shows the model proposed for changing similarities of co-twins' and siblings' personality characteristics as a function of waning family influences and increasing active genotype → environment effects.

Table 3.3 The similarity of co-twins and sibling's genotypes and environments for personality

		Correlations in the environments of related pairs	
	Genetic correlation	Negative passive genotype → environment effects in early development	Active genotype → environment effects in later development
MZ twins	1.00	Moderate	High
DZ twins	0.50	Moderate	Moderate
Biological siblings	0.50	Low	Low
Adopted siblings	0.00	Low	Low

If one were to guess what future studies will show, the best bet would be for increased resemblance among biological relatives when they no longer live together or when they have never lived together. As the present theory predicts, they will choose niches correlated with their own genotypes, environments that are also correlated with their family members' environments to the extent of their genetic correlations with those relatives.

IDENTICAL TWINS REARED APART

The most interesting observation is of the unexpected degree of resemblance between identical twins reared mostly apart. With the theory of genotype → environment effects, their resemblance is not surprising. Given opportunities to attend selectively to and choose from varied opportunities, identical genotypes are expected to make similar choices. They are also expected to evoke similar responses from others and from their physical environments. The fact that they were reared in different homes and different communities is not important; differences in their development could arise only if the experiential opportunities of one or both were very restricted, so that similar choices could not have been made.

According to previous studies (Newman, Freeman, & Holzinger, 1937; Juel-Nielsen, 1982; Shields, 1962) and the recent research of Bouchard and colleagues at the University of Minnesota (Bouchard, 1981), the most dissimilar pairs of MZ's reared apart are those in which one was severely restricted in environmental opportunity. Extreme deprivation and, perhaps unusual enrichment, can diminish the influence of genotype on environment and therefore lessen the resemblance of identical twins reared apart.

SUMMARY

In summary, the theory of genotype → environment effects proposed by Scarr and McCartney (1983) describes the usual course of human development in terms of three kinds of genotype–environment correlations that posit cooperative efforts of nature *and* nurture. Both genes and environments are constituents in the developmental system, but they have different roles. Genes determine much of human experience, but experiential opportunities are also necessary for development to occur. Individual differences can arise from restrictions in environmental opportunities to experience what the genotype would find compatible. With a rich array of opportunities, however, most differences among people arise from genetically determined differences in the experiences to which they are attracted and which they evoke from their environments.

The theory relies on the idea of individual differences in responsiveness to environments. This seems to me the essence of individuality. It is not just the familiar idea of reaction range but includes more active kinds of transactions between people and their surroundings. In addition, the theory accounts for seemingly anomalous results from previous research on twins and families. Most importantly, the theory addresses the issue of process in personality development. Rather than presenting a static view of individual differences through variance allocation, or relying on between-family differences that cannot possibly address the major sources of individuality, this theory hypothesizes processes by which genotypes and environments combine across development to make us both members of the human species and unique individuals.

REFERENCES

Ahern, F. M., Johnson, R. C., Wilson, J. R., McClearn, G. E., & Vandenberg, S. G. (1982). Family resemblances in personality. *Behavior Genetics, 12,* 261–280.

Bandura, A. (1982). The psychology of chance encounters and life paths. *American Psychologist, 37,* 747–755.

Bell, R. Q. (1968). A reinterpretation of the direction of effects in studies of socialization. *Psychological Review, 75,* 81–95.

Bersheid, E., & Walster, E. (1974). Physical attractiveness. In L. Berkowitz (Ed.), *Advances in experimental social psychology.* New York: Academic Press.

Boakes, R. (1984). *From Darwin to behaviorism.* New York: Cambridge University Press.

Bouchard, T. (1981, August). *The Minnesota study of twins reared apart: Description and preliminary findings.* Paper presented at the annual meeting of the American Psychological Association.

Bouchard, Jr., T. J. (1984). Twins reared together and apart: What they tell us about human diversity. In S. W. Fox (Ed.), *Individuality and determinism* (pp. 147–184). New York: Plenum Publishing.

Brackbill, Y., & Nichols, P. (1982). A test of the confluence model of intellectual development. *Developmental Psychology, 18,* 192–198.

Bugenthal, D. B., & Shennum, W. A. (1984). Difficult children as elicitors and targets of adult communication patterns: An attributional-behavioral transactional analysis. *Monographs of the Society for Research in Child Development, 49* (whole issue).

Buss, D. M. (1984). Toward a psychology of person-environment (PE) correlation: The role of spouse selection. *Journal of Personality and Social Psychology, 47,* 361–377.

Buss, A. H., & Plomin, R. (1984). *Temperament: Early developing personality traits.* Hillsdale, NJ: Lawrence Erlbaum Associates.

Campbell, D. P. (1974). *Manual for the Strong–Campbell Interest Inventory T325 (Merged Form).* Stanford, CA: Stanford University Press.

Carey, G., Goldsmith, H. H., Tellegen, A., & Gottesman, I. I. (1978). Genetics and personality inventories: The limits of replication with twin data. *Behavior Genetics, 8,* 299–313.

Carey, G., & Rice, J. (1983). Genetics and personality temperament: Simplicity or complexity? *Behavior Genetics, 13,* 43–63.

Chomsky, N. (1980). On cognitive structures and their development: A reply to Piaget. In L. Piatelli-Palmarini (Ed.), *Language and learning: The debate between Jean Piaget and Noam Chomsky,* Cambridge, MA: Harvard University Press.

Connolly, F. J., & Prechtl, H. F. R. (1981). *Maturation and development: Biological and psychological perspectives,* Philadelphia, PA: Lippincott.

Daniels, D., & Plomin, R. (in press). Differential experience of siblings in the same family. *Developmental Psychology.*

Daniels, D., Plomin, R., & Greenhalgh, J. (1984). Correlates of difficult temperament in infancy. *Child Development, 55,* 1184–1194.

Ernst, C., & Angst, J. (1983). *Birth order,* New York: Springer-Verlag.

Fischbein, S. (1984). Self- and teacher-rated school adjustment in MZ and DZ twins. *Acta Genet Med Gemellol, 33,* 205–212.

Galbraith, R. (1982). Sibling spacing and intellectual development. *Developmental Psychology, 18,* 2, 151–173.

Garmezy, N. (1983). Stress-resistant children: The search for protective factors. In J. E. Stevenson (Ed.), *Recent research in developmental psychopathology, Journal of Child Psychology and Psychiatry Book Supplement No. 4.* Oxford: Pergamon Press.

Gesell, A., & Ilg, F. L. (1943). *Infant and child in the culture of today,* New York: Harper and Brothers.

Gottlieb, G. (1976). The role of experience in the development of behavior in the nervous system. In G. Gottlieb (Ed.), *Studies in the development of behavior and the nervous system. Vol. 3: Development of neural and behavioral specificity.* New York: Academic Press.

Grotevant, H. D. (1978). Sibling constellations and sex typing of interests. *Child Development, 49,* 540–542.

Grotevant, H. D., Scarr, S., & Weinberg, R. A. (1977). Patterns of interest similarity in adoptive and biological families. *Journal of Personality and Social Psychology, 35,* 667–676.

Holland, J. L. (1966). *The psychology of vocational choices: A theory of careers.* Waltham, MA: Ginn.

Hopper, J. L., & Culross, P. R. (1983). Covariation between family members as a function of cohabitation history. *Behavior Genetics, 13,* 459–471.

Jensen, A. R. (1980). *Bias in mental testing.* San Francisco: Freeman.

Juel-Nielsen, N. (1982). *Individual and environment: Monozygotic twins reared apart.* New York: International University Press.

Kamin, L. J. (1974). *The science and politics of IQ.* Potomac, MD: Lawrence Erlbaum Associates.

Loehlin, J. C. (1982). Are personality traits differentially heritable? *Behavior Genetics, 12,* 417–428.

Loehlin, J. C., Horn, J. M., & Willerman, L. (1981). Personality resemblance in adoptive families. *Behavior Genetics, 11,* 309–330.

Loehlin, J. C., Horn, J. M., & Willerman, L. (in press). Aspects of the inheritance of intellectual abilities. *Behavior Genetics.*

Loehlin, J. C., & Nichols, R. C. (1976). *Heredity, environment, and personality.* Austin, TX: University of Texas Press.

Lytton, H. (1980). *Parent–child interaction: The socialization process observed in twin and single families.* New York: Plenum Press.

Maccoby, E. E. (1980). *Social development.* New York: Harcourt, Brace, Jovanovich.

Matheny, A. P., Jr., Wilson, R. S., Dolan, A. B., and Krantz, J. Z. (1981). Behavioral contrasts in twinships: Stability and patterns of differences in childhood. *Child Development, 52,* 579–598.

Newman, H. G., Freeman, F. N., & Holzinger, K. J. (1937). *Twins: A study of heredity and environment.* Chicago: University of Chicago Press.

Nichols, R. C. (1978). Policy implications of the IQ controversy. In L. S. Shulman (Ed.), *Review of research in education 6.* Itasca, IL: Peacock.

Piaget, J. (1980). The psychogenesis of knowledge and its epistemological significance. In M. Piattelli-Palmarini (Ed.), *Language and learning: The debate between Jean Piaget and Noam Chomsky.* Cambridge, MA: Harvard University Press.

Plomin, R., & Daniels, D. (1984). The interaction between temperament and environment: Methodological considerations. *Merrill-Palmer Quarterly, 30,* 2.

Plomin, R., DeFries, J. C., & Loehlin, J. C. (1977). Genotype–environment interaction and correlation in the analysis of human behavior. *Psychological Bulletin, 84,* 309–322.

Rowe, D. C., & Plomin, R. (1981). The importance of nonshared (E1) environmental influences in behavioral development. *Developmental Psychology, 17,* 517–531.

Scarr, S. (1981). *Race, social class, and individual differences in IQ: New studies of old issues.* Hillsdale, NJ: Lawrence Erlbaum Associates.

Scarr, S. (1985). Constructing psychology: Facts and fables for our times. *American Psychologist, 40,* 499–512.

Scarr, S., & Carter-Saltzman, L. (1980). Twin method: Defense of a critical assumption. *Behavior Genetics, 9,* 527–542.

Scarr, S., & Grajek, S. (1982). Similarities and differences among siblings. In M. E. Lamb & B. Sutton-Smith (Eds), *Sibling relationships* (pp. 357–381). Hillsdale, NJ: Lawrence Erlbaum Associates.

Scarr, S., & Kidd, K. K. (1983). Behavior genetics. In M. Haith & J. Campos (Eds.), *Manual of child psychology: Infancy and the biology of development, Vol. 2* (pp. 345–433). New York: Wiley.

Scarr, S., & McCartney, K. (1983). How people make their own environments: A theory of genotype → environment effects. *Child Development, 54,* 424–435.

Scarr, S., Scarf, E., & Weinberg, R. A. (1980). Perceived and actual similarities in biological and adoptive families: Does perceived similarity bias genetic influence? *Behavior Genetics, 10,* 445–458.

Scarr, S., Webber, P. L., Weinberg, R. A., & Wittig, M. A. (1981). Personality resemblance among adolescents and their parents in biologically-related and adoptive families. *Journal of Personality and Social Psychology, 40,* 885–898.

Scarr, S., & Weinberg, R. A. (1978). The influence of "family background" on intellectual attainment. *American Sociological Review, 43,* 674–692.

Shields, J. (1962). *Monozygotic twins brought up apart and brought up together.* London: Oxford University Press.

Thomas, A., & Chess, S. (1977). *Temperament and development.* New York: Brunner/ Mazel.

Wachs, T. D. (1983). The use and abuse of environment in behavior–genetic research. *Child Development, 54,* 396–407.

Wachs, T. D., & Gruen, G. (1982). *Early experience and human development.* New York: Plenum.

Watson, E. H., & Lowry, G. H. (1967). *Growth and development of children.* Chicago: Year Book Medical Publishers.

Zajonc, R. B., & Markus, G. B. (1975). Birth order and intellectual development. *Psychological Review, 82,* 74–88.

Zajonc, R. B., Markus, H., & Markus, G. B. (1979). The birth order puzzle. *Journal of Personality and Social Psychology, 37,* 1325–1341.

Zonderman, A. B. (1982). Differential heritability and consistency: A reanalysis of the National Merit Scholarship Qualifying Test (NMSQT) California Psychology Inventory (CPI) data. *Behavior Genetics, 12,* 193–208.

4

Personality Psychology: Back to Basics

Robert Hogan[1]

When evaluating another person's ideas, I like to know who or what influenced them. Should the reader share this curiosity, I can say that in my case, four major influences are reasonably clear. First, I have always been interested in natural history and biology. Reading Freud in high school, Darwin in college, and McDougall in graduate school convinced me that humans are biological animals and cannot, in principle, be understood outside the context of the evolutionary history of the species.

Second, reading Huizinga (*Homo Ludens,* 1955) and Mead (*Mind, Self, and Society,* 1934) persuaded me that there are important parallels between games and social living (e.g., social behavior is strategic, rule-governed, and some people are better at it than others), that personality is the product of social interaction, and that social maturity involves accurately attending to the legitimate expectations that others hold regarding one's behavior. As a Darwinian, Mead thought these tendencies were rooted in evolutionary history, and I believe he was correct.

Third, a number of modern philosophers (e.g., T. Mischel, Toulmin, Winch, Wittgenstein—cf. T. Mischel, 1969) caused me to doubt the merits of traditional explanatory models in psychology—psychoanalytic, humanistic, and behaviorist. They also convinced me that it is important to be explicit about one's assumptions regarding the nature of explanation. The

[1] I would like to thank Roy Baumeister, Steve Briggs, David Buss, David Funder, Douglas Kenrick, and Tod Sloan for their helpful comments regarding the original draft of this chapter.

newest writing in personality psychology (e.g., Buss & Craik, in press) reflects a sophistication about the problem of explanation that was not apparent 20 years ago.

Finally, my undergraduate engineering studies gave me a lifelong distaste for rationalism (the view that reason is sufficient unto itself as a means for acquiring knowledge about the world), for Platonism (the view that mathematics is somehow more real than everyday experience), and for the (historically false) notion that basic science is more important than, and necessarily precedes, achievements in technology. My empiricist leanings were reinforced by three marvelous years at the Institute of Personality Assessment and Research (IPAR) in Berkeley, where Donald MacKinnon, Harrison Gough, Kenneth Craik, Frank Barron, Ravenna Helson, and Wallace Hall showed me how these tendencies could be productively applied to personality measurement.

INTRODUCTION

At an informal meeting a few years ago, Silvan Tomkins remarked that more people were interested in personality theory outside psychology than in it. He was right, but he may have understated the case. Within academic psychology, personality theory does not have much status—it seems to be a source of vague embarrassment to the profession (cf. Fiske, 1974; Sechrest, 1976). On the other hand, there is intense interest in personality psychology outside academia; I find in interviews with law enforcement officials, CEO's of large organizations, and successful attorneys that they think psychologically, and they attribute much of their success to this ability. But they primarily read popular psychology, because our material is either irrelevant or inaccessible. Scholars who write biographies are also quite interested in personality. After documenting the facts of Newton's or Beethoven's life, they turn to personality psychology to make sense of these facts. Again, however, they seem to find our material unhelpful, and they appeal to psychoanalysis or other nonscientific sources for help.

How could a discipline with so much inherent appeal fall so far out of favor with so many people? One answer is that personality theory originated in the study of psychopathology and this tends to direct our attention to aspects of maladjustment—stress and coping, behavioral disorders, traumatic life changes, sexual abuse, depression, etc. Moreover, our data base is largely built on the study of circumscribed underclasses—students, neurotics, prisoners, and other captive populations. But what happens when we study real people—for example, adults who are gainfully employed? MacKinnon (1960) points out that one of the major discoveries of the Office of Strategic Services assessment team during World War II was that psychoanalysis is largely irrelevant as a means for understanding the lives of competent people. This finding turns up repeatedly in the various samples studied at the Institute of Personality Assessment and Research (IPAR) in Berkeley. That this should be the case seems obvious when one considers that the absence of psychopathology does not logically entail the presence of competence. More interesting, however, is the fact that Freud, Jung, Adler, and most of the early psychopathologists, at least in their theoretical writings, stigmatized high achievers—for Freud, they are father murderers; for Jung, they have formed a one-sided adaptation to reality; for Adler, they are compensating for feelings of inferiority. But most nonpsychologists who read personality—e.g., managers in business and government, biographers, intelligent adults, and a large number of our own undergraduates—are concerned about competence-related issues. They want to know about such issues as how to construct a relationship, how to raise a child, how to evaluate another person's reliability, and how to maximize their chances for vocational success. Consequently, they are likely to be frustrated by the answers contained in traditional (psychopathology-based) personality theory.

A second factor that may account for current ambivalence regarding personality psychology is the fact that, until recently, there was little consensus in the field regarding how personality was to be defined and, therefore, how it was to be operationally specified. Historically, virtually every personality theory has had its own preferred measurement procedure and set of variables: Psychoanalysis and the Rorschach; Murray's need system and the TAT; Jungian theory and the Myers–Briggs Type Indicator; Rotter's social learning theory and the locus of control scale; Kelly's personal construct theory and the Role Construct Reperatory Test; Interpersonal Theory and Schutz' FIRO-B; Allport's ideographic theory and the Study of Values. Two developments within the discipline since the early 1960s have the potential to remedy this disorderly state of affairs. On the one hand, the publication of such measures as the California Psychological Inventory, the Guilford–Zimmerman Temperament Survey, and Block's Q-sort shows that it is possible to construct reliable and valid measures of normal personality on pragmatic and empirical rather than theoretical or philosophical grounds; thus, one can develop personality measures that are not tied to particular definitions of personality. On the other hand, factor analytic research regarding the structure of trait ratings (cf. Tupes & Christal 1961, Norman, 1963) has converged on the view that personality can be described in terms of three to six broad dimensions (the three dimensions can be decomposed into the six). This finding, widely accepted within the personality research community (cf. Digmen & Tokemoto-Chock, 1981; Goldberg, 1981; McCrae & Costa 1987; Peabody, 1987), provides a systematic basis for deciding what variables to include in our measurement operations.

Scheibe (1984), in an interesting review of the history of the self concept since William James, concludes that, despite years of vigorous research, we have advanced our understanding of the self only marginally—because the research was predicated on a set of muddled ideas. Scheibe goes on to suggest that the model of the future will synthesize the views of Freud and Mead.

The same analysis holds true for personality psychology more generally; future progress will depend on getting our conceptual house in order. Although psychologists are often hostile to conceptual analysis, this tendency may be declining. For example, Robert White's (1981) keynote address at the initial conference in this series emphasized the need to expand the conceptual foundations of the field.

One possible means for expanding our traditional conceptual models is to take account of some of the very useful ideas in sociology. Along these lines, Marcuse (1958) proposed a (not entirely successful) synthesis of Freud and Marx. I would like to propose (á la Scheibe) a synthesis of Freud and Mead as an initial point of departure. Both theoretical traditions have some distinctive shortcomings [e.g., Mead was unconcerned with either individual differences or the problem of social change; Freud's motivational theory is inadequate, and his concept of repression is incoherent (Fingarette, 1969)]. Moreover, there are major points of disagreement between psychoanalysis and symbolic interactionism (e.g., Mead was a dissociationist, whereas Freud explicitly rejected the concept of dissociation; Mead thought integration into society promoted individual development, whereas Freud thought there was an inevitable and painful tension between personal development and the demands of society). Nonetheless, in those areas where both traditions agree, I believe there is theoretical gold rather than shared prejudice. The following are some crucial points of agreement (which I regard as axiomatic for modern personality psychology):

1. Personality theory must be based on evolutionary theory.

2. Personality develops through a set of identifiable stages.

3. Morality is defined in terms of social norms, rules, and values (*pace* Kohlberg), and a person's moral orientation forms the core of his/her personality.

4. Morality is the link between individual personality and the larger social order, and moral development accounts for the continuity of culture across the generations.

5. At the individual level, moral considerations normally override biological promptings.

6. Social interaction proceeds in terms of symbolic gestures that others must decode.

Mead began with the (valid) observation that there can be organized societies without individual personalities (e.g., the social insects) and concluded that the problem was to explain how individual personalities arise out of social interaction. Freud began with the (empirically false) observation that well-socialized adults are also neurotic and concluded that the socialization process, although necessary for individual survival, was also the source of individual neurosis (cf. Freud, *Totem and Taboo,* 1913). Freud was correct, however, that moral development lies at the core of personality. Modern anthropology and sociology contain two other generalizations that need explanation. The first is that people live in groups, and the second is that groups are always organized in status hierarchies. These are the starting points for socioanalytic theory. In my view, the goal of personality psychology is to analyze the factors that account for individual differences in the manner in which people integrate themselves into their social groups; an important component of this is the question of how they deal with the pursuit of status. I believe the problems that Freud and Mead set for themselves were special cases of this more general inquiry.

The rest of this chapter is organized in five sections. The next section presents the various assumptions underlying the model of personality that I have been developing. The following section offers some definitions of the subject matter. There then follows a discussion of personality dynamics and development, then a discussion of personality assessment. Finally, the chapter closes with some sample applications.

WHAT WE NEED

The futility of drawing up lists of human motives is pretty well recognized. Nonetheless, the logic of theory construction requires that one at least acknowledge one's motivational presuppositions (even Kelly, who was an outspoken critic of the concept, smuggles a set of motivational assumptions in the back door of his model—cf. Kelly, 1963, p. 157). I rely on three such assumptions, which, however, are in fact reasonably well grounded in past research. First, several lines of reasoning, including our evolutionary history as a group-living species, Harlow's research with Rhesus monkeys, and the maternal deprivation studies (Bowlby, 1969), suggest that we need attention and social acceptance (see also, Lovejoy, 1961, p. 107). In the same way, normal people find criticism, rejection, and ostracism immensely unpleasant. Second, studies of the experimental induction of neurosis from Pavlov to the present indicate that we also need structure and predictability—especially with regard to social rewards—and find uncertainty and randomness quite aversive. Third, I assume that most people are impelled (consciously or nonconsciously) to seek status, power, and influence in their social groups; failing that, they may change groups (recall Lucifer's line that it is better to be first in Hell than second in Heaven) or even drop out altogether. The notion that status-seeking tendencies are innate is consistent with the views of writers as different as White (1959) and Tedeschi and Norman (1985). DeWaal (1982) shows how free-living chimpanzees engage in constant ploying, maneuvering, and bargaining in the relentless pursuit of social position. Among humans, sibling rivalry, academic politics, and White House power struggles reveal that status seeking seems to be an inevitable (and often entertaining) aspect of human social behavior.

Discussions of human motivation should be placed in the context of evolutionary theory, and in that context fitness is the "bottom line." Fitness is defined in terms of the number of viable progeny that an individual leaves behind. Characteristics that contribute to fitness tend to be retained in a population's gene pool, and those that detract from fitness tend to disappear. Fitness requires reproduction, and this is the link to status. Status within a group confers upon the holder preferential opportunities for reproductive success—because status affords one a choice of mates, living sites, nutritional supplies, means of self-defense, etc. There is, therefore, a link between status and fitness. But one cannot simply lay claim to status; DeWaal (1982) demonstrates quite dramatically that among chimpanzees status is very carefully negotiated, over a long period of time, and it is a process that requires a great deal of patience, self-control, and luck.

The situation for people is even more complicated, and it turns on the notion of identity. Specifically, people depend on their groups for survival; groups, in turn, operate best when they are organized in terms of a sensible division of labor. From the perspective of group welfare, each person should contribute in some way to the ongoing maintenance of the collective. It follows that one normally should have a role to play in the economy of the group before one will be allowed to reproduce. A person's occupational identity is an index of his or her social and reproductive status, and this identity mediates individual fitness in human society. The establishment and maintenance of a successful social/occupational role, therefore, is a crucial problem in each person's development, and the solution to that problem is closely tied to social competence.

The foregoing discussion can be quickly summarized as follows. People are biological creatures. Human biology reflects our evolutionary origins as social animals. Although reproduction is the biological bottom line, reproduction normally depends on a person establishing a place for him- or herself in a human community. Human groups exist in concrete geographical environments that place specific demands on those groups, to which the successful ones manage to respond. Culture, to a large degree, reflects the kinds of adaptations a group has made to the demands of its environment. The shared values, goals, and aspirations of the group are the link between each person and his or her culture. People are all alike in terms of their basic human needs; groups differ in terms of the cultures they evolve in response

to environmental demands; people differ primarily in terms of the adaptations they make to their cultures. This is the functional context in terms of
which personality should be understood.

PERSONALITY DEFINED

There are two definitions of personality. They are overlapping but in-
commensurable, mutually translatable but deriving from different spheres of
experience. These are the perspectives of the observer and the actor, and
only confusion results when they are not distinguished. From an observer's
perspective, personality consists of an actor's reputation, his or her distinctive
social stimulus value. This reputation is not value-neutral; reputations are
explicitly evaluative and, *au fond,* they consist of an appraisal of the actor's
potential or demonstrated contribution to his or her social group. Every
culture has a vocabulary, a set of terms that it uses to make these evaluations,
and the structure of these vocabularies is much the same across cultures (cf.
White, 1980). These vocabularies are similar, because the natural environment puts many of the same demands on all human groups (e.g., every group
must find food, construct shelter, establish defenses, derive means for self-
regulation, instruct children, etc.). Moreover, this is an area in which personality psychologists have a major scientific finding to report. We now can
specify with some confidence the structure of the vocabulary that observers
use to describe actors—put another way, we have a replicable model of the
structure of personality from the viewpoint of an observer. In research
beginning with Allport (Allport & Odbert, 1936) and proceeding through
Cattell (1947), Tupes & Christal (1961), Norman (1963), Goldberg (1981),
Digman & Takemoto-Chock (1981), and Howarth (1980) there is now considerable agreement that observers' impressions can be expressed in terms
of about five dimensions. Everyone is evaluated by his or her family and peers
in terms of how bright they are, how self-confident they are, how dependable
they are, how much social space they occupy, and how rewarding they are to
deal with. Every person who reads this has a social reputation that his or her
peers can describe in terms of these five dimensions.

From the perspective of an actor—the reader—personality consists of the
inner psychological structures, qualities, and characteristics that cause him or
her to generate his or her unique reputation. We can speak with some
confidence about the parameters of a person's reputation. About the causes of
that reputation, however, we must be a good bit more cautious. Causes lie in
the domain of *verstehen,* of hermeneutics, of interpretation. This is the great,
uncharted frontier of personality psychology; it is the region of the self-
concept, of social aspiration and personal despair, of public claims and

private reservations, of hopes, doubts, and self-delusion. This domain presents formidable obstacles to scientific analysis because of its inherently ipsative or idiographic nature. But it is the domain to which virtually everyone's attention seems compulsively drawn, and we badly need to have something persuasive to say about it.

The distinction between these two definitions of personality has major conceptual and research implications which, I believe, have not been sufficiently appreciated. Let me mention four implications that come immediately to mind. First, the kind of research one will do depends on which definition one chooses. If one is concerned about personality from the observer's perspective, then one will study matters related to social perception (Cantor & Mischel, 1977) and social cognition in an effort to understand what qualities and behaviors of actors cause observers to form their varying impressions and what features of observers cause them to perceive actors as they do. Buss and Craik (in press), in their studies in act-frequency analysis, provide an excellent example of this kind of research. If one is concerned about personality from the actor's perspective, then one will investigate the relationship between an actor's temperament and developmental history and his or her values, aspirations, self-images, and social knowledge structures, and the subsequent relationship between the foregoing and his or her social behavior. Helson's (1985, in press) studies of the adult development of talented women is a fine example of this. The relationship between these two forms of personality is inherently ambiguous, because some observers are more perceptive than others and some actors are more aware than others of their own social stimulus value (cf. Mills & Hogan, 1978). Once again, let me note that it is terribly important to decide what one means by the word "personality" before one begins doing personality research.

Second, the distinction between personality from the actor's and the observer's perspectives is directly related to the often-ignored distinction between prediction and explanation (cf. Mischel, 1969). Trait terms, which reflect the observer's perspective, are invaluable as a means for predicting the behavior of actors. To know that someone has a reputation for being hostile and deceitful, for example, gives us invaluable information regarding what to expect of that person during future encounters. But knowing that the person is regarded as hostile and deceitful does not tell us why he or she has developed such a (self-defeating) reputation. Currently, there is considerable debate in sociology, anthropology, history, and political science regarding the merits of quantitative versus qualitative analyses; quantitative models are concerned with prediction, whereas qualitative analyses are concerned with explanation. The debate is largely wrong-headed, because both kinds of analyses are necessary. We need methods for forecasting important behaviors *and* methods for explaining why the forecasting models work as they do.

Consequently, we must systematically mine the latent knowledge of observers while at the same time exploring the intentions of actors as we pursue both prediction and explanation.

Third, personality assessment is a complex and highly evolved research methodology. Although criticized (and misunderstood) by many psychologists, it remains the methodology of choice for personality research. Despite the demonstrable predictive efficacy of personality assessment, it will never be more than a technical accessory to personality psychology until it successfully comes to terms with the actor/observer distinction. When a person responds to a personality measure, his or her purposes are normally different from the goals of the test user. Like observers everywhere, test users use test scores to ascribe traits to actors, who in this case are the test takers. Test scores are useful for predicting a person's behavior, but it is also important to ask why a person received his or her particular scores. It is entirely too facile to assume that the scores reflect the presence of in-dwelling traits; to do so confounds the observer's view with that of the actor.

Finally, the actor/observer distinction places the trait consistency controversy in a different light. Loosely put, critics of traditional personality psychology argue that, if there is a stable core to personality, then an actor's behavior should be consistent across situations. Note that this (behaviorist) argument, as it is normally phrased, avoids two crucial questions: (1) how to define a situation, and (2) how to define consistency. But if one takes account of the distinction between an actor's and an observer's perspective, then the core question (Do people behave consistently across "situations"?) turns into two very different questions: (1) Do actors have the same goals and social expectations in different social contexts?; and (2) Will observers describe actors consistently across different social contexts? From an actor's perspective, personality may change across social contexts; from an observer's perspective, actors seem rather similar in different contexts. In the absence of a clear definition of personality, the trait consistency controversy popularized by Mischel's (1968) book becomes essentially moot.

PERSONALITY DEVELOPMENT

From the perspective of an actor, personality consists of the methods and techniques that a person has developed to maximize status and predictable attention in his or her social groups. The structure of this private personality at any time reflects a kind of compromise between a person's temperament, his or her competencies and skills, and the expectations of the people with whom he or she must interact. For the first 18 months of life, children are relatively incompetent in social terms and depend on older caretakers to initiate and construct interactions with them. These early interactions are of a primitive, face-to-face variety, and place limited demands on a child's social skills.

When a child is about 18 months old, it becomes increasingly possible to construct interactions based on an external, make-believe focus, using complementary roles. One can, for example, sit with a child and "read" a book or magazine. The interaction consists of turning pages and remarking on their contents—note that in such a game, a child receives attention in a structured and predictable format. Some time around 20 months of age one may see "mother–baby" games, wherein a mother and a child will play at being mother and child—the mother will speak in an artificial voice, and the child may feign incompetence. Cheek (Hogan, Cheek, & Jones, 1984) thinks that role-distance begins in these episodes where infants self-consciously enact the roles that they actually occupy.

By 36 months many children, drawing on this early experience, are able to construct interactions with other children. These interactions typically take the following form: one child will say something like, "Pretend this teddy bear is sick, and we have to take care of it." The interaction will consist of ministering to the ailing bear. As with the earlier interactions, there is an external focus and mutual roles to play, but now there is a crucial difference—unless a child is able to draw another into the game, there will be no interaction. Play with peers, for the first time, puts demands on a child's social skills.

By 48 months some children seem to be as interested in playing with other children as they are in interacting with their parents. This trend normally continues until adolescence.

The biologically programmed concerns of adulthood begin to appear in adolescent peer interaction. There is a tendency to regard sexuality as the primary theme in adolescent interaction. But status issues also emerge at this time. Girls begin to compete (or at least make comparisons) in terms of clothes, popularity, and dates; boys begin to compete (or at least make comparisons) in physical and economic ways; and status issues powerfully constrain boy–girl relations—because, in general, boys are not allowed to date higher status girls. Status issues, as a result, are often logically prior to sexual matters. In any event, groping about in the firestorm of adolescent hormones, young people try out various identities on one another in an effort to achieve an acceptable level of status and popularity. All the familiar character types emerge: athlete, scholar, clown, rebel, deviant, artist, socialite. For some, these adolescent identities will harden and essentially typecast the person for life. For others, these adolescent roles will be stepping stones to surprisingly different adult identities.

There are five points to note about this process of identity negotiation in adolescence. First, the question is not whether a young person needs to develop an identity in order to interact with other young people; it is rather a question of what identity he or she will be able or allowed to adopt. Second, this process has been preceded by at least 10 years of practice; children bring to adolescent identity negotiation considerable experience and even skill at role-playing. Third, important psychosocial consequences attend the outcome of these activities, because the identities that young people establish for themselves can be scaled along the (correlated) dimensions of status and popularity. Fourth, all of this is a prelude to the task of finding a vocational identity in adulthood. And finally, identities are established and maintained through the process of self-presentation, through actions intended (often unconsciously) to tell others who one is and how one would like to be regarded.

Depending on the culture, a person may or may not move directly from the problems of adolescence to the problems of adulthood. Middle class children in industrialized societies are able to prolong adolescence (sometimes well into their 30s) through mechanisms that lead to what Erikson (1963) calls "psychosocial moritoria." Sooner or later, however, most people become concerned with establishing occupational identities, starting and maintaining families, and caring for the young. Some people are more successful in their chosen pursuits than others; this success is a function of family background, good sense, social skill, energy, ambition, and luck. Although establishing and maintaining a family and an occupation may seem prosaic and unchallenging, they are problems that a remarkable proportion of society seems unable to solve.

Some tennis players continue to improve their games throughout their career, usually by hard work, desire for improvement, and attention to coaching feedback; others reach plateaus and, for various reasons, remain there. And so it is with the game of life. Some people seem satisfied with the identities and corresponding lifestyles that they developed in adolescence. Others, for various reasons, continue to work on their life games—they evaluate their aspirations and achievements relative to their talents, they attend to social feedback, and they polish their social and interpersonal skills. Growth and change in adulthood, therefore, may owe more to such personal factors as concern for self-improvement and openness to experience than it does to biological programming. This, in turn, means that only some people will change over time. As to the mechanisms of change, one can only speculate. Changes in hormone levels, in neurological structures, and traumatic illnesses will explain some alterations in personality; other changes may result from alterations in how a person perceives him- or herself, and from desires for change in itself.

Whatever the larger developmental tasks of adulthood may be, life at the daily level consists of a nearly endless chain of interaction sequences, each with its separate agenda, players, and outcomes. In each interaction, observers have expectations with regard to an actor's likely behavior (as well as their own private agendas), and actors have views about the expectations of observers (as well as their own private agendas). Despite the shifting agendas, certain features of these interactions are constant—namely, actors have identities which they hope or expect observers will credit them with. These identities (which include claims about status, competency, and correlated rights and perogatives) are conveyed or expressed to others through self-presentational behaviors (cf. Schlenker, 1985). The related processes of self-presentation, impression management, and identity negotiation are the heart and core of everyday personality dynamics—which I call the politics of everyday life. And these processes turn out to be very complex indeed. The following three points hint at some of these complexities.

Character Structure and Role Structure

A person's audiences or counterplayers change over time and in predictable ways. Early on, one's audience is composed largely of family elders. During the school years, parents and parent surrogates (teachers) are joined by the peer group, which has very different expectations regarding one's social behavior. Finally, in adulthood, one's co-workers and the members of one's social network become the crucial counterplayers. The social expectations and forms of self-presentation that one develops in interaction with one's parents may be inappropriate and even maladaptive when dealing with one's teenaged peers, and the social behavior of adolescence may not work well in adulthood. Nonetheless, those behavioral programs and their associated social cues do not simply drop out of the psyche. Rather they continue to exist in psychic storage, and somewhere in that storage system, in a file next to the one marked "How to tie my shoes," is a file called "How to respond to unreasonable requests from authority." When in adulthood we are required to tie our own shoes, we nonconsciously execute a program of shoe-tying behavior. If, on another occasion, we must deal with an unexpected and unfriendly request from the Internal Revenue Service, we tend to execute our "response to unreasonable authority" program.

Each of us, then, has an array of attitudes, expectations, and interactional schemas that were acquired at an earlier point in development; they are stored somewhere in the memory system, they can be activated in the present, and they potentially can be inconsistent with current social knowledge structures and self-presentational methods. But the situation may be worse than that. The psychoanalysts argue that these early emotional and behavioral response patterns are often idealized—more highly prized—than the structures that replaced them and, therefore, may have a more urgent and compelling quality to them. The earlier structures form what I call "character structure," and the later ones what I call "role structure." Depending on the circumstances of one's life, there may be painful tensions between the earlier loyalties and the later obligations.

Sincerity and Competence

Some people object to the suggestion that interpersonal behavior consists of self-presentations. On the one hand, this evokes images of *quattrocento* Florentine skulduggery, a sinister, calculating approach to social life that they find distasteful if not dishonest. On the other hand they point out that actors *ought to be* candid, forthright, and open (this is a moral claim) and that they themselves are typically spontaneous, authentic, and sincere (cf. Buss & Briggs, 1984). This argument, with its naive faith in the perfectability of human relations, is charming and contains an important element of truth, but it also begs a number of questions.

The element of truth is the observation that we, as actors, only sometimes engage in conscious self-presentation, and as Buss and Briggs (1984) point out, it is important to specify the boundary conditions for intentional impression management. What might those be? Conscious self-presentation ordinarily occurs when one is involved in strategic interaction (Jones & Pittman, 1982), when one is trying to project a particular image, or otherwise defend one's reputation. Examples include TV interviews and comparable public performances, marriage proposals, contract negotiations, and other consequential bargaining situations. Some people are more continuously involved in self-presentation that others (Snyder, 1981), and some occupations require more impression management than others (e.g., politician vs. academic). Moreover, if one is preoccupied, ill, or otherwise self-absorbed and inattentive to social feedback (and some people seem always to be in this condition), then self-presentational considerations may never arise.

The problem with this argument concerns the issue of sincerity and authenticity. When social behavior is sincere and authentic, there is a correspondence between an actor's intentions and his or her behavior. But how are we to know when an actor is sincere? There is the problem that one person's sincerity may be another person's bad manners, that sincerity may be a mask for rudeness. In addition, the fact that an actor is not consciously engaged in self-presentation is no guarantee that he or she is not self-deceived (a hard-nosed Marine drill instructor may be merely doing his duty, but a psychologist might suspect that other, perhaps crueler, motives are sometimes at work). Nor is the fact that an actor believes that his or her performance is authentic a guarantee against self-deception. There is a curiously religious connotation to the concept of sincerity; the implicit assumption seems to be that there is a "real me" somewhere inside against which particular social performances may be compared for the purposes of evaluating their authenticity. But the "real me" is a negotiated identity which (within limits) can be renegotiated. In any case, if one feels compelled to make moral evaluations of individual social performances, accurate self-awareness may be a better criterion than sincerity.

But finally, it really does not matter whether an actor is consciously attending to the impression that he or she is creating in others, because observers will assume that the actions are intentional and evaluate the actor anyway. This is the particular curse of shy people (Jones, Cheek, & Briggs, 1985). Shy people seem to find unstructured interactions with casual acquaintances and strangers quite aversive, and most of their energy is apparently required to struggle through these interactions without fleeing in panic. Observers, however, assume that the awkward performances are intentional and typically judge shy actors to be rude, brusque, ill mannered, and even hostile. These evaluations are unfortunate—especially when they impede a shy person's career—but they are the inevitable and unavoidable consequences of the politics of everyday life. The point is that although we may only infrequently engage in conscious self-presentation, from the perspective of other observers it does not really matter; they normally and quite reasonably assume that our actions are sending them a message about what we think of them and how we ourselves want to be regarded.

Public and Private Selves

A person's social identity is largely a matter of public record. That social identity, however, is built upon and arises out of a private sense of identity—which is a complex amalgam of self-images and self-esteem that reflects each person's early developmental history (cf. Cheek & Briggs, 1982). From a phenomenological perspective, one's feelings of self-worth are more important, more vital, and more central than one's social identity; recall, however, that one's social identity mediates status in one's social group and, therefore, is directly tied to long-term success or failure in life. The two forms of identity exist in a kind of dialectical relationship; one's social and occupational failures and successes feed back into and influence one's feelings of self-regard, which, in turn, influence one's occupational successes.

Self-presentations are actions designed for two very different audiences; one's self and other people (Greenwald & Breckler, 1985). Competent people guide their actions by the anticipated expectations and evaluations of their audience. We sometimes guide our actions in anticipation of the evaluations of people who are not physically present; they may be elsewhere, they may be dead, they may even be nonexistent (dieties and other imaginary companions). But we also put on performances for ourselves, watch ourselves, and carry out interior monologues as a means of exploring, maintaining, or enhancing our private identities. A positive internal image makes hope and striving possible; a negative internal image is associated with despair and, in extreme cases, with illness and even death. To the degree that one must spend time working on one's internal image, energy is diverted from one's social or occupational goal. The blessed, the charmed, and the lucky need spend little time on inner work. More generally, however, we consciously and nonconsciously control our actions in response to the expected praise and blame of public and private others. Consequently, although we are not always engaged in self-presentation, the phenomenon is more pervasive than it seems when we first think about it.

PERSONALITY ASSESSMENT

Critics of traditional personality psychology (e.g., Gergen, 1981; Mischel, 1968; Nisbett, 1980) make two related claims. The first is the rather peculiar notion that there is no such thing as personality—more precisely, that there is no stable core to personality. (Parenthetically, this is one of those claims that an academic audience will entertain but which a real-world audience will find silly.) The second claim is that personality assessment is a pointless enterprise. This is so, in part, because traditional personality assessment is intended to measure something that the critics believe does not exist and, in part, because personality measures are alleged to account for only trivial amounts of the variance in meaningful, nontest criterion data.

This dispute breaks down into three related questions: (1) Does personality assessment work? (2) Why do people think that it doesn't? (3) What legitimate (as opposed to bogus) problems confront the field?

The most efficient way to answer the first question is to point to some examples. I will mention my three favorites. The first concerns creativity. Hall and MacKinnon (1969) compared three groups of architects ($N = 120$), who differed in terms of peer nominations for creativity, using their scores on a number of standard personality inventories. Cross-validated multiple correlations, based on various combinations of three variables, ranged between 0.38 and 0.61. This shows that an important aspect of real world performance can be predicted surprisingly well, and an inspection of the individual correlations tells us a good deal about the interpersonal qualities and features that distinguish the more from the less successful members of the architectural profession.

My second example concerns delinquency. Thirteen different samples from around the world (total $N = 10,296$) completed the socialization scale of the California Psychological Inventory (CPI) (Gough, 1975), which had been translated into seven different languages. The socialization scale discriminated felons from nonfelons in each sample. Moreover, in no one sample was the average score for delinquents higher than the score for nondelinquents in any other sample. But most significantly for our purposes here, the biserial correlation between socialization scores and the delinquent/nondelinquent criterion, over all samples, was 0.73.

My third example concerns adjustment to hazardous and confined working conditions. Each year the United States Navy and the National Science Foundation send teams of volunteers to staff research stations in the Antarctic. Although the volunteers undergo psychiatric screening, some people experience considerable subsequent difficulty adjusting to life and work in the very confined conditions necessary to sustain life during the long Antarctic winter. At the start of the summer in 1982, Biersner and Hogan (1984) gave 25 volunteers from two Antarctic research stations the Hogan Personality Inventory (HPI) (Hogan, 1986). They then asked members of each team to rate one another in terms of whether or not they would be willing to spend another winter with that person. A 54 item scale from the HPI correlated –0.50 with negative ratings and 0.57 with positive ratings in both samples.

The foregoing examples are by no means unique or isolated findings (cf. Hogan & Hogan, 1985), and they show that when done right, personality assessment yields significant, stable, and important correlations with meaningful, real-world criteria. But there is a larger point at stake here; it involves a problem in social justice about which critics of standard personality psychology may be unaware. The issue concerns whom to hire when one is choosing personnel. This is a core problem in Industrial Psychology and a topic to which personality assessment has a great deal to contribute. According to Hunter and Hunter (1984) and others, there is no alternative to intelligence testing as a method for personnel selection. The fact that intelligence tests *always* discriminate against certain minority groups is an unfortunate corollary of such practices, but one for which they believe there is no alternative. These people rely on standard criticisms of personality psychology (e.g., Mischel, 1968) for evidence that personality assessment is not a practical alternative to intelligence testing. In point of fact, however, competent personality measures yield validity coefficients with measures of job performance that are at least equal in magnitude to those provided by cognitive measures. Unlike intelligence tests, however, personality measures tend not to discriminate unfairly against minorities (Hogan, 1986). On the other hand, they do discriminate against people who are egocentric, immoral, intolerant, and hard to live with. Thus, the claim that personality assessment does not work is empirically false, and it contributes in a major way to the perpetuation of unfair hiring practices as well. Finally, it has been 20 years since the attack on personality assessment began, but we have yet to see the critics develop alternatives to traditional assessment that can be used in practical selection contexts.

Given the fact that some personality measures work quite well as means for predicting aspects of everyday social behavior, why do many psychologists believe that they lack scientific merit? One answer, sadly, is that some people do not read the evidence or simply ignore it; in their devotion to favored viewpoints and resistance to contrary evidence, however, psychologists are no different from any other group of scientists (cf. Kuhn, 1962).

A second answer has to do with the development of personality assessment itself. Historically, personality psychology has been a handmaiden to psychiatry. Personality theory was originally designed to explain the origins of certain forms of mental illness and to point to treatment methods. Personality assessment, in this model, is used as an aid to psychiatric diagnosis. Diagnostic measures of this type proliferated; some were projective (Rorschach, TAT, Bender–Gestalt, etc.) and some were "objective" (Bernreuter, Humm–Wadsworth, MMPI). In the minds of many people, these measures are the mainstream of personality assessment.

If this judgment were true, then personality assessment would indeed be in trouble because, at least since the milestone Kelly and Fiske (1951) assessment study of clinical psychologists, most personality researchers have recognized two points about psychiatrically oriented assessment. The first is that, in the absence of normal reliability estimates, the validity of projective testing is indeterminate if not undemonstrated (Entwisle, 1972). The second point is that objective measures of psychiatric syndromes are poor predictors of competent performance—a task for which they were never intended. To the degree that personality assessment is equated with psychiatrically oriented measurement procedures, it will be judged a failure; this is because such procedures do not work very well when put to purposes other than psychiatric diagnosis and the prediction of low base rate indices of abnormal functioning.

Once again, however, the mainstream of personality assessment research since the mid-1950s has been other than psychiatrically oriented, as shown by the publication of the California Psychological Inventory, the 16P-F, the Guilford–Zimmerman Temperament Survey, the Myers–Briggs Type Indicator, the Jackson Personality Inventory, the Hogan Personality Inventory, and many other tests. The evidence regarding the utility of these measures is altogether persuasive.

The critics of modern personality assessment may be wrong in their evaluations, but there are some residual problems in the field. What is not a problem is the topic of response sets, an issue that was firmly dismissed by Block (1965) and Rorer (1965) quite a while ago—although some textbook writers have yet to wake up to this reality. In my view, most of the problems in personality assessment stem from the fact that it tends to be an atheoretical enterprise and a number of important conceptual issues have yet to be resolved. I will mention two of these: item response theory and taxonomic theory.

Item Response Theory

What do scores on personality measures mean; what are people doing when they respond to items on a personality inventory? Many psychologists take a position of naive realism here—they believe that scale scores reflect the magnitude of in-dwelling traits and that item responses are self-reports. The model of interpersonal behavior presented in this chapter suggests an alternative way of thinking about these issues. Specifically, responding to items on a personality inventory can be seen as a kind of social behavior formally identical to any other; that is, actors, through the medium of the items on an inventory, often seek to tell an anonymous interlocutor how they want to be regarded. Valid scale scores, therefore, are means for predicting how a person will be regarded by observers. Gough (1975) has always advocated this (nominalist) view of the meaning of test scores.

The view that item responses are self-reports relies on the notion that memory is analogous to a stored video tape; when one is asked about his/her deportment in high school, for example, one replays a high school tape and decides about that deportment. But if we see memory as a construction organized around a set of self-images (Markus, 1977), then item responses may also be based on constructions—and they become statements designed to tell inner and outer audiences how the respondent wants to be regarded.

A self-presentational approach to item responses allows one systematically to analyze the problem of constraints on test validity. A very interesting literature has developed around this issue (Cheek, 1982; Johnson, 1981; Mills & Hogan, 1978; Wymer & Penner, 1985) which not only may permit us to squeeze more juice out of the psychometric turnip, but may also allow us to synthesize in a conceptual way measurement in personality and social psychology (attitude measures can also be interpreted in self-presentational terms). This seems to be a highly promising area of future research that has implications for personality measurement, attitude measurement, and survey methods.

Taxonomic Theory

Currently there is a surprising amount of research on taxonomies going on. The core question concerns what variables should be included in a reasonably comprehensive assessment of personality. Taxonomic research falls neatly into two traditions. The first, stimulated by Leary's (1957) pioneering book, is concerned with circumplexes. Perhaps the most fully elaborated circumplex model has been developed by Wiggins and Broughton (1985); it is an intricate and extremely interesting taxonomy of interpersonal behaviors organized around the dimensions of affection and status.

The second taxonomic effort concerns trait lists. The argument here concerns how many traits are necessary for a comprehensive list. Current evidence seems to favor a three-factor model (sociability, neuroticism, and impulse control), the factors of which can be decomposed into more specific elements (cf. Eysenck, 1978; Royce & Powell, 1983).

Residual questions concern how to link the circumplex with the trait-list tradition, how satisfactorily to reconcile the "big five" model (Digman & Takemoto-Chock, 1981; Goldberg, 1981) with the three-factor model, and what cross-cultural validity do these various models have? It seems clear, however, that the process of personality inventory construction will be permanently redirected by these various taxonomic endeavors.

PERSONALITY PRAXIS

Kurt Lewin is credited with the remark that "nothing is more useful than a good theory." It is also the case that in order to be good, a theory must be useful. In this section, I offer three examples of how the model of personality presented here can be used. These might be called examples of biographical explication, career management, and everyday survival. These are only illustrations; each is intended to point to uses of personality theory that may be of interest to persons other than academic researchers. Detailed presentations of these examples must wait until another day.

As a case of biographical explication, consider the life of Freud, a personage about whose history most readers will have some familiarity. Conventional treatments of Freud's biography tend to emphasize three themes: the development of his ideas; his relations with his family, colleagues, and disciples; and his self-analysis. Generally speaking, most writers locate the dynamic core of Freud's biography and the unifying theme of his life in his neurosis; this neurosis presumably drove his self-exploration, which then led to the announcement of psychoanalytic theory. This is a tidy story, but it ignores the most glaring and obvious aspect of Freud's biography—namely, his success. He was a world-famous man. Surely that fame did not come about by accident. I cannot imagine why Freud's biographers tend to regard this fact as a fortuitous by-product of an otherwise painful process of introspection.

An alternative and equally tidy story of Freud's life can be constructed on the basis of the ideas presented here. Consider first Freud's immense ambition. Lionel Trilling, in the introduction to his edition of Jones' biography, states that it is simply a fact—Freud was consumed and driven by intense aspirations for worldly acclaim. To fulfill these ambitions he needed a vehicle and a set of specific strategies. His family circumstances and personal predilections suggested a scholarly or scientific career was perhaps his most likely career choice. The specific strategies he developed concern the self-presentational techniques he used to support his scientist identity in his drive for recognition.

Freud's private correspondence is full of discussions of these matters. In a letter to his fiancee, he remarks that all of the imminent scientists in his circle had a distinctive interpersonal style and that he had decided to adopt the posture of rectitude and integrity to set himself off from the others. In a set of letters to Fliess, the two agreed that they would take on the roles of isolated, struggling geniuses. It is, therefore, a matter of public record that Freud gave considerable self-conscious attention to the question of how to present himself and what public posture would most effectively promote his career. It is also a matter of record that he had superb self-presentational skills—he was a compelling and dramatic lecturer and a "Viennese charmer" who paid fastidious attention to his personal appearance according to Allport. In this context it is easy to see Freud's famous self-analysis in the same terms as John Kennedy's famous torpedo boat incident—namely, as a superb marketing ploy. Bright, creative, intensely ambitious, and endlessly thoughtful about how to present himself and how to construct his career—these, it seems to me, are crucial details in Freud's life. To the degree that biographers focus on Freud's neurosis and self-analysis, they too have been taken in by this immensely clever man.

The second use for personality theory is in career management. The 1980 and 1984 American presidential elections provide nice examples of this process. Jimmy Carter and Walter Mondale are both bright, well-informed, hard-working, conscientious men with strong egalitarian values. Friends of farmers, labor, and education, they would seem to be, in principle, very attractive presidential candidates. Ronald Reagan, in contrast, has fewer technical qualifications for the job. He is not intellectually gifted, even his supporters admit that he does not work very hard, he has elitist values, and his policies (as predicted) have been less than advantageous for farmers, labor, and education. The record, however, is very clear; Ronald Reagan was a vastly more successful presidential candidate than either of his unusually able and well-informed opponents; he was, in fact, one of the most popular presidential candidates of the entire century. How do we account for this? The answer seems straightforward. The most powerful position in the free world was awarded on the basis of self-presentational skills. There are two additional points that I would like to emphasize. The first is that the process of identity negotiation through self-presentation is not a trivial party game or academic exercise—it is a process that has the most profound consequences for an individual career or the fate of a nation. Second, Jimmy Carter, Walter Mondale, and the rest of us apparently know about these things; the fact that we do not use this knowledge as successfully as Ronald Reagan does show how deeply rooted our self-defeating tendencies actually are. Our habitual methods of self-presentation are outside our awareness, often perverse, and powerfully resistant to change.

My final example comes from the world of law enforcement, whose practitioners rely on their knowledge of human nature as part of their work and as a tool for everyday survival. A couple of years ago I did a small bit of consulting with the FBI. The agent with whom I worked was reasonably senior and clearly on a fast career track. Over a two-day period, we talked a good bit about psychology, about human nature, and about its implications for his line of work. He regaled me with a number of fascinating stories, most of which would be suited for my purposes here. I mention the following incident because it is relatively brief. This particular agent went to the Miami airport one Sunday afternoon on a piece of government business. As he was about to leave, the airport security people informed him that his services were needed. A plane had just landed and three men on board were harassing the flight attendants and terrorizing other passengers—and this is a federal offense. He hurried to the gate in time to confront three large and formidably rough-looking men coming off the plane. He reported that he was frightened—he had no gun, no handcuffs, and no support other than three part-time airport security guards—but he assumed an angry, menacing look, drew himself up, and said "FBI! You three sit down here." To his great relief, the men sat down rather meekly on a row of chairs. The agent then turned to the airport police, who were gaping in amazement, and said, "Okay, you can handle this now," and walked off.

Virtually any experienced police officer can recount dozens of such stories, not all with happy endings. Law enforcement officials, trial lawyers, labor negotiators, military officers, and persons from a variety of other professions who have to deal with people rather than things tend to conduct their lives and think about other people in role-theoretical, dramaturgical, and self-presentational terms. This is especially true for the successful ones. For many people, earning a livelihood or simply staying alive depends on making accurate appraisals of other people and deciding correctly how to approach them. As Goffman (1958) remarked, all the world is not a stage and all the men and women are not merely actors, but the crucial ways in which they are not are hard to define.

CONCLUSION

I would like to conclude this chapter by briefly summarizing the most important points in the foregoing discussion. There are seven of these. The first point is that personality psychologists need to pay closer attention to the question of what a theory is intended to do. Some theories (e.g., factor analytic models) are descriptive; others are intended to be explanatory. In the latter case, we need to ask what is being explained. When we appeal to these explanatory models in order to understand or make sense out of some real life phenomena, we should ask if the theory is appropriate for the purposes to which we want to put it. In trying to make sense out of the lives of successful adults, for example, traditional psychoanalysis typically will not be appropriate. Worse than that, psychohistorical efforts such as *In Search of Nixon* (Mazlish, 1973), which offers a psychoanalytic portrait of Richard Nixon, sometimes turn out to be little more than pseudoscientific character assassinations. Such efforts are a discredit to all of us.

Second, despite the fact that Freud was concerned primarily with explaining hysterical disorders, there are some insights in psychoanalytic theory that are valuable for understanding normal behavior. Moreover, some of these insights were derived independently by Mead. This overlap is more than merely fortuitous. A modern synthesis of Freud's emphasis on biological and unconscious motives and Mead's analysis of social interaction may have possibilities for explaining individual differences in ordinary social competence.

Third, a key problem in human development is to establish a social and occupational identity for oneself. More precisely, we must negotiate our identities with other members of our society or culture. An individual's social competency strongly affects his or her efforts at identity negotiation. Social competency can be largely but by no means entirely defined in terms of individual differences in self-presentational skills. Self-presentation, then, is a major aspect of identity negotiation; as such individual differences in self-presentational skill can have fateful consequences for individual welfare.

Fourth, personality must be defined in two different ways. Both definitions have very different referents, and people need to be clear which definition they are using when they speak of personality. A great deal of confusion has resulted from the failure to distinguish these two perspectives. Personality in the first sense refers to a person's social reputation, and it can be specified in terms of three to six broad dimensions. Personality in the second sense refers to the intrapsychic factors that explain why actors create their unique reputations. Because these two concepts of personality derive from such different realms of experience, data based on these sources will not always converge. In fact, the relationship between data from these two sources will inevitably be problematic (Cattell & Digman, 1964).

Fifth, many people believe that Mischel's (1968) book largely discredited personality assessment. Hogan, DeSoto, and Solano (1977) point out that this view is empirically false; the utility of personality assessment is in fact well documented. Here I would like to make the additional point that failure to use established assessment procedures when they are appropriate can lead to major personnel errors, large costs to organizations, and perpetuation of the discrimination inherent in the use of "cognitive" measures as selection devices. That is, personality assessment not only works, it has a major contribution to make to the development of the national economy and to the promotion of fair employment practices. But it is also important to note that the test critics have brought forward no alternatives to replace the assessment procedures they have so roundly criticized. Consequently, the spate of anti-test criticism of the 1960s can be seen as either a watershed or a regressive movement—depending on one's attitude regarding the role of measurement procedures in the development of science.

Sixth, research since the late 1950s on the structure of the trait lexicon has converged, so that we now have the beginnings of a consensus regarding the dimensions that one must include if one wishes systematically to sample the personality domain. This consensus should bring about a revolution in research regarding how social context *and* personality combine to influence behavior (see Aronoff & Wilson, 1985, for a powerful summary of this research to date). We now have the outline of a periodic table for personality in terms of which the myriad of independent scales (F-scale, dogmatism, locus of control, self-monitoring) can be understood. This taxonomic effort also will bring some order to studies where groups are composed in terms of personality as a way of studying group process.

Finally, a biologically based role-theoretical analysis of personality holds out the prospect of putting the social back into personality, and personality back into social psychology. Snyder (1981) has demonstrated the importance of individual differences for social psychological experiments, Baumeister (1982) has shown that most of the classic social psychological experiments can be conceptualized in role-theoretical terms, and Wiggins and Broughton (1985), in a recent *tour de force,* dramatize the power of interpersonal models for integrating personality psychology. The parts are assembled for a major modern synthesis of personality and social psychology. I am personally quite optimistic about the future of the discipline. But it is also nice to know that some progress has been made since the publication of Murray's (1938) original masterwork.

REFERENCES

Allport, G. W., & Odbert, H. S. (1936). Trait names: A psycho-lexical study. *Psychological Monographs,* No. 211.

Aronoff, J., & Wilson, J. P. (1985). *Personality in the social process.* Hillsdale, NJ: Erlbaum.

Baumeister, R. F. (1982). A self-presentational view of social phenomena. *Psychological Bulletin, 91,* 3–26.

Biersner, R. J., & Hogan, R. (1984). Personality correlates of adjustment in isolated work groups. *Journal of Research in Personality, 18,* 491-496.

Block, J. (1965). *The challenge of response sets.* NY: Appleton-Century-Crofts.

Bowlby, J. (1969). *Attachment and loss.* NY: Basic Books.

Buss, A. A., & Briggs, S. R. (1984). Drama and the self in social interaction. *Journal of Personality and Social Psychology, 47,* 1310–1324.

Buss, D. M. & Craik, K. H. (in press). The act frequency approach and the construction of personality. In A. Angleitner, A. Furnham, & G. VanHeck (Eds.), *Personality psychology in Europe.* Lisse, The Netherlands: Swets & Zertlinger.

Cantor, N., & Mischel, W. (1977). Traits as prototypes: Effects on recognition memory. *Journal of Personality and Social Psychology, 35,* 38–48.

Cattell, R. B. (1947). Confirmation and clarification of primary personality factors. *Psychometrika, 12,* 197–220.

Cattell, R. B., & Digman, J. M. (1964). A theory of the structure of perturbations observer ratings and questionnaire data in personality research. *Behavioral Science, 9,* 341–358.

Cheek, J. M. (1982). Aggregation, moderator variables, and the validity of personality tests: A peer-rating study. *Journal of Personality and Social Psychology, 43,* 1254–1269.

Cheek, J. M., & Briggs, S. R. (1982). Self consciousness and aspects of identity. *Journal of Research in Personality, 16,* 401–408.

DeWaal, F. (1982). *Chimpanzee politics: Power and sex among the apes.* NY: Harper and Row.

Digman, J. M., & Takemoto-Chock, N. R. (1981). Factors in the natural language of personality: Re-analysis, comparison, and interpretation of 6 major studies. *Multivariate Behavioral Research, 16,* 149–170.

Entwisle, D. R. (1972). To dispel fantasies about fantasy-based measures of achievement motivation. *Psychological Bulletin, 77,* 377–591.

Erikson, E. H. (1963) *Childhood and society.* Second Edition. NY: Norton.

Eysenck, H. J. (1978). Super factors P, E, and N in a comprehensive factor space. *Multivariate Behavioral Research, 13,* 475–482.

Fingarette, H. (1969). *Self-deception.* London: Routledge & Kegan Paul.

Fiske, D. W. (1974). The limits for the conventional science of personality. *Journal of Personality, 42,* 1–11.

Freud, S. (1950/1913). *Totem and taboo.* NY: Norton.

Gergen, K. J. (1981). The functions and foibles of negotiating self-conception. In M. D. Lynch, A. A. Norem-Hebeisem, & K. J. Gergen (Eds.), *Self-concept: Advances in theory and research* (pp. 59–73). Cambridge, MA: Ballinger.

Goffman, E. (1958). *The presentation of self in everyday life.* NY: Doubleday.

Goldberg, L. R. (1981). Language and individual differences: The search for universals in personality lexicons. In L. Wheeler (Ed.), *Personality and social psychology review, Vol. 2* (pp. 141–165). Beverly Hills, CA: Sage.

Gough, H. G. (1975). *Manual for the California Psychological Inventory.* Palo Alto, CA: Consulting Psychologists Press.

Greenwald, A. G., & Breckler, S. J. (1985). To whom is the self presented? In B. R. Schlenker (Ed.), *The self in social life* (pp. 126–145). NY: McGraw-Hill.

Hall, W. B., & MacKinnon, D. W. (1969). Personality inventories as predictors of creativity among architects. *Journal of Applied Psychology, 53,* 322–326.

Helson, R. (1985). Which of those young women with creative potential become productive? Personality in college and characteristics of parents. In R. Hogan & W. H. Jones (Eds.), *Perspectives in personality* (pp. 49–80). Greenwich, CT: JAI.

Helson, R. (in press). Which of these young women with creative potential become productive? II. From college to midlife. In R. Hogan & W. H. Jones (Eds.), *Perspectives in personality, Vol II.* Greenwich, CT: JAI.

Hogan, R. (1986). *Manual for the Hogan Personality Inventory.* Minneapolis: National Computer Systems.

Hogan, R., Cheek, J. M., & Jones, W. H. (1984). Socioanalytic theory: An alternative to armadillo psychology. In B. Schlenker (Ed.), *The self and social life* (pp. 175–198). NY: McGraw-Hill.

Hogan, R., DeSoto, C. B., & Solano, C. (1977). Traits, tests, and personality research. *American Psychologist, 32,* 255–264.

Hogan, J., & Hogan, R. (1985). *Psychological and physical performance characteristics of successful explosive ordinance diver technicians.* Tulsa, OK: University of Tulsa.

Howarth, E. (1980). Major factors of personality. *Journal of Psychology. 104,* 171–183.

Huizinga, J. (1955). *Homo ludens.* Boston: Beacon Press.

Hunter, J. E., & Hunter, R. F. (1984). Validity and utility of alternative predictors of job performance. *Psychological Bulletin, 96,* 72–98.

Johnson, J. A. (1981). The self-disclosure and self-presentation views of item response dynamics and personality scale validity. *Journal of Personality and Social Psychology, 40,* 761–769.

Jones, W. H., Cheek, J. M., & Briggs, S. R. (Eds.) (1985). *A source book on shyness: Research and treatment.* NY: Plenum.

Jones, E. E., & Pittman, T. (1982). Toward a general theory of strategic self-presentation. In J. Suls (Ed.), *Psychological perspectives on the self, Vol. I* (pp. 231–262). Hillsdale, NJ: Erlbaum.

Kelly, G. A. (1963). *A theory of personality.* NY: Norton.

Kelly, E. L., & Fiske, D. W. (1951). *The prediction of performance in clinical psychology.* Ann Arbor: University of Michigan Press.

Kuhn, T. S. (1962). *The structure of scientific revolutions.* Chicago: University of Chicago Press.

Leary, T. (1957). *Interpersonal diagnosis of personality.* NY: Ronald.

Lovejoy, A. O. (1961). *Reflections on human nature.* Baltimore: Johns Hopkins University Press.

MacKinnon, D. W. (1960). The highly effective individual. *Teachers College Record, 61,* 367–378.

Marcuse, H. (1958). *Eros and civilization.* NY: Vintage.

Markus, H. (1977). Self-schemata and processing information about the self. *Journal of Personality and Social Psychology, 35,* 63–78.

Mazlish, R. (1973). *In search of Nixon.* Baltimore: Penguin Books.

McCrae, R. R., & Costa, P. F., Jr. (1987). Validation of the five-factor model of personality across instruments and observers. *Journal of Personality and Social Psychology, 52,* 81–90.

Mead, G. H. (1934). *Mind, self, and society.* Chicago: Chicago Press.

Mills, C. J., & Hogan, R. (1978). A role theoretical interpretation of personality scale item responses. *Journal of Personality, 46,* 778–785.

Mischel, W. (1968). *Personality and assessment.* NY: Wiley.

Mischel, T. (Ed.) (1969). *Human action.* NY: Academic Press.

Murray, H. (1938). *Explorations in personality.* NY: Oxford.

Nisbett, R. E. (1980). The trait construct in lay and professional psychology. In L. Festinger (Ed.) *Retrospections on social psychology.* NY: Oxford.

Norman, W. T. (1963). Toward an adequate taxonomy of personality attributes. *Journal of Abnormal and Social Psychology, 66,* 574–583.

Peabody, D. (1987). Selecting representative trait adjectives. *Journal of Personality and Social Psychology, 52,* 59–71.

Rorer, L. G. (1965). The great response-style myth. *Psychological Bulletin, 63,* 129–156.

Royce, J. R., & Powell, A. (1983). *Theory of personality and individual differences: Factors, systems, and processes.* Englewood Cliffs, NJ: Prentice-Hall.

Scheibe, K. E. (1985). Historical perspectives on the presented self. In B. R. Schlenker (Ed.), *The self and social life* (pp. 1–28). NY: McGraw-Hill.

Sechrest, L. (1976). Personality. In M. R. Rosenzweig & L. W. Porter (Eds.). *Annual review of psychology* (pp. 1-26). Palo Alto, CA: Annual Reviews.

Snyder, M. (1981). Impression management: The self in social interaction. In L. S. Wrightsman & K. Deaux, *Social psychology in the eighties* (3rd ed.) (pp. 90-123). Monterey, CA: Brooks/Cole Publishing Company.

Tedeschi, J. T., & Norman, N. (1985). Social power, self-presentation, and the self. In B. R. Schlenker (Ed.), *The self and social life* (pp. 293–322). NY: McGraw Hill.

Tupes, E. C., & Christal, R. E. (1961). *Recurrent personality factors based on trait ratings.* Technical Report ASD-TR-61-97, Personnel Laboratory USAF, Lackland Air Force Base.

White, R. W. (1959). The concept of competence: Motivation reconsidered. *Psychological Review, 66,* 297–333.

White, G. M. (1980). Conceptual universals in interpersonal language. *American Anthropologist, 82,* 75–81.

White, R. W. (1981). Exploring personality the long way: The study of lives. In A. I. Rabin, J. Arnoff, A. M. Barclay, and R. A. Zucker (Eds.) *Further explorations in personality.* New York: Wiley.

Wiggins, J. S., & Broughton, R. (1985). The interpersonal circle: A structural model for the integration of personality research. In R. Hogan & W. H. Jones (Eds.), *Perspectives in personality* (pp. 1–48). Greenwich, CT: JAI.

Wymer, W. E., & Penner, L. A. (1985). Moderation variables and different types of predictability: Do you have a match? *Journal of Personality and Social Psychology, 49,* 1002–1015.

5

Private Experience and Public Action: The Study of Ongoing Conscious Thought

Jerome L. Singer

> For most of us, our contextual selves are united by a continuously running
> autobiographical record. Just as we awaken in the morning knowing that we are the
> same person who went to sleep the night before, we are aware of the activities of
> our different selves. When our spouse self is activated, we can still remember what
> we did in our college-professor self or our jogger self and—equally important—we
> are aware of having shifted from one to the other and of why. In the final analysis,
> our personal histories provide for the continuity that is the essence of selfhood.
> (Kihlstrom and Cantor, 1984, p. 13)

Some time in the past 20 years I developed a new, recurring daydream, a
vivid private narrative not completely unrelated to my childhood fantasies but
definitely a new and pervasive feature of my thoughts in particular contexts.
The fantasy occurred especially when I was alone on long highway drives or
else in the shower. I developed an alter ego with a moderately elaborate
history as the world's greatest operatic tenor. In the safe privacy of my car or
shower, I pictured my character, a young American of course, singing to the
club of Italian millionaires who sponsored his career, performing in a wide
range of operas from *Don Giovanni* ("Il mio Tesoro"), *Trovatore* ("Di Quella
Pira"), *La Tosca* ("E Lucevan Le Stelle"), *Rienzi* ("Rienzi's Prayer"), to a new
opera on Goethe's last love which I conveniently wrote for him. I sang these
arias and many others (I even think my voice improved a bit from practice)
chiefly in such private settings or, occasionally, in the patient company of wife
and children present in the automobile with me. About 10 years ago during
an appearance on television's *Today Show* to talk about research on day-

dreams, Barbara Walters challenged me to describe a personal fantasy, and I mentioned this "tenor" story. She then offered me my chance to sing before the millions of viewers, but I immediately refused, saying, "I know the difference between fantasy and reality!"

I mention this experience in the hope of evoking some comparable experiences that my readers may identify in themselves. Such recurring fantasies, often, as mine, linked to specific settings, may continue for a lifetime alongside one's own awareness of the details of a specific personal history as child, student, worker, spouse, parent, etc. Indeed I can personally identify perhaps a half-dozen recurrent alter-ego fantasies most dating to middle childhood. Before you label me too hastily as a multiple personality along with Eve or Sybil, I urge you to consider whether you see such tendencies in yourselves and to reflect upon the possibility that, unlike these dramatic clinical cases, you retain a firm sense of personal continuity. I propose that what I call the private personality consists not only of our sense of individual continuity based upon memories of ourselves and important other people in various settings but also of a recurring series of more or less playful or, alas, sometimes threatening and guilt-provoking, daydreams as well as the awareness of the ongoing stream of our thoughts replete with plans, intentions, unfinished tasks, and long-standing yearnings, which we share only rarely, if ever, with other persons. While our public personalities as evident to others through our words, gestures, and actions reflect considerable variability depending on situational demands or our construal of such demands (Mischel & Peake, 1982), it is our private personality along with its extra baggage of potential or hopelessly unachievable alter egos that provides the deep sense of continuity that seems an inherent feature of the human condition (Hilgard, 1949; James, 1890).

I do not question the possibility that many of our thought processes occur outside conscious awareness. These include syntactic structures, musical organization, behavioral heuristics (Tversky & Kahnemann, 1980), attributions, inferences and generalizations (Nisbett & Ross, 1980), and a wide range of *overlearned* schemas, prototypes, scripts, personal constructs, or transferences (Meichenbaum & Gilmore, 1984; Singer, 1985; Turk & Speers, 1983). What I do believe needs more careful examination is the possibility that many of these influences upon our thought and action are not permanently unretrievable but that they recur regularly as part of the ongoing conscious stream in the form of fleeting thoughts, fantasies, and even the very extensive mentation identifiable in laboratory studies during sleep, only a fraction of which we happen to remember as the dreams with which we awaken in the morning (Arkin, Antrobus, & Ellman, 1978). I propose to highlight the encouraging possibility that research methods are increasingly available through which we can tap into ongoing thought. Perhaps we can begin to identify the numerous occurrences (which often go unnoticed because external situational demands preclude sufficient attention to such conscious thought for it to be labeled and stored for effective retrieval) in phenomenal awareness of imagery, fantasies, and interior monologues, which are often rehearsing or reshaping established schemas and personal scripts or gradually building new ones.

Curiously, Freud and many subsequent psychoanalytic theorists have paid surprisingly little attention to the structural characteristics of naturally occurring associative thought despite their dependence on the content of such material for drawing inferences about unconscious mechanisms. My own hypothesis, which someday I hope to elaborate, is that Freud's Victorian prudishness or his firm belief in the rationality of fully conscious thought led him to cast the childish, trivial, slimy, salacious, self-serving, and hostile qualities of ordinary conscious thought down to the limbo or hell of a preconscious or unconscious mind. Rather than confront the full absurdity of much of our ongoing consciousness he emphasized the secondary process or logical-sequential processes of ego-oriented consciousness and studied the primary processes as manifestations from the nether regions, discernible in occasional peremptory ideational upsurges, transference fantasies, and, especially, in night dreams. While psychoanalysis was forging its elaborate topography of the unconscious and general psychology was ignoring consciousness by recording overt behavior in rats and pigeons, the psychology of ongoing thought was explored primarily in the literary genre of stream of consciousness fiction. The ambitious, sweeping effort of James Joyce, especially, in capturing in richest detail the natural flow of the daily natural stream of consciousness evokes a shock of recognition from us. With honesty, introspection, and literary skill Joyce sets before us in *Portrait of the Artist as a Young Man* and *Ulysses* remarkable examples of human conscious thought which we can identify as often typical of our own stream of consciousness. The interior monologues, reminiscences, and occasionally playful fantasies of Herzog or Mr. Sammler in the novels of Saul Bellow, while designed for literary and aesthetic effect, also reflect qualities of ordinary waking consciousness that are quite comparable to the tape-recorded thought samples one obtains in the laboratory from participants in research (Pope, 1978).

COGNITIVE–AFFECTIVE PERSPECTIVE

It has become increasingly clear that our ways of knowing the world are intrinsically bound up with our ways of feeling or, indeed, our moral and aesthetic evaluations (Rychlak, 1977, 1981; Tomkins, 1962, 1963; Zajonc,

1980). Significant advances have been made in the past decade in empirical studies of the specific emotions with which we seem "wired." Excitement-interest and joy are positive emotions that, when invoked, are usually positively reinforcing. Fear-terror, distress-sadness, anger, and shame-disgust-guilt-humiliation are negative affects, generally serving as punishing experiences (Izard, 1977; Singer, 1974; Tomkins, 1962, 1963). Tomkins' proposal is that humans are inherently motivated by four implications of the positive and negative emotions: we maximize experiences we expect to generate positive affect and minimize the likelihood of experiencing negative affect; we experience and express emotions as fully as possible; and, finally, we control emotions as it becomes adaptively necessary. Since space limits a detailed exploration of the emotions, I will point here chiefly to their close link with the cognitive system and with the information processing sequence. In effect, in studying the private personality, we need to recognize that we can be startled and intrigued by our own thoughts, that waking as well as nocturnal fantasies can evoke the fear or terror we associate with nightmares, that recurrent fantasies of betrayal or humiliation may have important bodily feedback implications even if (or sometimes because) they are never translated into overt action. The quiet, "nonemotional" scholar can react with private experiences of intense joy to a humorous passage in one of Aristophanes' plays or with intense excitement at the realization of the relationship between two previously obscure readings of an ancient text. The hypertensive adult has been shown to be characterized specifically by recurrent aggressive daydreams (Crits-Christoph, 1984). The close tie between information processing on the one hand and emotional experience on the other pointed to by Tomkins (1962, 1963), Izard (1977), Mandler (1975), McClelland (1961), and Singer (1973, 1974) has greatly expanded our ability to relate motivation to cognition.

Cognitive theories often make the assumption that private experiences such as conscious thoughts, fantasies, or images provide an alternative environment to the continuous processing of material from the external world (Singer, 1974). Thoughts may be reshaped and reorganized and further acted upon by further thought in much the same way as our experience is modified by new inputs from the physical or social environment. Thus, there is a constant restructuring of material in the memory system; memory is never simply a process of passive storage.

Cognitive theories also assume that some attitudes, beliefs, or patterns of information are more central or self-oriented than others and, therefore, are more likely to evoke complex affective responses. The self can be regarded as an object of cognition or as a part of perceived experience rather than as an agent. Because our most personal schemas are associated both with a long background of memories from childhood and with our most recent experiences, they are linked to the most complex network of related images, memories, and anticipations (Kihlstrom & Cantor, 1984; Singer, 1984 a,b). Novel material that does not fit in with beliefs about the self will generate a sense of incongruity. In the face of persisting incongruity, an experience relating to the self will evoke greater intensities of distress or anger than a thought that relates to other persons or stems from news of other countries.

A young man coming home to his apartment house late one evening sees a couple kissing in the hallway. Ordinarily he might find this a bit surprising and mildly amusing as he walks past. If, however, he suddenly realizes that the woman is his wife, this new and surprising information arouses a great range of memories of closeness with this woman as well as anticipations and images of future closeness. All these anticipations and images are suddenly threatened. In addition, a whole set of private beliefs influencing his self-esteem that depend upon the fact that someone loves him and is faithful to him are suddenly incongruous with this new information. First, then, the man is startled. Then as the situation persists and the couple either keeps on kissing or refuses to explain what happened, the young man is confronted with a continuous incongruity between this new information and all his prior expectations and memories. He is likely to experience anger or despair. Certain events are clearly more central to this man's self, not because there is any inherent mystical quality about the self, but because of the greater network of private experiences relating to self-esteem and positive emotionality that are linked to his wife. Even without such a direct experience, some environmental cue, e.g., a scene in a film, may trigger a fantasy of such a kissing scene and evoke much the same sequence of emotional arousal as recent studies of jealousy suggest (Salovey & Rodin, 1986). The elaborate ACT model of Anderson (1982) seems to me also to suggest that self-related material can produce a complex and dense activation along associative pathways that would be reflected in strong emotional experience.

To summarize my general point of view, the human being is confronted regularly by two major sources of stimulation, the complex physical and social characteristics of the surrounding environment which makes demands for "channel space" on one's sensory system and an alternative, competitive set of stimuli generated by the brain that may also impact the sensory system although with somewhat less urgency when one is in the highly activated and aroused condition of wakefulness. A third source of stimulation, weaker in demand for conscious processing if often no less important, is the signalling system from the ongoing machinery of our bodies, a system of great importance in health but not yet well-enough researched and, certainly, except under great pain or fatigue, often ignored. We shall consider some of the implications of the link between bodily cues and the stream of consciousness later. What I would like to suggest is that as far as we can tell most people are carrying on some kind of ongoing interior monologue, a kind of gloss on the immediately occurring events as well as engaging in associations to these events. Kihlstrom (1984) has recently provided a profound review of the research literature in cognition and hypnosis, which supports a neodissociationist view that elaborate and complex parallel streams of thought may be possible, only one of which may be momentarily in phenomenal awareness. His analysis suggests that, even though parallel, these streams may be mutually influential.

Under circumstances in which the external stimulus field involves great redundancy or sufficient familiarity so that one can draw on automatized cognitive and motor processes, one may become aware of a continuing array of memories or fantasies unrelated to the immediate environment. Since, as I will argue below, much of our stream of thought is made up of unfinished intentions or long-standing as well as current concerns, the attention to such stimulation often provokes negative emotions of fear, sadness, shame–guilt, or anger and has a generally mildly aversive quality. Thus, we often prefer to put on the radio or television, do crossword puzzles, or, if in an elevator with a stranger, talk about the weather, rather than stay with a conscious thought sequence. There are great individual differences, however, in the extent to which people choose to control and indeed play along with their own ongoing thought stream or to engage in a more public self-monitoring (Snyder, 1979). The well-established psychometric dimension of introversion–extraversion identifies the range from those who like Walt Whitman "loaf and invite their souls" to those who constantly seek new external stimulation whether socially or from the electronic media in order to avoid self-awareness.

Attention to self-generated stimulation does seem to involve at least temporarily a shift to a different place and the use of the same sensory systems, sometimes in parallel, sometimes in sequential fashion (Antrobus, Singer, Goldstein, & Fortgang, 1970; Singer, Greenberg, & Antrobus, 1971). The complex interaction of both hemispheres of the brain necessary for such a mixture of sequential thought and automatic verbal-chain or intended action-sequence processing (left hemisphere) and for the more parallel, global, novelty-seeking, and perceptual orientation (right hemisphere) has been documented in an impressive review by Tucker and Williamson (1984) and recent suggestive experimental data are also available from Spence, Klein, and Fernandez (in preparation). Kihlstrom (1984) has argued convincingly for the position that primary activities of both hemispheres can be represented in consciousness but that communication about such experience may be hindered if the cerebral hemispheres are disconnected through commissurotomy.

EXPERIMENTAL LABORATORY STUDIES OF ONGOING THOUGHT: STIMULUS INDEPENDENT THOUGHT IN SIGNAL DETECTION STUDIES

Beginning in 1960, Antrobus and I developed a series of experiments designed to determine if we could in some way tap into ongoing thought. Our intention in effect was to capture the daydream or fantasy as it occurred, or come as close to doing so as possible. The model grew out of the vigilance and signal-detection studies developed in World War II to study how individuals could adjust to tasks that required considerable attention under monotonous conditions or environments of minimal complexity and stimulation.

In this model, the subject in effect has different degrees of demand made upon him or her for processing externally derived information under conditions of reasonably high motivation. Since the amount of external stimulation can be controlled, it remains to be determined by the study to what extent individuals will shift their attention from processing external cues in order to earn money by accurate signal detections, toward the processing of material that is generated by the presumably ongoing activity of their own brains. Our attempt was to determine whether we could ascertain the conditions under which individuals, even with high motivation for external signal-processing, would still show evidence that they were carrying on task-irrelevant thought responses (TITR) or stimulus-independent mentation (SIM).

Thus, if, while detecting auditory signals, an individual was interrupted periodically, say, every 15 seconds, and questioned about whether any stimulus-independent thoughts occurred, a "yes" response would be scored as SIM. By establishing in advance a common definition between subject and experimenter as to what constituted such task-irrelevant thought, one could have at least some reasonable assurance that reports were more or less in keeping with the operational definition established. A thought like the following, "Is that tone louder than the one before it? It sounded like it was," would be considered stimulus-dependent or task-relevant and would elicit a "no" response even though it was of course a thought. A response such as "I've got to remember about picking up the car keys for my Saturday night date" would be scored as stimulus-independent mentation. A thought about the experimenter in the next room, "Are they trying to drive me crazy?," even though in some degree generated by the circumstances in which the subject found him- or herself, was nevertheless scored as SIM, because it was not directly relevant to the processing of the signal that was defined for the subject as his or her main task but it could be considered as experiment-related TITR (see below).

By keeping the subjects in booths for a fairly lengthy time and obtaining reports of the occurrence of stimulus-independent thought, after 15 seconds of signal detection it was possible to build up rather extensive information on the frequency of occurrence of SIM, their relationship to the speed of signal presentation, the complexity of the task, and to other characteristics of the subject's psychological situation. Indeed, as Antrobus (1968) showed, it was possible to generate a fairly precise mathematical function of the relationship of stimulus-independent thought to the information load confronted by the subject in the course of ongoing processing.

By using periodic inquiries for content as well as for presence or absence of SIM, it was possible to examine the range and type of content available and to score this material along dimensions similar to those also used for night-dream research, e.g., vividness of imagery, modality of imagery, degree of personal content versus impersonal content, future or past references, etc. The alternative method of establishing content was to make use of continuous free association by the subject during a vigilance task (Antrobus & Singer, 1964).

In the latter study, it was possible to show that while subjects spoke continuously in a varied and undirected fashion (with white noise piped into their ears so they could not hear their own verbalization), they were more likely to maintain arousal during a lengthy session in a darkened booth detecting visual signals. In contrast, counting from one to nine repetitively during the same situation led to actual sleep, sleepiness, and, indeed, irritability and gross discomfort. The arousal effects of continuous free association were to some degree at the cost of accuracy, for when arousal was maintained artificially by periodically piping marching band music into the subject's ears, the accuracy rate of the counting condition was significantly greater than for the free-association condition. In other words, responding to one's inner experiences provides to some extent a varied internal environment that maintains moderate arousal under conditions of a fairly routine or boring task. This is at the cost, however, of some inaccuracies. If external situations are sufficiently arousing, then a restricted internal focus of attention, as in the counting task, may actually lead to more accurate response to the environment. In a sense, then, daydreaming may be one way we maintain interest and arousal in boring or redundant situations with the likelihood that because the situations are so redundant we will not miss too much of what happens. The situation is analogous in many ways to that of driving on a well-known, relatively untraveled highway where we may often drift into daydreaming or listening to music for long periods and yet handle the car safely. Clearly, under conditions of driving in heavy traffic in a midtown area, daydreaming would be less functional than concentration almost completely on the physical environment. Experimental research with driving simulators to test out some of these implications remains to be done, however. There is intriguing data that prior mental rehearsal can play a useful role along with perceptual-motor practice in improving actual driving skills and make driving performance more automatic (Lewin, 1982).

A number of generalizations have emerged out of the signal-detection experiments. It was possible to indicate that stimulus-independent thought could be reduced significantly if the amount of reward paid subjects or the complexity of the task was systematically increased. As a matter of fact, although significant reductions did occur, it turned out to be difficult to reduce reports of stimulus-independent thought to zero unless signals came at such irregular intervals that subjects could not apparently learn to pace themselves. While this would suggest that the general pattern of dealing with stimulus-independent thought involves a sequential style, there has been evidence in a study by Antrobus, Singer, Goldstein, and Fortgang (1970) that, under certain circumstances, it is possible to demonstrate parallel processing, that is, reports of stimulus-independent thought occurring even as the subject was accurately processing signals. These data are also congruent with studies of parallel automatic learning studies and related quasihypnotic phenomena (Hirst, Spelke, Reeves, Caharzck, & Neisser, 1980; Kihlstrom, 1984).

When new, potentially personally relevant information is presented to the subjects just prior to a signal detection "watch," there is a greater likelihood of an increase in stimulus-independent thought. Errors, however, may not necessarily increase for some time. It is as if in many instances for tasks of this kind subjects are not using their full channel capacity for processing private as well as external cues.

The signal-detection model also permits the study of some degree of individual differences. Antrobus, Coleman, and Singer (1967) were able to show that subjects, already by self-report predisposed to be imaginative, were more likely as time went on to report more stimulus-independent thought than subjects who reported on a questionnaire that they were little given to daydreaming. The differences between the two groups increased over time and indeed so also did the number of errors. Initially, the high daydreamers reported a considerable amount of stimulus-independent thought without differing in the level of errors from the low daydreamers. As time went on, however, there was suggestion that they seemed to be preferring to respond to stimulus-independent mentation and their error-rate increased significantly compared with the relatively stable rate of errors for the subjects who showed relatively little stimulus-independent mentation.

The cognitive processing model has a great many other implications that have not been examined fully. In addition to individual differences and to studies of the very process or relationship of information load from the external environment to self-generated material, we can look also at the task of processing in relation to the kind of priorities the individual may set more generally for processing in life situations, whether to stress internally generated material or externally generated signals, and we can also look at the role of private material in generating specific emotional reactions. Thus, the same signal detection task has been used in several studies to which we will refer below for establishing the implications of positive and negative affect.

In various studies directed by Antrobus and myself, we have consistently found evidence that even when persons are paid for correct signal detections, penalized for errors, forced to maintain a rapid pace of response (e.g., 1 per second), they show a fairly consistent rate of stimulus-independent thought (Antrobus et al., 1970).

An attempt was made to observe the relative frequency of two types of thought content both unrelated to an immediate task (auditory signal detections). Four persons participated in 11 consecutive daily two-hour signal detection watches with interruptions after each 16-second trial for reports of occurrence of task-irrelevant thought. Subjects maintained an 80% accuracy detection level throughout. They reported the occurrence of stimulus-independent thought in more than 55% of the trials, a figure that was remarkably stable across the 11 daily sessions. Within the category of stimulus-independent thought, thoughts of a general nature about the experiment (but not about the detection of signals, e.g., "I'm imagining what the experimenters are doing in the next room while I'm in here") are experiment-related but task irrelevant; they may be compared with more remote task-irrelevant thoughts such as "I'm picturing meeting my roomate's sister next week." While experiment-related thought constituted up to 40% of all task-irrelevant thought in the first four sessions, it dropped off drastically during the remaining days, while more remote thought increased considerably (Antrobus, Fein, Goldstein, & Singer, in preparation) (see Figure 5.1.) In yet another study, reports of stimulus-independent thought characterized somewhat more than 50% of 80 trials of random lengths in four daily signal-detection watches. Female participants reported a higher overall level of such responses; both males and females reported *more* task irrelevant thought when the experimenter was of the *opposite sex,* but the effect was greater for females (Algom & Singer, 1984).

Controlled studies of ongoing thought during signal-detection watches afford a continuing rich opportunity for estimating the determinants of the thought stream. We know that the introduction of unusual or alarming information prior to entry into the detection booth (overhearing a broadcast of war news) can increase the amount of stimulus-independent thought even though accuracy of detections may not be greatly affected. A series of studies directed by Horowitz (1978) has demonstrated that specific emotional experiences of an intense nature prior to engaging in signal detections lead to emergence of material in the form of stimulus-independent ideation when thought is sampled during the detection period. Such findings have suggested a basis for understanding clinical phenomena such as "unbidden

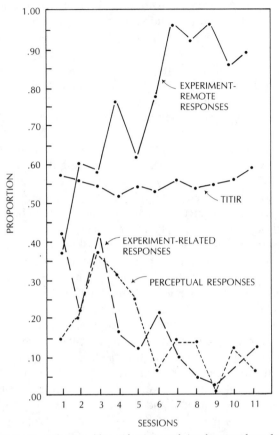

FIGURE 5.1. Mindwandering: Time-sharing task-irrelevant thought and imagery with experimental tasks. Proportion of experiment-remote, experiment-related, perceptual responses, and TITIR as a function of sessions.

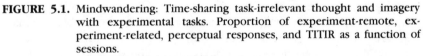

From Antrobus, Fein, Goldstein, and Singer, in preparation.

images" (Horowitz, 1978) or "peremptory ideation" (Klein, 1967). I believe, however, that we can go even further with such a procedure and begin to develop a systematic conceptualization of the determinants of the stream of consciousness.

EXPERIMENTAL INTERVENTIONS AND THOUGHT SAMPLING

While the signal detection procedure gives us a powerful control over the environmental stimulus input and affords an opportunity to estimate very precisely the lengths of specific stimulus-independent thought sequences, here are somewhat less artificial methods of thought-sampling that have been increasingly employed in the development of an approach to determining the characteristics and determinants of waking conscious thought. These involve (1) asking participants to talk out loud over a period of time while in a controlled environment and then scoring the verbalization along empirically or theoretically derived categories; (2) allowing the respondent to sit, recline, or stand quietly for a period of time and interrupting the person periodically for reports of thought or perceptual activity; (3) requiring the person to signal by means of a button press whenever a new chain of thought begins and then to report verbally in retrospect or to fill out a prepared rating form characterizing various possible features of ongoing thought.

Klinger (1977a, b, 1978, 1981) has employed thought-sampling in the above forms to test a series of hypotheses about ongoing thought. He has made an interesting distinction between operant thought processes and respondent thought processes. The former category describes thoughts that have a conscious instrumental property—the solution of a specific problem, analysis of a particular issue presently confronting one, examination of the implications of a specific situation in which one finds oneself at the moment. Operant thought is active, directed, and has the characteristics of what Freud called "secondary process thinking." As Klinger has noted, it is volitional, it is checked against new information concerning its effectiveness in moving toward a solution or the consequences of a particular attempted solution, and there are continuing efforts to protect such a line of thought from drifting off target or from the intrusion of distraction either by external cues or extraneous, irrelevant thought (Klinger, 1978). Operant thought seems to involve a greater sense of mental and physical effort, and it probably has the property that the neurologist Head (1926) called "vigilance," Goldstein (1940) the "abstract attitude," and Pribram and McGuinness (1975) "effort," a human capacity especially likely to suffer from massive frontal brain damage. Klinger's research involving thought-sampling methods has suggested that operant thought is correlated to some degree with external situation-related circumstances. It involved higher rates of self-reports about thought evaluation progress toward the goal of the thought sequence as well as of efforts to resist drift and distraction (Klinger, 1978).

Respondent thought in Klinger's terminology involves all other thought processes. These are nonvolitional in the sense of conscious direction of a sequence, and most are relatively noneffortful (Bowers, 1982). Respondent processes include seemingly unbidden images (Horowitz, 1970) or peremptory thought (Klein, 1967), which are the mental distractions one becomes aware of when trying to sustain a sequence of operant thought e.g., analyzing the logic of a scientific or legal argument) or trying to concentrate on writing checks to pay bills. Most of what we consider daydreams and fantasies (and, of course, nighttime dreams) are instances of respondent thought.

One can, of course, further classify ongoing thought as stimulus-dependent or independent (Antrobus et al., 1970; Singer, 1966); thought identifiably relevant to external cues or to processing environmentally operated cues is at least to some degree stimulus-dependent. In a sample of 285 reports from a dozen subjects, Klinger reported a significant correlation between the environmental setting and reports of operants or directed thought, but a goodly percentage of the variance of both operant and respondent thought seemed independent of the physical or social milieu. We shall return to this point later when we relate waking thought to night dream reports.

The use of thought-sampling in a reasonably controlled environment also permits evaluation of a variety of conditions that may influence or characterize ongoing consciousness. One can score the participants' verbalizations on dimensions such as (1) organized-sequential vs. degenerative, confused thought; (2) use of imagery or related episodes or event memory material vs. logical-semantic structures; (3) reference to current concerns and unfulfilled intentions; (4) reminiscence of past events vs. orientation towards future; (5) realistic vs. improbable content, etc. A study by Pope (1978) demonstrated that longer sequences of thought with more remoteness from the participants' immediate circumstances were obtained when the respondents were reclining rather than walking freely and when they were alone rather than in an interpersonal situation. Zachary (1983) evaluated the relative role of positive and negative emotional experiences just prior to a thought-sampling period. He found that intensity of experience rather than its emotional nature, and, to a lesser extent, the relative ambiguity versus clarity of the material, determined recurrence in the thought stream.

Studies reviewed by Klinger, Barta, and Maxeiner (1981) point to the relative importance of current concerns as determinants of the material that emerges in thought-sampling. Such current concerns are defined as "the state of an organism between the time one becomes committed to pursuing a particular goal and the time one either consummates the goal or abandons its objective and disengages from the goal" (Klinger et al., 1981). Such current concerns as measured by a well-thought-out psychometric procedure make up a useful operationalization of the Freudian wish in its early (prelibido theory) form (Holt, 1976). They may range from unfulfilled intentions to pick up a container of milk on the way home to long-standing unresolved desires to please a parent or to settle an old score with a parent or sibling. In estimating current concerns at a point in time prior to thought-sampling sessions, one obtains scale-estimates of the valences of the goals, the relative importance of intentions in some value and temporal hierarchy, the person's perception of the reality of goal achievement, etc. It seems clear that only after we have explored the range and influence of such current consciously unfulfilled intentions in a sampling of the individual's thoughts and emotional and behavioral responses can we move to infer the influence of unconscious wishes or intentions.

The possibilities for controlled, hypothesis-testing uses of laboratory thought-sampling can be exemplified in a recent study on determinants of adolescents' ongoing thought following simulated parental confrontations (Klos & Singer, 1981). In this study, we set up a hierarchy of experimental conditions prior to a thought-sampling that were expected to yield differential degrees of recurrence in the consciousness of the participants. We proposed that even for beginning college students parental involvements were likely to prove especially provocative of further thought. We chose to evaluate the relative role of (1) generally fulfilled versus unresolved situations, the old Zeigarnick effect (Lewin, 1935); (2) a mutual nonconflictual parental interaction; (3) a confrontation or conflict with a parent that involved, however, a collaborative stance by the adult; and (4) a comparable confrontation in which the parent's attitude was clearly coercive rather than collaborative. We proposed that exposure (through a simulated interaction) to each of these conditions would yield differences in the later recurrence of simulation-relevant thoughts in the participants' consciousness. For example, we believed in general that unresolved situations would be more likely to recur than resolved ones but that, in general, the incompletion effect would be less powerful than (1) a collaborative confrontation and, especially, (2) a coercive confrontation. We hypothesized that the coercive parental conflict simulation when unresolved would lead to the highest frequency of recurrence in the thoughts of the adolescents. We went a step further, however, in the light of the research just mentioned on current concerns. We proposed that a history of long-standing stress with parents would be reflected as a major current concern and that this factor would amplify the effect on later thought of the simulated parent interactions. Thus, frequency of occurrence in later thought of a simulated parent interaction would be highest for those participants with a history of long-standing parental conflict simulating a coercive confrontation that was left unresolved.

A total of 96 men and women participated in the study and were assigned (after having, some weeks earlier, reported on parental stress among other questionnaires) to one of six conditions:

1. collaborative decision-making with parent, resolved
2. collaborative decision-making with parent, unresolved
3. collaborative confrontation with parent, resolved
4. collaborative confrontation with parent, unresolved
5. coercive confrontation with parent, resolved
6. coercive confrontation with parent, unresolved

Participants engaged in carefully developed imaginary simulated interactions with one of their parents (seated in an "empty chair") while an experimenter read a predeveloped parental script appropriate to each situation. Three rather typical parent–child situations were used in each simulation condition. Subsequent to the simulations subjects were taken to another room and over a period of 20 minutes thought samples were obtained at 20 random-interval interruptions (45 to 75 seconds). Their reports were taperecorded and then scored by experimentally naive judges who rated whether verbalized content was related to definitions of the simulation settings. The participants had also made ratings of their involvement in the task, the specific emotions experienced and their relative vividness of imagery during simulation, their perception of the relative similarity of simulations to their own early experience with parents, etc. Manipulation checks failed to suggest in-condition differences other than those experimentally defined and supported the relative involvement and "reality" of the experience for this sample.

Figures 5.2 and 5.3 provide a graphic means of evaluating the findings. First of all, Figure 5.2 is included to demonstrate how meaningful estimates of emotion can be obtained in thought-sampling. While the conditions differed in the directions expected with respect to emotions such as joy and discomfort (distress), the emotion of anger showed a specific relationship to the coercive confrontation conditions and to the subjects' history of stress with a parent (see Figure 5.2).

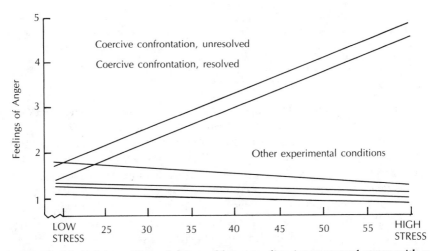

FIGURE 5.2. Adolescent's evaluation of long-standing interpersonal stress with a parent. Regression lines showing the interaction of coercive confrontation and long-standing interpersonal stress or anger arousal (Feelings of Anger is a self-rating immediately after the simulation on a 5-point scale from "Not at all angry" to "Very angry").

From D. S. Klos and J. L. Singer, Determinants of the adolescent's ongoing thought following simulated parental confrontation. *Journal of Personality and Social Psychology,* 1981, *41*(5), 975–987. Copyright © 1981 by the American Psychological Association. Reprinted by permission of the publisher.

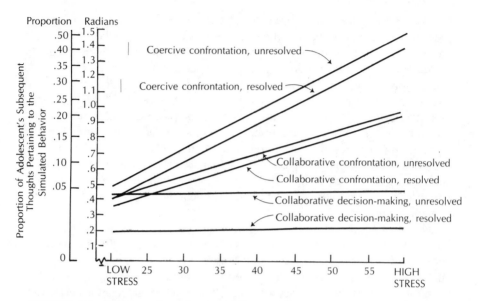

FIGURE 5.3. Adolescent's evaluation of long-standing interpersonal stress with a
parent. Regression lines showing the interaction of confrontation
process and long-standing interpersonal stress on subsequent
thoughts about the simulation. (Proportion (*p*) of subject's 20
thoughts, sampled during 20 minutes subsequent to simulation. Ra-
dian is a 2 arcsine $\sqrt{p}$ transformation to stabilize the variance of *p*.)

From D. S. Klos and J. L. Singer, Determinants of the adolescent's ongoing thought following
simulated parental confrontations. *Journal of Personality and Social Psychology*, 1981, *41*(5),
975–987. Copyright © 1981 by the American Psychological Association. Reprinted by permission
of the publisher.

Figure 5.3 provides clear support for our major hypotheses. The frequency
of recurrences of simulation-condition related thoughts occur in the predicted order with the effects clearly amplified by a history of long-standing interpersonal stress with a parent. The incompletion effect is a modest
one, mainly in evidence in the nonconflictual situation. It is overridden to
some degree by the increasing coerciveness of the imaginary conflict situations. Of special interest is the fact that, once exposed to a simulated parent conflict, those young people who had a history of stress showed as
much as 50% of their later thought reflecting this brief, artificial incident.
One might surmise that, if we generalize from these results, the thought
world of adolescents who have had long-standing parent difficulties may be a
most unpleasant domain since many conflictual chance encounters or even
film or television plots might lead to recurrent thoughts to a considerable
degree. The implications of a method of this kind (combined with estimates
of personality variables or of other current concerns) for studying various
groups, clinical, postsurgical, hypertensives, etc. seem very intriguing.

THOUGHT AND EXPERIENCE SAMPLING IN DAILY LIFE

It is obvious that laboratory-based methods present some difficulties because of their artificiality and also because the very controls on physical movement and restrictions on novel sensory input that are necessary for their effectiveness may lead to overestimations of the naturally occurring fantasy and daydreaming. An approach to thought-sampling that circumvents some of these problems calls for participants to carry signalling devices in pockets, purses, or on pants belts as physicians do. These beepers go off at random during the ordinary activities of participants, and they at once fill out a special card that asks for reports of activity just prior to the signal, the environmental setting, and their current thoughts and emotional state. Typically these are carried for a week, and they go off on the average of two-hour intervals permitting an accumulation of about 50 to 60 reports per participant. Studies by Klinger (1978), Hurlburt (1979, 1980), McDonald (1976), and a whole series directed by Csikszentmihalyi (1982; Csikszentmihalyi & Graef, 1980; Csikszentmihalyi & Kubey, 1981; Csikszentmihalyi & Larson, 1984) all demonstrate the feasibility of this method and its potential for reliable results and suitability for hypothesis testing as well as for accumulation of normative data. In a recent study with 75 adolescents in a suburban community, self-reports were obtained for 69% of the signals sent leading to an accumulation of almost 4,500 reports. Missed signals were chiefly attributable to travel outside the 50-mile signal range, beeper malfunctions, or sleep. Reports included such potentially censorable events as parental quarrels, sexual intimacies, or drug and alcohol abuse. Evidence for consistency and reliability are impressive in most of these studies.

Figure 5.4 presents a sample information sheet one can use in such studies modified from Csikszentmihalyi and Larson (1984). By including specific references to a limited group of emotions and to *types* of operant and respondent thought processes, one can apply such an activity sheet to a large sample of respondents and to clinical patients as well and thus accumulate data on ongoing private experience as well as public action. The implications of such a monitoring procedure for developing both normative and idiographic data in the health field seem very exciting. Elaborate code sheets for scoring self-reports using trained judges are available but one can also simplify the participants' task (at the risk of some data loss) by providing them with empirically derived categories for checking off their experiences as predefined for them in training sessions.

Johnson and Larson (1982) used the experience sampling method with bulimics and a normative group and demonstrated that bulimics showed more dysphoric moods and also greater mood variability. They spent far more time alone at home where they reported their highest levels of distress.

FIGURE 5.4 Random Activity Information Sheet

Date: _____ Time Beeped: _____ am/pm   Time Filled Out: _____

AS YOU WERE BEEPED

What were you thinking about? _____

_____

Where were you? _____

What was the MAIN thing you were doing? _____

_____

Why were you doing it? ( )I had to ( )I wanted to ( )Nothing else to do

What other things were you doing? _____

_____

	not at all		some- what		quite		very

How well were you concentrating?
+ --- + --- + --- + --- + --- + --- + --- + --- + --- +

Was it hard to concentrate?
+ --- + --- + --- + --- + --- + --- + --- + --- + --- +

How self-conscious were you?
+ --- + --- + --- + --- + --- + --- + --- + --- + --- +

Were you in control of the situation?
+ --- + --- + --- + --- + --- + --- + --- + --- + --- +

Were you enjoying what you were doing?
+ --- + --- + --- + --- + --- + --- + --- + --- + --- +

Do you wish you had been doing something else?
+ --- + --- + --- + --- + --- + --- + --- + --- + --- +

How worried were you feeling?
+ --- + --- + --- + --- + --- + --- + --- + --- + --- +

0   1   2   3   4   5   6   7   8   9

Describe your mood as you were beeped:

	very	quite	some	neither	some	quite	very	
alert	●	○	·	—	·	○	●	drowsy
happy	●	○	·	—	·	○	●	sad
suspicious	●	○	·	—	·	○	●	trusting
strong	●	○	·	—	·	○	●	weak
angry	●	○	·	—	·	○	●	friendly
active	●	○	·	—	·	○	●	passive
want to be with others	●	○	·	—	·	○	●	want to be alone
detached	●	○	·	—	·	○	●	involved
free	●	○	·	—	·	○	●	constrained
interested	●	○	·	—	·	○	●	bored
open	●	○	·	—	·	○	●	closed
confused	●	○	·	—	·	○	●	clear
relaxed	●	○	·	—	·	○	●	tense

From Csikszentmihalyi & Larson, 1984.

In a European investigation employing a variation of this method, 24 house-wives who had already taken personality tests were studied over a month. The attributions of causes of moods in various settings could be ascertained as a function of the personality characteristics of the respondent and the situation. Thus, imaginative women attributed the causes of their moods to themselves; self-confident women were more likely to attribute positive moods to their own actions rather than to others (Brandstatter, 1983). In another study, participants whose Thematic Apperception Tests pointed to greater motiva-tion for intimacy showed more interpersonal thoughts and more positive emotional responses in interpersonal situations than did low intimacy motive scores based on a week-long accumulation of eight daily reports (McAdams & Constantian, 1983). The relationship between accumulated daily reports about thought patterns and a self-report questionnaire, the Imaginal Pro-cesses Inventory (Singer & Antrobus, 1972) was evaluated by Hurlburt (1980). He reported significant correlations between the retrospective ques-tionnaire scales for frequent daydreaming, acceptance of daydreaming, and low distractibility and the accumulated daily reports of daydreaming based on two days of dozens of interruptions. The scale on the IPI of sexual daydreams was significantly correlated ($r = +0.40$) with the accumulated record of sexual fantasies. Similarly, those persons who reported more future-oriented daydreaming on the IPI questionnaire scale actually were significantly more often likely to be engaging in such fantasies of the future ($r = +0.39$) when interrupted by the electronic pager during the two days sampled.

PSYCHOMETRIC ASSESSMENTS

Estimating Current Concerns

Another approach to estimating patterns and content of the private thought stream has emerged from using self-reports by participants who, in effect, summarize their accumulated experience in this domain through responses to carefully designed questionnaires. Mention has already been made of Klinger's Concern Dimensions Questionnaires, which have proven useful in predicting how much time people actually spend thinking about something (Klinger, Barta, & Maxeiner, 1981). Respondents list "things" thought about in the past few days, rank them in terms of how much time they estimate they've spent on the subjects, and then rate the thoughts on four factor-analytically derived dimensions: (1) valence (positive or negative); (2) value (emotional investment in goal or general affective intensity); (3) probability of successful goal attainment; and (4) imminence of goal or of resolution of the situation. A beeper study with 11 participants who were interrupted at about 40-minute intervals for the day following completion of one of these questionnaires provided evidence that at least 62% of the thoughts obtained from the sample were judged by "blind" raters as semantically related to the questionnaire-derived thoughts, especially those given highest rank. An even more intriguing study using this procedure (and linked to the relation between daytime thought and night dream content, which will be discussed below) was the finding that sleeping subjects given verbal cues during Stage 1, REM sleep were more likely to incorporate current concern related cues into their dream content (determined from later ratings of similarity from their laboratory awakening dream reports) than cues about thought material not listed by themselves but by other respondents (Hoelscher, Klinger, & Barta, 1981).

A more ambitious effort to establish lists of significant current concerns, assign them to major life area categories such as "home and family," "love and sex," etc., determine valences, values, personal estimates of probabilities of success, etc., involves a self-administered Interview Questionnaire (Klinger, Barta, & Maxeiner, 1981).

A device like this provides a wealth of information about conscious current wishes and their apparent importance to the individual. While the research and clinical possibilities of such a procedure seem to be great, there is as yet little systematic evidence available. The assessment of current concerns and their valences, values, proximity to resolution, and subjectively estimated probability of attainment seems an important basis for evaluation of the conscious content of thought linked to a fairly sophisticated quantitative motivational theory such as thought of Heckhausen (1977). It also points up the necessity for a systematic exploration of conscious content, Freud's "day residues," from whose workings out in fantasy and night dreaming we may attempt to infer unconscious schema or scripts. Indeed, it seems likely that only after we have thoroughly explored the potential of these methods for tapping conscious thought will we be free to assert that *unconscious* motives or intentions are primary determinants of lifespan personality variation.

Identifying Patterns of Daydreaming and Attention to Private Experience

Another approach to describing private experience is to rely upon the self-awareness of each individual's own continuing thought patterns. These self-reports can be accumulated in the psychometric questionnaire format that has served personality researchers fairly well when properly employed. I will mention just a few of many possible research approaches in this area.

Factor analyses with large numbers of respondents generally yield three second-order factors that seem to underlie scales characterizing inner experience (Imaginal Processes Inventory; IPI) (Giambra, 1980; Huba, 1980; Huba, Singer, Aneshensel, & Antrobus, 1982; Isaacs, 1975; Segal, Huba, & Singer, 1980; Singer & Antrobus, 1972). One factor can be labeled "Positive-

Constructive Orientation of Inner Experience": It includes scales tapping positive emotions and events in daydreams, an acceptance and enjoyment of daydreams, vivid visual and auditory imagery in fantasies, and a generally future-oriented and problem-solving quality to fantasy. A second dimension can be characterized as Guilty-Dysphoric daydreams or unpleasant, emotionally toned fantasies. Scales such as Guilty content in daydreams, Hostile-Aggressive Daydreams, Fear of Failure fantasies, and so forth load highest in this factor. The third pattern that we identify really represents a negation of an extended, elaborated inner experience. Instead, it reflects Poor Attentional Control and is characterized by high loadings of such scales as Distractability, Susceptibility to Boredom, and other scales suggesting an inability to sustain an extended skein of private imagery or, for that matter, to maintain a prolonged internally oriented concentration without reaction to the continuous stimulation in the physical environment.

Some examples of correlates of these daydreaming styles can be cited briefly. Maddi (1976) proposed a tridimensional personality classification, High–Low Activation, High–Low Active–Passive Control, and Internal–External Event Orientation. Data from a sample of 1,000 respondents using the Jackson Personality Research Form, Zuckerman's Sensation-Seeking scales, the Imaginal Processes Inventory, and Rotter's Locus of Control Inventory seemed to offer evidence of at least two of Maddi's combinations: High-Activation, Internal Focus, Active Control and Low Activation, Passive, Internally Oriented (Segal et al., 1980). In another study employing Fenigstein, Scheier, and Buss's (1975) scales of Public and Private Self-Consciousness and Tellegan and Atkinson's Absorption Scale, a distinct cluster of measures including Positive-Constructive Daydreaming, Guilty-Dysphoric Daydreaming, Private Self-Consciousness, and Absorption emerged, suggestive of Thinking Introversion. Poor Attentional Control, Public Self-Consciousness, and Social Anxiety formed a separate cluster reflecting something more like an emotional instability dimension (Barrios & Singer, 1981). In studies of hypnotic susceptibility or of the use of daydreaming scales to predict waking imagery methods of helping people to overcome creative blocks, there is further evidence that a predisposition to positive, playful daydreaming is consistently tied to measures of absorption, imagery vividness, and hypnotic responsiveness (Barrios & Singer, 1981; Crawford, 1982). Golding and Singer (1983) reported on data linking Guilty Daydreaming to one style of depression (self-critical and guilt-oriented depression) and Poor Attentional Control to another (dependency and shame-oriented depression).

The three patterns of experience constitute a separate domain of measurable psychological response from personality trends and more public behavior, but they are linked systematically to such behaviors, probably in a transitional two-way interactive fashion (Segal et al., 1980). Recent studies by

McIlwraith and Schallow (1983a, b) found that adults and children who were heavy viewers of television and especially of the more violent programming were also characterized by higher scores on the Guilty-Dysphoric Daydreaming dimension. The data are correlational and cross-sectional, but other evidence suggests that persons with unpleasant and distressing inner experiences may seek distraction and passive escape from such thoughts in television (Csikszentmihalyi & Kubey, 1981). Once exposed to the violence and disaster that characterize daily television fare, they may find their later conscious experience increasingly characterized by frightening, hostile, or fearful fantasies (Kubey, 1982).

With the availability of psychometric instruments such as the IPI, Bowers' (1982) Effortless Experiencing Scale (which taps perhaps somewhat related aspects of respondent thought), the Public and Private Self-Consciousness Scales, the Absorption Scale, a complex questionnaire and thought-sampling method designed to estimate alternate states of consciousness (Pekala & Levine, 1981, 1982), and a number of other new and promising questionnaires for scoring imagery vividness and control (Cartwright, Jenkins, Chavez, & Peckar, 1983; Tower & Singer, 1981), we can set up experiments or naturalistic studies that examine such long-standing predispositions along with thought samples and measures from outcomes of experimental interventions.

Other Methods for Estimating Private Experiences

Johnson and Raye (1981) in a thoughtful paper reflecting a cognitive experimental orientation have identified a process they term "reality monitoring." It refers to the relative ability of individuals to identify events as having occurred in the "real world," that is in their physical environment, e.g., words or pictures shown them by an experimenter, and the same stimuli as generated by their own imagery and memory systems. They point to specific processing and structural differences that lead to correct differentiation of such experiences up to a week following occurrence. They do not, however, examine patterns of individual differences in imagery vividness, attention to or enjoyment of self-generated processes.

The patterns of questionnaire responses described above or data from a burgeoning group of new questionnaire or assessment devices (Bowers, 1982; Pekala & Levine, 1982; Tower & Singer, 1981) suggest that many individuals learn over their lifetime to tune attention in and out of the private stream of thought, to direct or control it, and to engage in a variety of cognitive operations that may actually help them make more precise discriminations between "reality" and "fantasy" or at least control their priorities for inner attention. Indeed, it has been argued that one major outcome of the subtle training one undergoes in psychoanalysis or in the more explicit rehearsal procedures of cognitive therapies is to learn to "rerun" the mental "film" of a series of experiences, identifying gaps, moments of anger or anxiety, and, ultimately, the overlearned cognitive structures (schemas, scripts, or transferences) that may represent the unconscious motivations for thought or behavioral sequences (Meichenbaum & Gilmore, 1984; Singer, 1974). Measures of imagery vividness abilities, controllability, self-monitoring (Snyder, 1979), absorption in one's experiences, etc. provide an exciting possibility for identifying those persons who may prove especially adept at monitoring their thought streams or benefitting quickly from training in this area and those persons who may show real difficulties in identifying or controlling their thought patterns. This latter group is of special interest in view of some evidence that "repressors" or "alexeithimics" may be more susceptible to a variety of health difficulties (Jensen, 1984; Lesser, 1981; Schwartz, 1983).

An area of relevance in relation to measurement of absorption in fantasy is that of hypnosis. A good deal of evidence is accumulating to suggest that measures of hypnotic susceptibility and some of their cognitive or childhood correlates are also associated systematically with the capacity for vivid imagery, the enjoyment and use of daydreams in a positive manner, etc. (Barber, 1984; Barrios & Singer, 1981; Crawford, 1982; Spanos & Radtke, 1981–1982; Wilson & Barber, 1983). Indeed, one might take the position today, building upon Hilgard's (1965, 1977) extensive research on hypnosis, that entering a "deep" hypnotic state may not reflect a weakness or even a "susceptibility," to use the term still current, but a basic human capacity.

It was once thought that introverted subjects, persons given to imagery and fantasy, were less hypnotizable, but I propose the hypothesis that a necessary intervening variable to test such a view would involve evaluation of personal beliefs that "being hypnotized" represented a human weakness, a surrender of autonomy. Introverts could distract themselves by tuning out the phrases of the hypnotist and attending to their private thought stream, thus not accepting the psychological "contract" of the trance situation. Once having modified their fear of hypnosis, such persons ought to be the best candidates for hypnosis since, in effect, they often already engage in the self-hypnosis of extended reverie states or absorptions in books (Singer & Pope, 1981).

In summary, there seems a considerable and growing availability of reasonably sophisticated measures for assessing ongoing thought in laboratory or in the field and for estimating for individuals and groups through questionnaires the trait-like patterns of current concerns, styles of daydreaming, imagery use, and absorption capacities in private experience even to the point of trance-like states. What we have not done yet is to examine in more systematic ways the links between these data derived from conscious report and the kinds of inferred unconscious schema, motivational structures, and special processing patterns beneath awareness that have made up the bulk of the clinical literature on the unconscious dimension of human experience.

ONGOING THOUGHT IN THE FORMATION AND MAINTENANCE OF SCHEMAS, SELF-CONCEPTS, AND ACTION-SCRIPTS

Methods are increasingly available for capturing ongoing thought as it occurs or for identifying personality variations in the styles of ongoing thought and the relative emphasis on verbal or visual imagery, vividness, controllability, future orientation, positive or negative affective quality, etc. (Langer, 1983; Tower & Singer, 1981). Indeed, we have good support now for the possibility of using concurrent physiological measurement to identify bodily correlates of some mental activity through cardiovascular measures (Bowen, 1984; Schwartz, Weinberger, & Singer, 1981; Weinberger, Schwartz, & Davidson, 1979; Qualls, 1982–1983), facial muscle activity (Brown, 1978; Ekman, Levenson, & Friesen, 1983), and brain-wave patterns (Ahern, 1982). Of special interest is the evidence that we can identify a group of individuals, sometimes termed "repressors," whose conscious reports that they do not feel anxious, worried, or tense are belied by strong physiological patterns suggestive of fear and distress. These physiological reactions, indeed, are similar to or even greater than those obtained from participants who admit consciously to a good deal of anxiety (Weinberger, 1983; Weinberger, Schwartz, & Davidson, 1979). We shall shortly consider some of the health implications of this repressive style.

Let me now outline some major speculations, hypotheses, and possibilities for research that stem from my emphasis on the importance of the ongoing stream of consciousness.

Implications for Affect and Cognition

Following up on Tomkins' (1962) theoretical proposals I have suggested that most people are motivated to enhance circumstances for experiencing positive emotions. The two major positive emotions are (1) interest-excitement, generated by a *moderate* level of novel stimulation or complexity and ambiguity in one's environment and (2) the joy one experiences by matching or assimilating such novel or complex information with previously well-established schema. I propose that one major function of ongoing consciousness may be to react to new information by reflection and matching against previous schema. The duplication of experience through imagery and an interior monologue may reduce the fear associated with extreme novelty but allow for a curious, interested continued search until the information is fully assimilated. Broadbent (1958) has described two forms of processing styles: "short-processing" in which each stimulus is reacted to with the most immediate previous or nearly automatic overlearned association, thus yielding a rapidity of reaction, while "long-processing" involves an extended reaction involving a fuller survey of possible long-term memory match-ups before a response is produced. I have elsewhere proposed some links between extraversion, the cognitive style of field-dependence, the "neurotic" style of hysteria (Horowitz, Marmar, Krupnick, Wilner, Kaltreider, & Wallerstein, 1984) and short-processing and thinking introversion, field-independence, the obsessional neurotic pattern, and long-processing (Singer, 1984a, b). It is my hypothesis that reflective awareness and longer processing may slow down reactivity, lead to some loss of information (but most of our environments are highly redundant), and establish a sense of *control* over input, which maintains an emotional stance of interest and even excitement or of joy. The inner environment of the short processor may lack a complexity and richness of or depth of processing, which may lead to a lack of complicated emotionality but, perhaps, a vulnerability through lack of preparatory rehearsal of material, to sudden fear or distress when extremely novel or complex *external* information is presented.

The practiced long-processor may show less fluctuation in mood but may face more continuing blends of the interest and joy of controlled processing with the mildly dysphoric awareness through reflection of one's unfinished business, unfulfilled intentions or of the various inherent tragedies (e.g., death, nuclear war, injustice) that any serious sequence of associations will lead to. Studies by Linville (1982) suggest that persons identified as showing self-complexity do demonstrate less variability in mood over several days' samplings. Self-complexity refers to a measure of more differentiated self-description, acceptance of somewhat contradictory beliefs, recognition of weaknesses as well as strengths, etc. It is my proposal that such a more differentiated belief structure about one's self emerges from greater reflection and mental replay in the form of ongoing rumination, in effect, a habitual or stylistic pattern of long-processing. Such a pattern in a normal personality configuration can be recognized as an adaptive form of a thinking introversive or (in Witkin's extensive research) field-independent cognitive style (Witkin & Goodenough, 1981). In its more pathological extreme such an elaborate set of self-beliefs may be a feature of the obsessive-compulsive style described by Horowitz (1976).

The patterns of response to stimuli from long-term memory as they emerge spontaneously (especially in less novel, "busy," or life-endangering physical and social environments) may also reflect the styles of long- and short-processing and the attempt to maintain a positive affective tone either by exploration, search, and "play" with thought (the long-processing mode) or by rapid shifts of attention to new external material (the short-processor's method). Such styles involve the individual in differential amounts and quality of rehearsal of current concerns and projections of self into different situations, and gradually become the basis for forming sets of organized beliefs about the self or about the environment that have special properties that, I believe, link the conscious representations of the stream of thought to the unconscious schemas, scripts, and prototypes that unroll automatically to expedite cognitive matching and information-processing.

Knowledge Structures: Schemas[1] and Scripts About Self and Others

Although the concept of schemas as organizational structures that encapsulate knowledge about self or the world are traceable in psychology to the concepts of Piaget, Lewin, Tolman, and Kelly ("Personal Constructs") and, of course, reflect as well the psychoanalytic notions of unconscious fantasy, object representations (Blatt & Wild, 1976) and transference, it is only during less than the last decade that systematic efforts at operationalizing and experimenting with such notions have proliferated (Hollon & Kriss, 1984; Turk & Speers, 1983). Schemas may serve to filter the complex new information our senses confront, but they are also continuously strengthened when similar information is processed ("dogs bark when someone is at the door") or when one reflects on new, slightly divergent information ("why isn't Fido barking when the bell rings? Is he sick?").

Self-schemas as operationalized and investigated systematically by Markus (1977), Bandura (1977), and, in work with depressed patients, by Beck, Rush, Shaw, and Emery (1979) represent a special case of beliefs about one's self. Beliefs about other people, fuzzy set prototypes such as "a typical businessman" or "the usual politician" have also been identified and studied (Cantor & Mischel, 1979). The term "scripts," originally proposed by Tomkins (1962, 1963), has been developed by researchers in artificial intelligence in a specialized way to define organized belief-systems about action-sequences in the "real world," sequences that unroll relatively automatically like well-programmed series (Schank & Abelson, 1977). Indeed, a model for a similar schema in dealing with the imaging process was developed by Minsky (1975). The recent theorizing of Tomkins has proposed that scripts about self or about especially important interpersonal interactions have been organized out of often fairly specific childhood "scenes" that were associated with either strong positive or negative emotions (Tomkins, 1979). The work of Carlson

---

[1] I have chosen to use the Anglicized plural for schema rather than the ancient form at the suggestion of George Mandler.

(1981) and Carlson and Carlson (1984) exemplifies the way in which positive or negative affective "scenes" and scripts are differentially influential in current behavior and in the interpretation of new information. The semantic and practical relationship of schemas, scripts, and prototypes to the transference phenomena identified in psychoanalytic sessions deserves much more extensive attention. It is increasingly clear that the long-standing dilemma of social psychology, "why don't attitudes predict behavior?," has been resolved when careful measurement of schemas about self and about others are considered separately and combined to predict overt actions (Kreitler & Kreitler, 1976, 1982).

This very brief review of a major area of development in the lively field of social cognition is designed to suggest that if we wish to understand unconscious processes we will, first of all, have to seek them in the relatively automatic unrolling of scripts, the filtering processes of schemas, or in the inherent rules for evaluating information and making judgments described as *availability, representativeness,* and *anchoring with adjustment* heuristics by Tversky and Kahnemann (1974). Yet, so far such patterns of relatively automatic sequences have been explored chiefly in the framework of assigning individuals rather specific tasks to accomplish or problems to solve. The thrust of my earlier presentation leads me to propose that schemas, scripts, or prototypes are not static, if moderately well-organized structures. They are constantly subject to reexamination and reshaping during waking conscious thought or even in the course of rumination about night dreams, especially if one approaches such a process, as a psychotherapy patient might, with a particular schema for interpretation. If we are ultimately to understand the workings of the "unconscious" we will have to "unpackage" the various individual schemas, prototypes, scripts, "core organizing principles" (Meichenbaum & Gilmore, 1984), or behavior heuristics through some types of systematic questioning or through various forms of thought sampling that can permit us to observe how they are used in ordinary daily life. Of course, psychoanalysis has been engaged in such a task but, I suggest, in an often unwitting and diffuse fashion. More recently, cognitive behavior therapists have begun addressing this task quite directly in treatment (Meichenbaum & Gilmore, 1984; Singer, 1974). Luborsky's (1977) demonstration of reasonably reliable methods for identifying "core conflictual themes" (surely close relatives of schemas and scripts) within psychoanalytic sessions could also be applied to more extensive samples of nontherapeutic ongoing thought sequences in daily life or in laboratory settings as well as to samples of patients' communication in various forms of psychotherapy.

In view of the great importance assigned to beliefs about self by both psychoanalysts oriented towards object relations theory and cognitive researchers, special attention should be paid to how such schemas become organized through ongoing interior monologues. Tomkins' notion of positive or negatively laden nuclear scripts (which usually involve the self) implies differential filtering processes for new information in relation to expectancies based on such scripts, e.g., *hypersensitivity*, to possible analogies in new settings for negative nuclear scripts or efforts to "reshape" new information to *enhance* its similarity to positive nuclear scenes. Can we identify such processes through extended samples of thought or self-monitoring procedures? Certainly no one would seriously claim nor could they prove that the "objects" of psychoanalytic object relations are permanently crystallized in the original pregenital schemas. Very likely they emerge again and again into conscious ruminations, tested and elaborated in mental rehearsals or reminiscences and also "acted out" in transferential encounters in daily life as well as in analysis (Singer, 1985). Indeed, as we shall consider in the next section, they may also be replayed and reshaped further in what we remember of our sleep mentation. An individual stylistic variable worth exploring may be that "repressors" may have developed long-standing strategies to avoid extended attention to ongoing thought and thus may have differentiated and reshaped earlier schemata, prototypes, and scripts less than other individuals with the result that when such material emerges into consciousness it may indeed (1) surprise them more or seem alien and peremptory and (2) remain more global, child-like, and rigid in structure. Recent and as yet unpublished work by Bowen suggests that such undifferentiated patterns may also be evident in their cardiovascular response to emotional arousal.

One of the most intriguing recent studies in the emerging field of lifespan explorations of personality has been the work by Helson, Mitchell, and Moane (1984) on the "social clock." This term suggests both a social group's agreement about when certain events ought occur in one's life (e.g., marriage before age 30) and one's own more personal set of goals (or "script") for achieving such states as intimacy, childbearing, career success, or financial security. In a 20-year follow-up of female college graduates, it was possible to identify those women adhering to a traditional feminine social clock, those willing to postpone but not give up such expectations of marriage and childrearing, and those women who early eschewed such a script or who, by age 28, had chosen career lines that conformed in the 1960s to a "masculine" social clock. The data point up the long-term predictive effect of scales on the California Personality Inventory and of personal social clocks in suggesting the patterns of adherence to these early scripts over the years and also the reactions of the women who, despite adherence, experienced divorce or other disruption of these scripts.

Space does not permit a review of the richly suggestive data of this study. Such research based on a few questions about conscious life goals and responses to a standard inventory make it clear how much more we could gain in exploring ongoing intentions and personal schemas or scripts by recurrent sampling.

Waking Thought and Dream Content

I have already suggested that we begin to structure the content and organization of sleep mentation in the "day residues" or, as Klinger (1971) has proposed, in the current concerns of waking life. While Freud regarded the dream as the royal road to the unconscious, I suggest that increasing evidence we have from comparisons of daydream and nightdream samples (Starker, 1978) or from accumulation and analysis of sleep mentation reports in REM, EEG Stage 1 and nonREM, EEG Stage 2 from laboratories points to a continuity between dream and conscious thought. The studies of Breger, Hunter, and Lane (1971) indicated how even specific phraseology occurring in presleep verbalizations emerged as presumably visual images in subsequent dream reports of participants who slept in the laboratory. Recent careful work by Antrobus (1983) and his co-workers has shown that very precise quantitative analyses of REM and NREM sleep mentation reports point much more to continuities and similarities rather than to differences between these stages in content or patterns of thought as reported. Antrobus' analysis of the metaphoric structure of waking thought and how metaphors may be formed through semantic generalization in dreams further suggests a continuity of day and sleep mentation (Antrobus, 1987). In a recent and, I believe, very important analysis, Antrobus, Reinsel, and Wollman (1987) have compared night dream reports from Stage 1, REM and Stage 2, NREM with reports obtained from waking subjects in a normally stimulated environment and in one in which sensory input is relatively reduced. They hypothesized that two properties of Stage 1, REM sleep might account for the major difference consistently obtained between dream reports from that sleep stage and those from Stage 2, NREM: a higher level of cortical activation (that is, a more wakeful brain) and a higher perceptual threshold for awareness of one's physical surroundings. Indeed, this combination has led to the general term "paradoxical sleep" for Stage 1, REM. In the waking state, even in relatively understimulated environments, one usually is processing external material, and daydream material seems, therefore, to lack the vividness, sense of reality, and figure-ground differentiation of the nightdream report. The findings of this study indicated that the major differences between the reports obtained from a series of participants was that Stage 1, REM and sensory-restricted wakeful free associations were characterized by more words used, longer sequences of thought, and less reference to the physical environment. One might surmise that the long story-like quality of the "classical" Stage 1, REM dream is a function of an extended response to long-term memory material uninterrupted by any notice of the participants' surroundings, e.g., bed, laboratory. Such references are more frequent in both the waking "noisy" environment reports and the Stage 2, REM reports. Similarly, the waking mentation reports in a less busy setting reflect extensive response to self-derived thought and minimal reaction to the physical environment. Comparable waking data of longer sequences of thought, more remote from present concerns, as situation of the respondent was reduced in terms of social contact were obtained in a thought-sampling study by Pope (1978). A remarkable literary demonstration of this result can be seen in Molly Bloom's soliloquy in bed at the end of James Joyce's *Ulysses* (Humphrey, 1968; Steinberg, 1973).

What these data of the comparability of waking reverie and nightdreaming suggest is again an extended continuity between conscious mentation and night dream content. I propose that the images and metaphors of many dreams are already prepared in waking rumination but, often, such thoughts are forgotten because we have no purpose in remembering them. Dream interpretation in psychoanalysis draws on after-the-fact associations. What would we find if we sampled the patients' thoughts beforehand?

Here is an example of such an instance presenting first the dream and then the prior thought samples of an individual who carried a pager for a week:

> I am in Canada visiting Bill, a younger former associate of mine. We are on an extremely steep mountain. There are dozens of skiers who are coming down this incline with great speed, often taking long leaps before coming back down to earth. Bill points upwards and says, "Let's keep walking up there, and we can get some skis and ski down." I find myself appalled as I see the steepness of the mountain. As we climb higher I become more and more aware that I am not a good enough skier to come down at the rate of other skiers.
>
> I put on some skis and am trying in my slow fashion to cut slowly sideways across the mountain face rather than schussing straight downhill. I notice my friend Bill whizzing by with great confidence. Suddenly, however, he takes a very bad fall and lies in the snow obviously having hurt his leg.
>
> Later I am visiting Bill and another even younger man who now shares an apartment with him. I realize that both Bill and his new roommate have recently had marital problems and are living bachelor lives. I say to them that while I appreciate some of the advantages of bachelorhood I am really quite happy with my wife after 20 years of marriage.

A surprising number of details from this man's recent prior waking thoughts turned up in the dream. The dreamer was a middle-aged man who was an executive in a well-established engineering company. He seriously questioned his ability to master the required technology ("to schuss downhill") as the firm moved into new areas of engineering. He had also been examining in his thoughts the value of his intensive work for the company. He wondered whether he could keep up the pace, considering his apparently diminishing physical strength and skill.

Several events in recent days had triggered some of these thoughts. In one of them, he and his wife had set out on a quiet walk on a marked trail in the woods. They took the wrong path and ended up climbing a mountain; they then had to retrace their steps down a steep incline. Despite what seemed at times an impossible climb, they both emerged none the worse. He had also been watching the Olympic games on television, with many thoughts and conversations about the intensity and determination required for the athletes to reach the levels of skill necessary for international competition.

The man's dream can be understood as a representation in visual form of a whole series of questions and thoughts that had been going on in his conscious mind. These included intense emotions as well as unfinished business and current concerns. There were fears and doubts associated with the difficulty of maintaining his standards of scientific work as his company moved toward more technological development. This thought brought to mind his former colleague, Bill. Though younger, Bill had always seemed more technically competent, but in recent years he had suffered setbacks at work and in his personal life. A newly employed younger colleague (who also figures in the dream) also seemed likely to have greater professional skills, but again (and here the dream fades to a wish, perhaps) the older man can say, "Well, I can still climb that mountain, and I can also say that I have a more fulfilled personal life than these younger men."

Thus, the symbolism of the dream was probably not created completely within the dream but was already anticipated in the man's daytime thoughts. Usually, psychologists do not have daytime records and samples of ongoing thought as in this case. And, in a psychotherapy session, a patient's associations to a dream are after the fact. The likelihood is that many of our daytime thoughts contain symbolic or allegorical associations, which we may store together and think about further during the day. But the press of daily affairs may prevent us from noticing how much time we spend in self-reflection. Having forgotten that we thought metaphorically we are surprised later by the symbolism and imagery of our dreams (Singer, 1984a).

THOUGHT AND HEALTH: SOME RESEARCH DIRECTIONS

Let me, finally, point to some implications for physical health that have been emerging from studies of thought. I have already indicated that the ongoing machinery of the body represents a signalling system that competes weakly (except for massive pain or severe stress or fatigue) for channel space at the focus of conscious awareness with environmental stimuli and reverberating material from long-term memory. The process is cyclical and interactive. As systems theorists point out our mental awareness of body signals produces thought sequences that, if in the form of pleasant, relaxing imagery or in the form of frightening scripts about serious illness, surgery, or death may generate quite specific neurotransmitter reactions in the central nervous system and particular autonomic, muscular, or cardiovascular reactions (Schwartz, 1982). Researchers are increasing their efforts to identify general kinds of self-communications that aid people in coping with particular kinds of pain or physical stress and that may also promote longer-term strategies of adherence to medical regimens, self-care, or disease preventive life-styles (Turk, Meichenbaum, & Genest, 1983).

Probably the most persuasive evidence of how some form of thought activity can almost at once influence physiological functions or disease processes has come from clinical and experimental studies with hypnosis. A recent review by Barber (1984) documents dozens of examples of bodily changes produced by suggestion and intense imagery absorption.

There is a sizable and growing literature linking major illness, either in onset or in course, to particular psychological orientations. I will mention here only a few instances of studies in which specific thought processes have been linked to such illness or their outcomes. A very careful recent study by Crits-Christoph (1984) examined the thought patterns (based on questionnaire responses) of normal individuals whose blood pressure was determined and clinical hypertensives. For these groups, contrary to some early beliefs, it could be shown that a history of consciously experienced anger, not suppression or repression of anger, predicted hypertension. Anxiety, direct or suppressed, served as a control emotion measured and did not predict hypertension. Thus, the effect was specific to a particular emotion and was even more specifically linked to hostile, angry fantasies as measured from the Imaginal Processes Inventory.

A more extensive study carried out by Jensen (1984) sought to determine if psychological measures could predict the course of neoplastic disease, specifically malignant breast cancer. Very carefully matched groups of women who were cancer-free, women with malignant breast cancer but who remitted for two years, and women with breast cancer recently diagnosed were set up. Matching on a very extensive array of physical, hereditary, and sociocultural and treatment variables was carried out. An array of psychological tests as well as extensive physiological and blood chemistry measures were administered, and the groups were followed for two years. In conformity to a good number of earlier studies, both cancer groups showed a greater proportion of women who could be classified as repressors, that is, persons who report little anxiety but who score higher on a measure of social conformity or defensiveness than the control group. The repression variable proved to be a strong predictor of a poor treatment course for the patients along with a measure of Positive Daydreaming. The latter variable was especially predictive for non-repressors; that is, women who did not show a repressive style but who reported a good deal of positive, playful, or escapist daydreaming obtained as poor scores on disease status after two years as did the repressors. The psychological variables were as good or better as predictors as the blood chemistry measures. The implications of these findings (in conformity with clinical reports) is that better health outcomes may emerge, at least for some forms of cancer, if the patient concentrates on angry and resolute fantasies rather than denying concern or escaping into pleasant fantasy. A recent study by Felton and Revenson (1984) also found a poor outcome for escapist, wish-fulfilling fantasy in chronic illness, and other evidence in cancer further supports the link between a repressive personality style and disease onset or poor prognosis (Kneier & Temoshok, 1984). In the words of Dylan Thomas to his dying father, "Do not go gentle into that good night . . . Rage, rage against the fading of the light."

Note the contrast between the two studies cited. In one, angry fantasies seem correlated with pathological trends; in the second, the absence of conscious anger, determination, and concern seems more associated with a disease process. In a study just completed by Polansky (1985), images involving the patient's fantasy of healthy changes in the immune system of asthmatics were specifically associated with subsequent *actual* improvements in the immune system, if not nearly so strongly with symptomatic relief. We will need a great deal more careful work, it appears, tying the specific kinds of self-generated images to specific ongoing physiological changes. An exciting opportunity lies ahead. Are conscious thoughts functioning like ideomotor suggestions, or are they merely translating into conscious reports some as yet not understood "body machinery" communication? Are the relatively automatic, out-of-awareness operations of our body scripts and schemas crucial here, or are conscious reports the critical factors? I believe that research may support the latter option.

From the standpoint of personality patterns we see numerous reports from clinical studies and some fairly well-controlled investigations pointing to greater susceptibility to illness in persons who show the repressive style or who are sometimes termed alexithymics, those with an inability to find words (or, I would add, "images," to describe feelings). We need considerably more work pinning down such constructs as alexithymia or repressive defensiveness, perhaps through recurrent thought sampling, so that we can observe how elaborate memories, body signals, future fantasies as well as worries or angry thoughts are avoided. What are the differential implications of regular private thoughts of a continuing worrisome nature as in hypochondria and obsessive rumination? What situational variations mesh with predispositional thinking styles to yield more or less adaptive responses? I believe we will need to do more frequent measurements and more temporally extended sampling of thoughts, situations, and overt actions as part of our attempt to identify the links between private experience, body processes, and public action.

An intriguing hypothesis proposed by Kobasa (1979) and elaborated in a longitudinal study of the health of a group of business managers by Kobasa,

Maddi, and Courington (1981) describes a personality style resistant to illness, which is termed "hardiness." Based on questionnaires and interviews they identify the hardy personality as someone accepting commitment, seeking challenges, and believing in personal control of events. Such persons have a good deal of curiosity, find their experiences meaningful and interesting, value their imagination, and believe they can be influential through their thoughts and actions. They confront new situations not as threats but as challenges to imaginative thought and action. Even when prior illness history is controlled for, hardiness (along with constitutional predisposition) accounts for continuing good health, while stressful life events do not enter significantly into the equation. The hardy personality style may transform stress into challenge.

Again, we need more regular measurements of the ongoing thoughts and the recurring schemas and scripts of hardy or (at the opposite pole) alienated personalities in the face of a series of more or less stressful life situations if we are to be certain about the process. I would propose the hypothesis that the hardy personality has a greater tendency to play with situations in consciousness and to work at active transformation of them before moving to active, committed behavior. Can we identify recurring personal schemas or nuclear scripts that fashion a style like hardiness or repressive defensiveness? Clearly there is much yet to be done in the field of the links between personality style and health, but the prospect is challenging and exciting, especially for those of us who are truly hardy personalities.

CONSCIOUS AND UNCONSCIOUS THOUGHT: SOME PROPOSALS

While I have been stressing the importance of conscious thought, or, in other words, phenomenal awareness of one's memories, intentions, schemas, scripts, and prototypes, I do not wish to be misunderstood as minimizing unconscious processes in organismic functioning. Clearly, millions of words, images, and more abstract propositions are stored in some way out of our ordinary awareness. The forms of syntax, procedural and behavioral strategies such as attribution rules, representative or availability heuristics, etc. all operate out of awareness as do thousands of scripts and schemas that have been overlearned so that they guide our ordinary motor activities and many of our social interactions to function smoothly. When, however, new situations occur not fully anticipated by previous schemas, we are startled or intrigued if we do not carry around a metacognitive strategy (Meichenbaum & Gilmore, 1984) that says, "Reexamine your scripts or schemas or personal constructs!" We may either be paralyzed by fear or respond at once, relying on an automatized script and rue our impulsive actions later. The willingness to search for, retrieve, reexamine, and reshape our schemas in the face of new information (an activity in many ways reflecting Freud's early description of the function of the ego) necessitates a conscious awareness, some form of imagery replay or verbal interior monologue. It is, I believe, through such conscious processes that we enhance our decision-making abilities, deal more effectively with the unexpected, and evoke our more creative potentialities. Consciousness gives us a second chance at events, and it may be a key to control and to self-correction. Of course, excessive consciousness risks awkwardness, slowness of response, and social detachment. Perhaps the art of adaptive and exciting living necessitates our learning to value and to use our capacity for conscious thought, to be willing to reexamine our constructs, replay our guiding schemas or nuclear scripts, and, yet, to do so rapidly and smoothly so that we move quickly to action. Just as our human condition presents us continuously with a tension between autonomy and social communion, it also confronts us with the dilemma of conscious thought at the risk of delay and awkwardness or action that may be smooth and fast but guided by irrelevant or inaccurate scripts. I think future research using some of the methods I have outlined for sampling ongoing thought may help us ascertain how some of us manage an artful balance between a rich, varied consciousness and effective action.

REFERENCES

Ahern, G. L. (1982). *Differential lateralization for positive and negative emotion in the human brain: EEG spectral analysis.* Unpublished doctoral dissertation, Yale University, New Haven, CT.

Algon, D., & Singer, J. L. (1984). Interpersonal influence on task-irrelevant thought and imagery in a signal-detection task. *Imagination, Cognition and Personality, 4.*

Anderson, J. R. (1982). *Cognitive psychology and its implications.* San Francisco: Freeman.

Antrobus, J. S. (1968). Information theory and stimulus-independent thought. *British Journal of Psychology, 59,* 423–430.

Antrobus, J. S. (1983). REM and NREM sleep reports: Comparison of word frequencies by cognitive classes. *Psychophysiology, 20,* 562–568.

Antrobus, J. S. (1987). Cortical hemisphere activity and sleep mentation. *Psychological Review,* in press.

Antrobus, J. S., Coleman, R., & Singer, J. L. (1967). Signal detection performance by subjects differing in predisposition to daydreaming. *Journal of Consulting Psychology, 31,* 487–491.

Antrobus, J. S., Fein, G., Goldstein, S., & Singer, J. L. (in preparation). *Mindwandering: Time-sharing task-irrelevant thought and imagery with experimental tasks.* Manuscript submitted for publication.

Antrobus, J. S., Reinsel, R., & Wollman, M. (1987). Dreaming: Cortical activation and perceptual thresholds. In S. Ellman & J. S. Antrobus (Eds.), *The mind in sleep* (2nd ed.). Hillsdale, NJ: Erlbaum.

Antrobus, J. S., & Singer, J. L. (1964). Visual signal detection as a function of sequential task variability of simultaneous speech. *Journal of Experimental Psychology, 68,* 603–610.

Antrobus, J. S., Singer, J. L., Goldstein, S., & Fortgang, M. (1970). Mindwandering and cognitive structure. *Transactions of the New York Academy of Sciences (Series II), 32,* 242–252.

Arkin, A., Antrobus, J. S., & Ellman, S. (1978). *The mind in sleep.* Hillsdale, NJ: Erlbaum.

Bandura, A. (1977). Self-efficacy: Toward a unified theory of behavioral change. *Psychological Review, 84,* 191–215.

Barber, T. X. (1984). Changing "unchangeable" bodily processes by (hypnotic) suggestions: A new look at hypnosis, cognitions, imaging, and the mind-body problem. In A. A. Sheikh (Ed.), *Imagination and healing* (pp. 69-128). Farmingdale, NY: Baywood Publishing Co.

Barrios, M., & Singer, J. L. (1981). The treatment of creative blocks: A comparison of waking imagery, hypnotic dreams, and rational discussion techniques. *Imagination, Cognition and Personality, 1,* 89–116.

Beck, A. T., Rush, A. J., Shaw, B. F., & Emery, G. (1979). *Cognitive therapy of depression.* New York: Guilford Press.

Blatt, S. J., & Wild, C. M. (1976). *Schizophrenia: A developmental analysis.* New York: Academic Press.

Bowen, W. (1984). *Cardiovascular rigidity and flexibility: Relationship to affect and cognition.* Unpublished doctoral dissertation, Yale University, New Haven, CT.

Bowers, P. B. (1982). On *not* trying so hard: Effortless experiencing and its correlates. *Imagination, Cognition and Personality, 2,* 3–14.

Brandstatter, H. (1983). Emotional responses to other persons in everyday life situations. *Journal of Personality and Social Psychology, 45,* 871–883.

Breger, L., Hunter, I., & Lane, R. W. (1971). *The effect of stress on dreams.* New York: International Universities Press.

Broadbent, D. (1958). *Perception and communication.* London: Pergamon Press.

Brown, S. L. (1978). *Relationships between facial expression and subjective experience of emotion in depressed and normal subjects.* Unpublished doctoral dissertation, Yale University, New Haven, CT.

Cantor, N., & Mischel, W. (1979). Prototypes in person perception. In L. Berkowitz (Ed.), *Advances in experimental psychology, Vol. 12.* New York: Academic Press.

Carlson, R. (1981). Studies in script theory: I. Adult analogs of a childhood nuclear scene. *Journal of Personality and Social Psychology, 4,* 533–561.

Carlson, L., & Carlson, R. (1984). Affect and psychological magnification: Derivations from Tomkins' script theory. *Journal of Personality, 52,* 36–45.

Cartwright, D., Jenkins, J. L., Chavez, R., & Peckar, H. (1983). Studies of imagery and identity. *Journal of Personality and Social Psychology, 44,* 376–384.

Crawford, H. J. (1982). Hypnotizability, daydreaming styles, imagery vividness, and absorption: A multidimensional study. *Journal of Personality and Social Psychology, 42,* 915–926.

Crits-Christoph, P. (1984). *The role of anger in high blood pressure.* Unpublished doctoral dissertation, Yale University, New Haven, CT.

Csikszentmihalyi, M. (1982). Toward a psychology of optimal experience. In L. Wheeler (Ed.), *Review of personality and social psychology, Vol. 3.* Beverly Hills, CA: Sage.

Csikszentmihalyi, M., & Graef, R. (1980). The experience of freedom in daily life. *American Journal of Community Psychology, 8,* 401–414.

Csikszentmihalyi, M., & Kubey, R. (1981). Television and the rest of life: A systematic comparison of subjective experience. *Public Opinion Quarterly, 45,* 317–328.

Csikszentmihalyi, M., & Larson, R. (1984). *Being adolescent.* New York: Basic Books.

Ekman, P., Levenson, R. W., & Friesen, W. V. (1983). Autonomic nervous system activity distinguishes among emotions. *Science, 221,* 1208–1210.

Felton, B. J., & Revenson, T. A. (1984). Coping with chronic illness: A study of illness controllability and the influence of coping strategies on psychological adjustment. *Journal of Consulting and Clinical Psychology, 52,* 343–353.

Fenigstein, A., Scheier, M., & Buss, A. H. (1975). Public and private self-consciousness: Assessment and theory. *Journal of Consulting and Clinical Psychology, 43,* 522–524.

Giambra, L. M. (1980). Sex differences in daydreaming and related mental activity from the late teens to the early nineties. *International Journal of Aging and Human Development, 10,* 1–34.

Golding, J. M., & Singer, J. L. (1983). Patterns of inner experience: Daydreaming styles, depressive moods, and sex roles. *Journal of Personality and Social Psychology, 45,* 663–675.

Goldstein, K. (1940). *Human nature in the light of psychopathology.* Cambridge, MA: Harvard University Press.

Head, H. (1926). *Aphasia and kindred disorders of speech* (2 vols.). Cambridge: Cambridge University Press.

Heckhausen, H. (1977). Achievement motivation and its constructs: A cognitive model. *Motivation and Emotion, 1,* 283–329.

Helson, R., Mitchell, V., & Moane, G. (1984). Personality and patterns of adherence and nonadherence to the social clock. *Journal of Personality and Social Psychology, 46,* 1079–1096.

Hilgard, E. R. (1949). Human motives and the concept of self. *American Psychologist, 4,* 374–382.

Hilgard, E. R. (1965). *Hypnotic susceptibility.* New York: Harcourt Brace and World.

Hilgard, E. R. (1977). *Divided consciousness: Multiple controls in human thought and action.* New York: Wiley.

Hirst, W., Spelke, R., Reeves, C. S., Caharzck, G., & Neisser, U. (1980). Dividing attention without alternation of automaticity. *Journal of Experimental Psychology: General, 109,* 98–117.

Hoelscher, R. J., Klinger, E., & Barta, S. G. (1981). Incorporation of concern- and nonconcern-related stimuli into dream content. *Journal of Abnormal Psychology, 90,* 88–91.

Hollon, S. D., & Kriss, M. (1984). Cognitive factors in clinical research and practice. *Clinical Psychology Review, 4,* 35–76.

Holt, R. R. (1976). Drive or wish? A reconsideration of the psychoanalytic theory of motivation. In M. M. Gill & P. S. Holzman (Eds.), *Psychology versus metapsychology: Psychoanalytic essays in memory of George S. Klein* (pp. 158-197). *Psychological Issues, Monograph 36.* New York: International Universities Press.

Horowitz, M. J. (1970). *Image formation and cognition.* New York: Appleton-Century-Crofts.

Horowitz, M. J. (1976). *Stress response syndromes.* New York: Aronson.

Horowitz, M. J. (1978). *Image formation and cognition.* New York: Appleton-Century-Crofts.

Horowitz, M., Marmar, C., Krupnick, J., Wilner, N., Kaltreider, N., & Wallerstein, R. (1984). *Personality styles and brief psychotherapy.* New York: Basic Books.

Huba, G. J. (1980). Daydreaming. In R. H. Woody (Ed.), *Encyclopedia of clinical assessment.* San Francisco: Jossey-Bass.

Huba, G. J., Singer, J. L., Aneshensel, C. S., & Antrobus, J. S. (1982). *The Short Imaginal Processes Inventory.* Port Huron, MI: Research Psychologists Press.

Humphrey, R. (1968). *The stream of consciousness in the modern novel.* Berkeley, CA: University of California Press.

Hurlburt, R. T. (1979). Random sampling of cognitions and behavior. *Journal of Research in Personality, 13,* 103–111.

Hurlburt, R. T. (1980). Validation and correlation of thought sampling with retrospective measures. *Cognitive Therapy and Research, 4,* 235–238.

Isaacs, I. (1975). *Self reports of daydreaming and mindwandering: A construct validation.* Unpublished doctoral dissertation, City University of New York, New York.

Izard, C. E. (Ed.) (1977). *Human emotions.* New York: Plenum.

James, W. (1890/1950). *The principles of psychology* (2 vols.) New York: Dover Publications.

Jensen, M. (1984). *Psychobiological factors in the prognosis and treatment of neoplastic disorders.* Unpublished doctoral dissertation, Yale University, New Haven, CT.

Johnson, C., & Larson, R. (1982). Bulimia: An analysis of moods and behavior. *Psychosomatic Medicine, 44,* 341–351.

Johnson, M. K., & Raye, C. L. (1981). Reality monitoring. *Psychological Review, 88,* 67–85.

Kihlstrom, J. F. (1984). Conscious, subconscious, unconscious: A cognitive perspective. In K. S. Bowers & D. Meichenbaum (Eds.), *The unconscious reconsidered* (pp. 149-211). New York: Wiley

Kihlstrom, J. F., & Cantor, N. (1984). Mental representations of self. In L. Berkowitz (Ed.), *Advances in Experimental Social Psychology, Vol. 17.* New York: Academic Press.

Klein, G. (1967). Peremptory ideation: Structure and force in motivated ideas. In R. R. Holt (Ed.), *Motives and thought* (pp. 1–61). New York: International Universities Press.

Klinger, E. (1971). *Structure and functions of fantasy.* New York: Wiley.

Klinger, E. (1977a). *Meaning and void: Inner experience and the incentives in people's lives.* Minneapolis: University of Minnesota Press.

Klinger, E. (1977b). The nature of fantasy and its clinical uses. *Psychotherapy: Theory, Research and Practice, 14.*

Klinger, E. (1978). Modes of normal conscious flow. In K. S. Pope & J. L. Singer (Eds.) *The stream of consciousness* pp. 226–258). New York: Plenum.

Klinger, E. (1981). The central place of imagery in human functioning. In E. Klinger (Ed.), *Imagery, Volume 2: Concepts, results, and applications* (pp. 3–16). New York: Plenum.

Klinger, E., Barta, S., & Maxeiner, M. (1981). Current concerns: Assessing therapeutically relevant motivation. In P. Kendall & S. Hollon (Eds.), *Assessment strategies for cognitive-behavioral interventions* (pp. 161–196). New York: Academic Press.

Klos, D. S., & Singer, J. L. (1981). Determinants of the adolescent's ongoing thought following simulated parental confrontations. *Journal of Personality and Social Psychology, 41,* 975–987.

Kneier, A. W., & Temoshok, L. (1984). Repressive coping reactions in patients with malignant melanoma as compared to cardiovascular disease patients. *Journal of Psychomatic Research, 28,* 145–155.

Kobasa, S. C. (1979). Stressful life events, personality and health: An inquiry into hardiness. *Journal of Personality and Social Psychology, 37,* 1–11.

Kobasa, S., Maddi, S., & Courington, S. (1981). Personality and constitution as mediators in the stress-illness relationship. *Journal of Health and Social Behavior, 22,* 368–378.

Kreitler, H., & Kreitler, S. (1976). *Cognitive orientation and behavior.* New York: Springer.

Kreitler, H., & Kreitler, S. (1982). The theory of cognitive orientation: Widening the scope of behavior prediction. In B. Maber (Ed.), *Experimental personality research.* New York: Springer.

Kubey, R. (1982). *Recuperative leisure and the psychic economy: The case of television.* Unpublished doctoral dissertation, University of Chicago, Chicago.

Langer, E. (1983). *The psychology of control.* Beverly Hills, CA: Sage.

Lesser, I. (1981). A review of the alexithymia concept. *Psychosomatic Medicine, 43,* 531–543.

Lewin, K. (1935). *A dynamic theory of personality.* New York: McGraw Hill.

Lewin, I. (1982). Driver training: A perceptual motor skills approach. *Ergonomics, 25,* 917–924.

Linville, P. W. (1982). Affective consequence of complexity regarding the self and others. In M. S. Clark & S. T. Fiske (Eds.), *Affect and cognition: 17th Annual Carnegie Symposium on Cognition.* Hillsdale, NJ: Erlbaum.

Luborsky, L. (1977). New directions in research on neurotic and psychosomatic symptoms. In I. L. Janis (Ed.), *Current trends in psychology. Readings from the American Scientist.* Los Altos, CA: Kaufmann.

Maddi, S. (1976). *Personality Theories: A comparative analysis.* Homewood, IL: Dorsey.

Mandler, G. (1975). *Mind and emotion.* New York: John Wiley.

Markus, H. (1977). Self-schemata and processing information about the self. *Journal of Personality and Social Psychology, 35,* 63–78.

McAdams, D., & Constantian, C. A. (1983). Intimacy and affiliation motives in daily living: An experience sampling analysis. *Journal of Personality and Social Psychology, 4,* 851–861.

McClelland, D. C. (1961). *The achieving society.* Princeton: Van Nostrand.

McDonald, C. (1976). *Random sampling of cognitions: A field study of daydreaming.* Unpublished master's predissertation, Yale University, New Haven, CT.

McIlwraith, R. M., & Schallow, J. (1983a). Adult fantasy life and patterns of media use. *Journal of Communications, 33* 91–99.

McIlwraith, R. M., & Schallow, J. (1983b). Television viewing and styles of children's fantasy. *Imagination, Cognition and Personality, 2,* 323–331.

Meichenbaum, D., & Gilmore, J. B. (1984). The nature of unconscious processes: A cognitive-behavioral perspective. In K. Bowers & D. Meichenbaum (Eds.), *The unconscious reconsidered* (pp. 273–298). New York: Wiley.

Minsky, M. (1975). A framework for representing knowledge. In P. H. Winston (Ed.), *The psychology of computer vision.* New York: McGraw-Hill.

Mischel, W., & Peake, P. (1982). Beyond *déjà vu* in the search for cross-situational consistency. *Psychological Review, 89,* 730–755.

Nisbett, R. E., & Ross, L. D. (1980). *Human inference: Strategies and short-comings of informal judgment.* New York: Prentice-Hall.

Pekala, R., & Levine, R. (1981). Mapping consciousness: Development of an empirical-phenomenological approach. *Imagination, Cognition and Personality, 1,* 29–47.

Pekala, R., & Levine, R. (1982). Quantifying states of consciousness via an empirical-phenomenological approach. *Imagination, Cognition and Personality, 2,* 51–71.

Polansky, W. H. (1985) *Psychological factors, immunological function and bronchial asthma.* Unpublished doctoral dissertation, Yale University, New Haven, CT.

Pope, K. S. (1978). How gender, solitude, and posture influence the stream of consciousness. In K. S. Pope & J. L. Singer (Eds.), *The stream of consciousness* (pp. 259-301). New York: Plenum.

Pribram, K., & McGuinness, D. (1975). Arousal, activation and effort in the control of attention. *Psychological Review, 82,* 116–149.

Qualls, P. J. (1982–1983). The physiological measurement of imagery: An overview. *Imagination, Cognition and Personality, 2,* 89–101.

Rychlak, J. (1977). *The psychology of rigorous humanism.* New York: John Wiley.

Rychlak, J. (1981). Logical learning theory: Propositions, corollaries, and research evidence. *Journal of Personality and Social Psychology, 40* (4), 731–749.

Salovey, P., & Rodin, J. (1986). The differentiation of social-comparison jealousy and romantic jealousy. *Journal of Personality and Social Psychology, 50,* 1100–1112.

Schank, R. C., & Abelson, R. P. (1977). *Scripts, plans, goals, and understanding.* Hillsdale, NJ: Erlbaum.

Schwartz, G. E. (1982). Cardiovascular psychophysiology: A systems perspective. In J. T. Cacioppo & R. E. Petty (Eds.), *Focus on cardiovascular psychopathology.* New York: Guilford.

Schwartz, G. E. (1983). Disregulation theory and disease: Applications to the repression/cerebral disconnection/cardiovascular disorder hypothesis. *International Review of Applied Psychology, 32,* 95–118.

Schwartz, G., Weinberger, D., & Singer, J. A. (1981). Cardiovascular differentiation of happiness, sadness, anger and fear, following imagery and exercise. *Psychosomatic Medicine, 43,* 343–364.

Segal, B., Huba, G. J., & Singer, J. L. (1980). *Drugs, daydreaming and personality: A study of college youth.* Hillsdale, NJ: Erlbaum.

Singer, J. L. (1966). *Daydreaming.* New York: Random House.

Singer, J. L. (Ed.) (1973). *The child's world of make-believe.* New York: Academic Press.

Singer, J. L. (1974). *Imagery and Daydreaming. Methods in psychotherapy and behavior modification.* New York: Academic.

Singer, J. L. (1984a). *The human personality: An introductory text.* San Diego, CA: Harcourt Brace Jovanovich.

Singer, J. L. (1984b). The private personality. *Personality and Social Psychology Bulletin, 10,* 7–30.

Singer, J. L. (1985). Transference and the human condition: A cognitive-affective perspective. *Psychoanalytic Psychology, 2* (3), 189-219.

Singer, J. L., & Antrobus, J. S. (1972). Daydreaming, imaginal processes, and personality: A normative study. In P. Sheehan (Ed.), *The function and nature of imagery* (pp. 175-202). New York: Academic Press.

Singer, J. L., Greenberg, S., & Antrobus, J. S. (1971). Looking with the mind's eye: Experimental studies of ocular mobility during daydreaming and mental arithmetic. *Transactions of the New York Academy of Sciences, 33,* 694–709.

Singer, J. L., & Pope, K. S. (1981). Daydreaming and imagery skills as predisposing capacities for self-hypnosis. *The International Journal of Clinical and Experimental Hypnosis, 29,* 271–281.

Snyder, M. (1979). Self-monitoring processes. In L. Berkowitz (Ed.), *Advances in experimental social psychology.* New York: Academic Press.

Spanos, N. P., & Radtke, H. L. (1981–1982). Hypnotic visual hallucinations as imaginings: A cognitive-social psychological perspective. *Imagination, Cognition and Personality, 1,* 147–170.

Spence, D. P., Klein, L., & Fernandez, R. J. *Size and shape of the subliminal window.* Manuscript in preparation.

Starker, S. (1978). Dreams and waking fantasy. In K. S. Pope & J. L. Singer (Eds.), *The stream of consciousness: Scientific investigations into the flow of human experience* (pp. 302-320). New York: Plenum.

Steinberg, E. R. (1973). *The stream of consciousness and beyond in Ulysses.* Pittsburgh: University of Pittsburgh Press.

Tomkins, S. S. (1962). *Affect, imagery, consciousness, Vol. 1.* New York: Springer.

Tomkins, S. S. (1963). *Affect, imagery, consciousness, Vol. 2.* New York: Springer.

Tomkins, S. S. (1979). Script theory: Differential magnifications of affects. In H. E. Howe, Jr. & R. A. Dienstbier (Eds.), *Nebraska symposium on motivation, 1978.* Lincoln: University of Nebraska Press.

Tower, R. B., & Singer, J. L. (1981). The measurement of imagery: How can it be clinically useful? In P. C. Kendall & S. Hollon (Eds.), *Assessment strategies for cognitive-behavioral interventions* (pp. 119-160). New York: Academic.

Tucker, D. M., & Williamson, P. A. (1984). Asymmetry neural control systems and human self-regulation. *Psychological Review, 91,* 185–215.

Turk, D. C., Meichenbaum, D., & Genest, M. (1983). *Pain and behavioral medicine: A cognitive-behavioral perspective.* New York: Guilford Press.

Turk, D. C., & Speers, M. A. (1983). Cognitive schemata and cognitive processes in cognitive-behavioral interventions: Going beyond the information given. In P. C. Kendall (Ed.), *Advances in cognitive-behavioral research and therapy, Vol. 2.* New York: Academic Press.

Tversky, A., & Kahnemann, D. (1974). Judgment under uncertainty: Heuristics and biases. *Science, 135,* 1124–1131.

Tversky, A., & Kahnemann, D. (1980). Causal schemas in judgments under uncertainty. In M. Fishbein (Ed.), *Progress in social psychology.* Hillsdale, NJ: Erlbaum.

Weinberger, D. A. (1983). *Distress, suppression of desire and the classification of personality style.* Unpublished doctoral dissertation, Yale University, New Haven, CT.

Weinberger, D. A., Schwartz, G. E., & Davidson, J. R. (1979). Low-anxious, high-anxious, and repressive coping styles: Psychometric patterns and behavioral and physiological responses to stress. *Journal of Abnormal Psychology, 88,* 369–380.

Wilson, S. C., & Barber, T. X. (1983). The fantasy-prone personality: Implications for understanding imagery, hypnosis, and parapsychological phenomena. In A. A. Sheikh (Ed.), *Imagery: Current theory, research, and application* (pp. 340-390). New York: Wiley.

Witkin, H. A., & Goodenough, D. R. (1981). *Cognitive styles: Essence and origins.* New York: International Universities Press.

Zachary, R. (1983). *Cognitive and affective determinants of ongoing thought.* Unpublished doctoral dissertation, Yale University, New Haven, CT.

Zajonc, R. B. (1980). Feeling and thinking: Preferences need no inferences. *American Psychologist, 35,* 151–175.

6

Script Theory

Silvan S. Tomkins

If personology is to fulfill the aspirations of Murray's *Explorations in Personality,* it must match the depth and scope of that pioneering vision. It must ground personality in an evolutionary biological base that provides the foundations for a model of the human being at a general psychological level, which is in turn embedded in a historical, sociocultural, and civilizational matrix. The human being is born a biological entity, whose destiny it is to die a socialized, acculturated advocate or adversary of a civilization at a particular historical moment. If personology is to become a science for all seasons it must assume the daunting burden of analyzing and resynthesizing the particular and the abstract, the historic and the ahistoric, the micro components and the macro fields and contexts, origins and terminals, continuities and discontinuities, rapid changes and slow changes, stable equilibria and unstable equilibria. We must study personality not only the long way developmentally, but also the deep way biologically and the broad way historically (Tomkins, 1979, 1981a, b). I offer script theory as a first approximation in such a quest.

OVERVIEW OF SCRIPT THEORY

Script theory, as a theory of personality, is built upon a particular theory of the innately endowed nature of the human being (Tomkins, 1962, 1963a, b, 1979). Script theory assumes that the basic unit of analysis for understanding

Inasmuch as I object equally to gender bias and to gender blindness, but even more to the impersonal, neutered, and abstract circumlocution, I have adopted the less than optimal device of alternating attribution of gender in succeeding sections of this chapter.

persons, as distinguished from human beings, is the scene and the relationships between scenes, as ordered by sets of rules I have defined as scripts.

Some scripts are innate, but most are innate and learned. The learned
scripts originate in innate scripts but characteristically radically transform the
simpler, innate scripts.

The earliest (neonatal) observed script is the birth distress cry and flailing
arms and limbs, in response either to the excessive stimulation of change of
scene or to the slap on the behind. The second observed innate script is the
excitement-driven visual tracking of the utterly novel face of the mother.
Much later to be observed is the enjoyment-driven scene of relaxation of the
face (in a smile) and of the body, in correlated reduction in tonus, to the
reappearance of that new face, suddenly recognized as the same, familiar
face. Next to be observed are the rage scripts driven by excessive stimulation,
e.g., from hunger, which are similar to the distress scripts except that they are
more intense in both stimulus and in response. We are so accustomed to
regard motivation as goal-directed responsiveness that it is difficult to regard
the crying, flailing, just-born neonate either as motivated or as emitting
rule-governed responses. I describe these as innate scripts, because they
connect stimuli and responses by imprinting *both* with the same abstract
analogic quality and thus amplify both, as well as amplify, connect, and make
similar to each other.

The innate affect mechanisms structurally embody rules for differential
resonance to every major *abstract* profile of neural firing in terms of its *level*
of change or its *rate* of change. Thus, we inherit a variety of ways of caring
about every major contingency within the internal environment that is correlated by transmission with the external environment. It is a change-amplifying
mechanism and a correlating mechanism, imprinting, as it does, both its own
activator (making it more-so) and *whatever* response is recruited or being
executed at that time. So, the angering stimulus is guaranteed an enraged
response equal in amplification to its origin. That response is originally not
necessarily either instrumental or goal-directed; nor is it necessarily motor;
but whether that response is motor or cognitive, it is amplified, enhanced,
and *made* more analogous to its stimulus, as the stimulus is made more
similar to the response it evokes as amplified by the same affect. So, an
angering stimulus is also made a "hittable" stimulus.

We are richly endowed with a number of variously scripted alternative
scenes that we do not have to learn, but from which we continue to learn. It
is extraordinarily improbable that *any* human being will emerge from his/
her earliest years innocent of having enacted *exciting scenes,* responded to
rapidly and with increased tonus; *enjoyment scenes,* responded to with
equally rapid but relaxed responses, with decreased tonus; *surprise scenes,*
responded to with the most rapid increase of startle; *terrifying scenes,* responded to with very rapid increased tonus in escape or avoidance; *distress-*

ing scenes, responded to with increased level of tonus; *enraging scenes,* with an even more increased level of tonus; *disgusting scenes,* responded to with literal or analogous distaste responses and expulsion; *dismelling scenes,* responded to with literal or analogous removing the nose from the offending bad-smelling source; and finally, *shaming (and/or guilt-inducing) scenes,* responded to with partial and temporary reduction in either the increase or decrease in the rate of response (i.e. in interrupted excitement or enjoyment).

But to respond with excitement to "something happening quickly" with "some equally quick response" may strike the reader as at once too vague or general or abstract or incomplete to be properly defined as a script, or a set of rules for the interpretation and response to sets of scenes. One wonders what precisely it *is* that is so exciting and precisely *how* one does respond to that specific sense of excitement. Despite the speed of exciting stimuli and the speed of exciting responses, surely there is much more going on in different kinds of exciting scenes that is *not* innately scripted. This is of course true, but also irrelevant. Scripts may vary radically in their completeness of specification of rules or in their particularity or abstractness of rules, as well as in an indefinitely large number of other possible distinctive features of rules for dealing with scenes. All scripts are incomplete in varying degrees and depend on auxiliary information to particularize the script. What is distinctive about innate scripts is not the incompleteness and abstractness of their rules, but rather the imposed identity and similarity of their strict *correlation* between stimulus and response. Not even a reflex has *this* property. This invariance has been masked by the variable learned particularities in which these scripts are co-assembled and embedded.

But if it is improbable that anyone will not have enacted any of the innate scripts—amplifying scene and response equally and in kind—it is equally improbable that anyone will have experienced them alike either in their frequency or in all their particularity. The innate scripts are enacted momentarily in specific scenes. Learned scripts have been generated to deal with *sets* of scenes. This entails a difference I have defined as that between *amplification* and *magnification.* A single affect is scripted innately to amplify its own activator in a single momentary scene. But when amplified scenes are *co-assembled,* as repeated, the resulting responses to such a set represent magnification, or amplification, of the already separately amplified scenes. Now it is the *set* of such co-assembled scenes that is then amplified by fresh affect, and which I am defining as magnification, in contrast to the simpler script involved in any innate amplification of the single scene. Co-assembly of scenes need not be limited to either repeated scenes or to repeated scenes of the same affect, and the affect to co-assembled scenes need not be identical with the affect of the co-assembled scenes. Further, the co-assembled scenes include scenes projected as possibilities in the future, with or without co-assembly of past scenes, repeated or sharply contrasted in quality. What is essential for magnification is the *ordering* of sets of scenes by rules for their interpretation, or evaluation, or production, or prediction, or their control, so that these scenes *and* their rules are themselves amplified by affect.

Consider one of the earliest human scenes, the hungry infant in the arms of her mother. As a human being, she carries as standard equipment the rooting reflex—by which she turns her head from side to side in front of the breast—and the sucking reflex—by which she manages to get the milk from her mother's breast once her lips have found and locked onto her nipple. By any conception, this is a good scene. She appears to herself, as to her mother, to be utterly competent (and that without even trying), to make the world her oyster, to reduce and appease her hunger, and at the same time to reap the rewards of drive satisfaction. As a bonus, this reward is further amplified by bursts of the positive affects of excitement followed by the positive affect of enjoyment at satiety.

Is there any reason to expect trouble in such a paradise? Everything is in the best imaginable working order. And yet the newborn infant is *not* fundamentally happy with this state of affairs. Her behavior, soon after birth, seems to tell us, "I'd rather do it myself! I may not be able to do it as well as those reflexes do it, but I might be able to do it better, and I'm going to try." The experiments of Bruner (1968) have shown that very early on, the infant will replace the reflex sucking by beginning to suck voluntarily, and this is discriminably different from reflex sucking. If she succeeds, she will contin- ue. If it doesn't work too well, she falls back on reflex sucking. This is a prime example of what I have called *autosimulation* or imitation of one's own reflexes. The same phenomenon occurs with the orienting reflex and the several supporting ocular motor reflexes. Although the eye is innately equipped to track any moving stimulus in a reflex way, I have observed apparently voluntary moving of the head and neck very early on to bring visual tracking under voluntary control.

Psychological magnification begins, then, in earliest infancy when the infant imagines, via co-assembly, a possible improvement in what is already a rewarding scene, attempts to do what may be necessary to bring it about, and so produces and connects a set of scenes that continue to reward her with food and its excitement and enjoyment and also with the excitement and enjoyment of remaking the world closer to the heart's desire. She is doing what she will continue to try to do all her life—to command the scenes she wishes to play. Like Charlie Chaplin, she will try to write, direct, produce, criticize, and promote the scenes in which she casts herself as hero.

Not all amplified scenes are magnified. I have defined transients as scenes that occur with varying degrees of amplification, but zero or minimal magnification. Thus, the sound of a passing automobile blowing its horn loudly and unexpectedly may startle but never again enter into the plot of a life. The number of transients in the course of an individual's lifetime might be very large. As craft union scientists, we have had minimal interest in the density of transients. The individual who suffers an excessive density of unconnected transients may however suffer from the experience of lacking connectedness and/or magnification in her life.

The major difference between how an individual governs herself in an isolated scene without script, and with a script, is that in the former case she may experiment with alternative responses to the scene until she is either more satisfied or less dissatisfied than with the scene at its beginning. But such an amplified scene may have no consequences for her future, in fact or in intention. It is only when a set of such scenes is co-assembled, thought about, and used as a base for designing strategies and/or tactics for increasing or decreasing and/or for changing the responses to that family of scenes that we have a script and its magnification. The script is itself subject to plurideterminate experimentation and confirmation or disconfirmation or change, but it is the script itself that is increasingly at issue rather than any individual scene.

I define magnification as the advantaged ratio of the simplicity of ordering information to the power of ordered information times its affect density:

Magnification Advantage = (Power of Ordered Information × Affect Density)/ Simplicity of Ordering Information

The concept of magnification advantage is the product of information advantage and affect density (intensity × duration × frequency). Information advantage as I am defining it is that part of the above formula minus the affect. It is fashioned after the concept of mechanical advantage in which the lever enables a small force to move a larger force or, as with a valve, by which small energy forces are used to control a flow of much larger forces, as in a water distribution system. Informational advantage is an analogue. Any highly developed theory possesses great informational advantage, being able to account for much with little via the ratio of a small number of simple assumptions to a much larger number of phenomena described and explained that constitutes its power. The helix possesses very great informational advantage capable as it is of vast expansion properties of guidance and control.

But information advantage is not identical with magnification. Consider the difference between the information advantage of what I have described as the valley of perceptual skill, the ability of an individual to "recognize" the presence of a familiar face at varying distances or directions, with varying alternative small samples of the whole. To see the chin, or the nose, or the forehead, or any combination is quite enough to enable skilled expansion of these bits of information so that one "knows" who the other is. It is an "as if" information with minimal (but accurate) awareness *and* minimal affect. All habitual skills operate via *compressed* information with minimal ratio of conscious reports to messages and with minimal affect. Thus, one may cross a busy intersection "as if" afraid, looking up and down, for possible danger from passing automobiles, but characteristically without *any* fear, and with minimal awareness of scanning. Contrast the informational advantage of a husband and wife "recognizing" the face of the other with the recognition of the same face in the midst of their initial love affair. When the lover detects the face of the beloved as a figure in a sea of other faces as ground, there is no less informational advantage involved in that recognition of the newly familiar face, but there is a radical magnification of consciousness and affect that together with all the significances attributed to the other make it an unforgettable moment.

In our proposed ratio for script magnification, the denominator represents the compressed (smaller) number of rules for *ordering* scenes, whereas the numerator represents the expanded (much larger) number of scenes, both from the past and into the indefinite future, which are *ordered* by the smaller number of compressed rules. In the numerator, there are represented both the scenes that gave rise to the necessity for the script as well as all the scenes that are generated as responses to deal with the initial co-assembly of scenes, either to guarantee the continuation of good scenes, their improvement, or the decontamination of bad scenes, or the avoidance of threatening scenes. The compressed smaller number of rules guide responses that, in turn, recruit amplifying affect as well as samples of the family of scenes either sought, interpreted, evaluated, produced, and expanded.

Because there is a *mixture* of informational advantage and affect-driven amplification, the individual is characteristically much less conscious of the compressed rules than of their expansion scenes, just as one is less aware of one's grammar than of the sentences one utters. Although the compression of rule information in the denominator always involves information reduction and simplification, there may be varying quantities of information in the number of co-assembled scenes that gave rise to the scripted responses in scenes yet to be played, as well as varying intensities, durations, and frequencies of affect assigned to these scenes and to the scripted response scenes. Thus, a low degree of magnification script may involve a small number of scenes to be responded to by a small number of scripted scenes with moderate, relatively brief, affect. In contrast, a high degree of magnification script may involve a large number of scenes to be responded to by a large number of scripted scenes with intense and enduring affect. The magnification *advantage* ratio of either script might nonetheless be low or high, depending on the ratio of ordering rules to rules ordered.

Further, any of the values in such equations are susceptible to change. Thus, in the midst of a heart attack (in a case reported to me by an English physician about himself), there was a rapid review of many scenes of his past life, their relationship to the present and future, a deep awareness that his life could never again be quite the same, and gradually a return to the status quo in which that whole series of reevaluations became attenuated and eventually segregated to exert diminishing instructions on how he conducted his life. Again, a central much magnified script involving someone of vital importance may be first magnified to the utmost via death and mourning and by that very process be ultimately attentuated, producing a series of habitually skilled reminiscences that eventually become segregated and less and less retrieved. Mourning thus retraces in reverse the love affair and is a second edition of it, similar in some ways to the mini-version of these sequences in jealousy, when a long quiescent valley of perceptual skill may be ignited by an unexpected rival.

The most magnified scripts require minimal reminders that the present is vitally connected to much of our past life and to our future and that we must attend with urgency to continually act in such a way that the totality will be as we very much wish it to be and not as we fear it might be. Between such a script and scripts I have labeled "doable" (in which one may pay one's bills as a moratorium in the midst of a task that is critical but, for the time being, "undoable" by any conceivable path) are a large number of scripts of every degree of magnification and type, which we will presently examine in more detail.

GENERAL FEATURES OF SCRIPTS

Before examining specific scripts I will now present some of the general features of all scripts:

1. Scripts are *sets of ordering rules* for the interpretation, evaluation, prediction, production or control of scenes.

2. They are *selective* in the number and types of scenes which they order.

3. They are *incomplete* rules even within the scenes they attempt to order.

4. They are in varying degrees *accurate* and *inaccurate* in their interpretation, evaluation, prediction, control, or production.

5. Because of their selectivity, incompleteness, and inaccuracy, they are *continually reordered* and changing, at varying rates, depending on their type and the type and magnitude of disconfirmation.

6. The coexistence of different competing scripts requires the formation of *interscript,* scripts.

7. Most scripts are *more self-validating than self-fulfilling.* Thus, a mourning script validates the importance of the lost relationship, but in the end frees the individual from that relationship. A nuclear script that attempts to reduce shame validates the self as appropriately shame-worthy more than it succeeds in freeing the individual of his burden. A commitment script validates the importance and necessity of the struggle, but the achievement of the commitment may erode it or require its redefinition to continue. A

hoarding script validates the danger of insufficiency more than it guarantees against its possibility. A power script validates the danger of powerlessness more than it guarantees the adequacy and perpetuation of power. A purity script validates the impurity of the individual more than it guarantees his purity.

8. The incompleteness of scripts necessarily requires *auxiliary* augmentation. This may be gained via *media mechanisms* (e.g., vision), which provide relevant contemporary information that cannot be entirely written into any script except in a general way. Even the simplest habitual skilled scripts require them; e.g., shaving requires a mirror; driving a car requires constant monitoring no matter how skilled the driver. One cannot begin to use any script without much information that cannot be scripted in advance. Further, one normally requires auxiliary media information gained by use of the arms and legs to reach further information as well as to alter perspectives. Again one requires *speech* and/or *written* language as auxiliary sources of information, past as well as present. These are also media mechanisms, but culturally inherited media. Next one requires as auxiliaries, compressed information in the form of *theories,* lay and professional, about causal relationships, signs or omens, intentions, and consequences. Next, one requires the memorially supported *plot,* which is a sequentially organized series of scenes of the life one has led and the lives others have led. Next, one requires *maps,* which are spatio-temporal schematics that enable the plots to be handled more economically. We possess maps of varying degrees of fineness of texture, normally generated by their usefulness for different scripts. The difference between a duffer and professional tennis player is reflected not only in the differences between their families of tennis scripts, but also in the detail of the maps of their opponent's past performances. Finally, one script may use another *script as auxiliary.* Thus, Calvinism used the entrepreneurial activity of the economic competition script to increase the probability of grace in warding off the hell fires of their vivid version of the life hereafter.

9. Scripts contain *variables as alternatives.* Variables are those rules that as alternatives depend on auxiliary information to further specify. A script,thus may, for example, differentiate strategy and tactics, conditional upon variable auxiliary information. Thus, a child may learn to script a relationship with a parent in which he extorts as much as is possible just within the limits of the patience and power of the indulgent but irascible other. The auxiliary information need, however, not be limited to external information. Thus, an otherwise deeply committed individual may nonetheless exempt himself from his major concern should he become ill or seriously disturbed or depressed. Very few scripts are conceived as completely unconditional, since they are designed to deal with variable selected features of selected scenes. When unanticipated conditions are encountered, the individual has the option of further adding to the script "not when I'm sick" or "no matter what I

must keep at it." Indeed, as we shall presently see, it is just such encounters and their absorption that are critical in the deepening of a commitment script.

10. Scripts have the property of *modularity.* They are variously combinable, recombinable, and decomposable. The separate scripts may be aggregated and *fused,* as when a career choice combines scripts that enable an individual to explore nature, to be alone, and to express himself through writing, as in the case of Eugene O'Neill who chose to live at the ocean's edge in solitude as he wrote his plays. Compare such a set of component subscripts with that of a lumberjack who enjoys nature, but in the company of others and also in exercising his large muscles. Contrast both with an archaeologist who is enchanted with the rediscovery of the past, with others, in very special remote nature sites. Not only is each component of a single script endlessly combinable and recombinable, but so are scripts themselves, as when addictive scripts for cigarettes, eating, and drinking are combined in a bottoming-out nuclear script.

Scripts may also be *partitioned,* as in the classic neurotic split libido and in the characteristically French separation of family and mistress, one cherished for enjoyment and continuity, the other for novelty and excitement.

If scripts are combinations of modular components, we will now describe some of the major modular components of any script. Not all scripts include all kinds of component rules, although many different kinds of scripts may include the same distinctive kinds of component rules, but with different particular values, as two sentences might include similar and different letters or words. Following is a sample of modular rule components.

(a) Specifications of quantities, ratios, and directionality of positive and negative affects. How much positive and how much negative affect is anticipated and enacted and in what ratio? How much are scripted scenes rewarding and punishing, how optimistic and how pessimistic are expectations, and in what ratio and in what sequential direction?

(b) Specification of quantities, ratios, and directionality of specific positive and negative affects. For example, is excitement greater than enjoyment? Does distress lead to anger?

(c) Specification of different loci of affect magnification. Is there excitement about time, place, people, psychological functions (such as thinking, feeling, perceiving, imagining, remembering, speaking, acting), events, props, specific settings (such as work, family, church, army, school), near or remote settings?

(d) Specifications of affect salience. Is there a quest for pure excitement as such or for excitement as a *scene derivative,* e.g., to hear an exciting symphony, or for excitement as a scene *system derivative,* e.g., on the whole an exciting way of life?

(e) Specifications of relations between origin-source-affect-response-target in families of script sequences. Which parts of a sequence in a script are defined as dependent, which as independent, which as interdependent? Thus, if anger is defined as independent, then neither its source (e.g., the anger of another) nor the origin of that (a careless remark by the self) will influence the individuals' aggressive response, which is defined as dependent. Such an individual will warn others not to make him angry, because he is scripted to strike out in aggressive response to his own anger. In contrast if it is the anger of the other as source that is scripted as independent then one's own response might be scripted as dependent and conciliatory in aim, whether or not one was angry, if the script had been formed in response to overwhelming anger and aggression brought to bear upon an intimidated child. In socialization that was more democratic, more interdependence and systematic tradeoffs might eventually be scripted in mutually angering scenes.

(f) Specifications of different strategies of relating risks, costs, and benefits such that they are either minimized/maximized, optimized, or satisfied. In the first case, one strives for the greatest benefits and least costs at least risks. In the second case, one strives for the optimal benefits and costs at a moderate level of risk. In the final case, one strives for modest benefits with modest costs and modest risks.

(g) Specifications of clarity of distance and direction of scripted responses. In the monistic script, there may be complete clarity about what must be done or varying degrees of uncertainty about directionality and distance of how to proceed. In the dualistic script, there is conflict in distance and direction such that approach in one direction increases the distance from the other wish. In the pluralistic turbulent script, there is ambiguity and multiple conflicts of distances and directions, as, e.g., in the identity problem of plural "selves," or in schizophrenic confusional states.

(h) Specification of interscript relations. Scripts are defined as much by their explicit relations to other scripts as by their rules for ordering their own family of scenes. Is the script entirely orthogonal, e.g., a hobby, in that no other script is presumed to have any jurisdiction over these scenes? Is it in a hierarchical relationship of priority over some scripts and subordination to other scripts, e.g., in family and work scripts? Is it mutually supportive and supported by other scripts, e.g., so that one works to support a family and the family works together in a farm or business?

These components of scripts are a sample of some of the major modules that form scripts, but they are necessarily as incomplete as would be any attempt to exhaustively enumerate all possible words, phrases, and sentences in a language, or for that matter all elementary molecules, atoms, and elementary particles in physics and chemistry. Psychological reality is inherently more complex and, therefore, more modular than either the physical or biological reality in which it is nested. According to the quantum principle in physics, there exists a threshold of excitation for any dynamical system, whose threshold becomes higher as the dimensions of the system decrease, thus accounting for the apparent independence of the laws of atomic nuclear and subnuclear particle physics. Complexity arises from any increase in dimensionality, which represents an increase in independent variability within and between components of a complex system. Any script modular component therefore coexists with more elementary modular components and with more complex contextual modular components in ever changing coassemblies.

The consequences of such complexity for understanding and describing the scripts within any single personality or between personalities, or between a single personality at different developmental phases, or under variations in inner or outer environmental conditions are therefore both daunting and inherently capable of progress but without determinable limit, what Kant called a *Grenzbegriff,* a limiting concept.

Any script theoretical description is *inherently* too abstract or too particular, too analytic or too contextual to finally converge on the reality of our concern, but it is *also* capable of approaching closer and closer to convergence on that reality or going off in a less promising direction and to be so demonstrated. We can ask for no more, and script theory will offer no more guarantees against limited imagination and blatant error than will any other type of personality theory. Its structure would, however, protect us against both overevaluation and underevaluation of the validity and power of our constructs. It would render moot many of the classic concerns of personality theory, the reality of traits, of interactionism, of cognitive versus perceptual versus behavioral versus affective versus drive imperialisms, of historic versus ahistoric controversies, of analytic versus contextual priorities. It is not that these are unimportant issues but rather that they must be incorporated into script models and integrated rather than posed as either/or polarities or as eclecticisms.

Thus, to describe a personality in terms of the modular component of the ratio of positive to negative affect is neither entirely appropriate nor inappropriate. *Some* personalities *are* very optimistic or very pessimistic in general, but some are neither, because these rules are dependent on too many other rules themselves dependent on and reponsive to auxiliary information that is not itself scripted, as in the case of unpredictable good or bad luck, gratuities, or accidents. Or because the variance of good or bad outcomes is controlled by scripted partitioning, such that if he is optimistic only if alone or with others; or with elders or with peers; or with large groups or with small groups; or in intimate or distant interaction; or with same or with opposite sex; or with angry scenes or with distressing scenes; or in the past or in the present or in the projected future, in his home town or away; or when he is reading or when he is speaking; or when he is perceiving or when he is acting, or when he is imagining; or when he is with his family or at school, or at business, or in the army; when he is reaching for the moon or for more reachable goals or for very modest goals; when he is single-mindedly pursuing one goal, or two or many; when he is in quest of pure affect, e.g., "kicks" or when he is pursuing an exciting person or idea, or when he is balancing several scripts; or focused on one particular script at a time, in hot pursuit of a scene, or the morning after when the disregarded weight of the rest of his scripts reasserts itself. Any modular rule has the properties of a word or phrase in a sentence.

It may be as complete as in the one word sentence "Stop," but more often its meaning will depend on the other modules with which it is variously co-assembled. As any particular modular component *becomes* magnified, its consequences for other modular components as dependent and less magnified are fateful and constitute the central features of the personality. *What* rules *are* so consequential, is the major question for any theory of personality. It is the advantage of script theory to provide the framework for the pursuit of such rules and to caution against the perennial vulnerability to prematurity of closure of these questions.

DIFFERENTIAL MAGNIFICATION OF RATIO OF POSITIVE–NEGATIVE AFFECT

I will now examine some of the consequences of the differential magnification of the modular component of the quantity, ratio, and directionality of positive and negative affect *for* the differential magnification of other modular components. What happens when we *fix* this quantity, this ratio, at particular values of extreme or intermediate density and ratio of positive to negative affects?

First, let us briefly address the question of how varying values of the density and ratio of positive to negative affect may be fixed. There is no royal road to psychological affluence or poverty, although there are many alternative roads. Neither the biological inheritance of a vigorous healthy, agile, beautiful, intelligent nervous system and body will guarantee a happy life, nor their opposite a miserable life. Neither the psychosociocultural inheritances or achievements of individual and national economic wealth, political status and privilege, social privileged status, knowledge and literacy, social stability and tolerable rates of change, openness of opportunity for age, gender, and class, or rewarding socialization via optimal mutuality, modeling, and/or mirroring will guarantee an optimal balance of positive over negative affect, nor will their opposites guarantee the reverse ratio.

One must however inherit and achieve *some* gratuities in sufficient quantities to attain a critical mass for a good and rewarding or bad and punishing life, or for some intermediate mixture thereof. Note that we have contrasted a good life and rewarding life with a bad life and a punishing life. This is because of the variable interdependence of judgments of evaluation and effectiveness (by the self and by others) and the experienced ratio of the density of positive and negative affect. If one has enjoyed one's life it is more probable that one (and others) will also judge that it has been good, effective, and fulfilling. But nothing is more common than the judgment and evaluation of a life as good and effective but which failed to yield the expected and believed deserved rewards of excitement and enjoyment. Similarly if one has suffered excessively, one is likely to judge one's life ineffective and bad, but one may judge one's life to have been relatively ineffective and bad but not to have suffered negative affect in equal amount. Hence suicide among the "affluent" and joy among the "impoverished" is by no means rare, whether that affluence be measured in economic, political, social, psychological, or biological terms.

Not only must there be an optimal *set* of inheritances and achievements of affluence of many but not all kinds, but there must be an optimal interdependence between "causes" and "effects" of affluence or of poverty. The rich must learn to *become* and *remain* richer, as the poor must learn the other skills. This is a special case of what I have called plurideterminacy, that the effects of any cause are indeterminate until they are continually validated by further magnification or attenuated. Any gratuity must be built upon to reward in the long run; any threat must be elaborated by further action to become traumatic. Thus, a mugging may be shrugged off as a transient or built upon as a way of life if one elects to hire a bodyguard. Thus, some of the major kinds of modular script components, e.g., the clarity of distance and direction, the quantity strategies of optimizing versus satisficing versus mini-maximizing are at once criteria of positive and negative scripts as well as their causes and supports. When, however, the density of the ratio of positive to negative affect reaches a critical level, then it can become a relatively *stable equilibrium,* both self-validating and self-fulfilling. At that point the possibility of radical change, though always present, becomes a diminishing probability requiring ever more densely magnified countervailing forces of positive or negative affect.

Let us now briefly examine the consequences of affluence over poverty for a sample of the major varieties of scripts.

All human beings require and generate scripts of *orientation* consisting of abstract spatiotemporal *maps,* more dense *theories,* and special *instrumental skills* of how to talk, move, persuade, construct, what we must, to live in the world whatever its reward or punishments. The more affluent we are, however, the more such instrumental skills, maps, and theories are both rewarding rather than punishing and the more positive features of that world are differentiated in texture and generalized in scope. Because scripted sources of orientation are more positive in reward, they also enable the development of greater skill. It is much more difficult for the very frightened, ashamed, disgusted, distressed, or enraged to write, speak, move, manipulate, or observe with great skill.

Consider next scripts of *evaluation*. All human beings in all societies must acquire not only orientation but also discriminate moral, aesthetic, and truth values, what to believe is good and bad, beautiful and ugly, true or false. These are *ideological* scripts, widely inherited, first of all, as religious scripts as well as a variety of national secular ideologies. These are scripts of great scope that attempt an account, guidance, and sanctions for how life should be lived and the place of human beings in the cosmos. They conjoin affect, values, the actual, and the possible in a picture of the "real." As such they represent *faith*, whether religious or secular.

Since all ideologies contain evaluation *and* orientation and delineation of both positive and negative scenes, their relative salience in the life of the affluent is biased toward the positive components compared with the life of the impoverished, even when they inherit the *same* ideology. Some Calvinists were more certain they would be elected, and others more certain that they would suffer eternal damnation. Still other Christians believed themselves destined for the midway of Purgatory before entering heaven.

Next are *affect* scripts, concerned primarily with the control, management, and salience of affect. No society and no human being can be indifferent to the vicissitudes of affect per se, quite apart from other human functions and other characteristics of the world in which we live. This is because of their extraordinary potency for amplification and magnification of *anything*, their seductiveness, their threat, and not least their potentiality for contagion and escalation. *Affect control* scripts regulate the consciousness of affects, their density, display, communication, consequences, and their conditionality. The affluent are characteristically the recipients of rewarding socialization of both positive and negative affects, which is tolerant rather than intolerant toward consciousness of affect, toward the density of affect rather than its attenuation (e.g., "simmer down"); toward the display of affect rather than its suppression (e.g., "stop whining"); toward the communication of affect rather than its suppression (e.g., "don't ever raise your voice to me"); toward affect-based action rather than its suppression (e.g., "don't ever hit me again"); toward the tolerable consequences of affect based action rather than the intolerable consequences (e.g., "when you get so excited you give Mommy a headache"); toward their specificity and conditionality rather than their abstractness and generality (e.g., "don't get too loud and excited when we have guests" versus "nobody likes a noisy kid").

In *affect management* scripts, negative affects are sedated by specific actions quite apart from their instrumental consequences. Thus, cigarettes are smoked to "feel better" whether they help otherwise or not. As sedation becomes more urgent it is transformed into an addictive script in which smoking becomes an end in itself and displaces all its original sources as the primary source of deprivation affect. As the density of negative to positive affect grows, such dependences shift from purely positive savouring scripts to sedative scripts, to preaddictive scripts (e.g., "I cannot answer the telephone without a cigarette"), to addictive scripts, with fateful consequence for their compulsion and freedom to relinquish, which we will trace later.

Affect salience scripts address the questions of how directly or indirectly one should aim at affect and how much weight one should assign to affect in the whole family of scripts. When affect per se becomes focal as a script, we seek "kicks" or "peace" or "terror" or "rage" or "sadness." Persons and activities are judged primarily by their affect payoff. In contrast, in derivative affect scripts, a person, a place, or an activity is rewarding *because* that one is a competent or nurturant or good person, because that activity is socially productive, because that place has extraordinary vistas or architecture. In affect systematic scripts, affect becomes one of *many* criteria for script guidance and many scripts are considered as part of one system for evaluation. As affluence increases, focal affect scripts are subordinated to derivative affect scripts, which are in turn subordinated to affect systematic scripts.

Finally, consider that large class of scripts defined by *risk, cost, benefit components.* Here we have distinguished four general types of script, with several subtypes within each general type. First are *affluence* scripts, which are those which govern predominately positive affect scenes. Second are *limitation-remediation* scripts, which govern negative affect scenes that are attempted to be transformed into positive affect scenes, with varying degrees of success. Third are *contamination scripts,* which govern ambivalent and plurivalent scenes that resist complete and enduring decontamination. Fourth are *antitoxic scripts,* which govern purely negative affect scripts with limited success. The basis of this classification is the varying ratios of density of positive to negative affect and the assumption that the effectiveness of coping with this ratio is dependent upon its absolute and relative *quantities* of positive and negative affect. As negative affect density increases, scripts move from affluence to remediation to enduring ambivalence and plurivalence to limited antitoxic outcomes, with recurrent threats and dangers.

All individuals enjoy *some* scenes via scripts of affluence, remedy some negative scenes, are plagued with some continuing ambivalence and plurivalence, and are threatened with toxic scenes via scripts that are precarious and fragile at best. The critical question raised by the modular component of the relative density and ratio of positive to negative affect is how general and extreme this ratio is and how it may be partitioned.

Risk, cost, benefit scripts address the systematic tradeoffs in specific scenes, or for families of scenes or for all scenes, about what relative quantities of probability there may be for quantities of costs versus benefits of payoff, of script enactment that are to govern choices, decisions, and planning for one's life—whether in a family, or in work, or in solitude, or as a citizen, as a friend, as actor, observer, critic, or producer.

Although these scripts may be characterized by their decisions concerning the risks one intends to take for varying probabilities of reward and punishment (and therefore also for positive and negative affect), their complete set of rules would necessarily include the specification of the *specific* positive and negative affects differentiated, so that one individual might be committed to a script of creative *excitement* of discovery, as a scientist, whereas another might be committed to a script of the *enjoyment* of teaching science to a younger generation. Further, the same commitment script must be differentiated not only by the specific affects involved, but also by the specific *loci* of affect investment, such that one is committed to science, another to art, another to business, another to politics, all equally committed to risk for a gain of benefit over costs to be absorbed. When we speak of a commitment script as one type of limitation remediation script, we do not prejudge its more specific affects nor its more particular loci of affect investment.

Let us now consider some varieties of scripts of affluence and their interaction with a high ratio of dense positive over negative affect. As this ratio becomes more positive it becomes a more stable equilibrium so that scripts of affluence assume a central influence in the personality. Empirically this is a relatively rare state of affairs, as is its mirror image: the inverse ratio and the consequent centrality of scripts of toxicity for some individuals.

There are numerous types of affluence scripts, apart from their varieties of specific positive affects, and apart from their varieties of specific loci of positive affect investment. A very high density and magnification of positive affect could *not* be achieved from a life lived as a series of unconnected transient positive, even "peak" scenes, since magnification, in contrast to amplification, requires co-assembly of *sets* of scenes and scripted *further responses* to them, either to be repeated, to be sought, to be improved upon, to be produced, or created anew. Magnification of scripts of affluence can neither consist of isolated scenes nor of scenes sought exclusively for pure positive affect, such as pure excitement or pure enjoyment without regard to their source. The irrelevance and absence of evaluation (other than pure affect as criterial) would improverish the critical and discriminating skills of the individual to such an extent that the magnification of positive affect would itself be jeopardized. Such a one could only say, "I know what excites or pleases me," but not exactly why, or why it ceases to excite or please if and when it does so. Such an individual would be too easily uninterested, bored, or displeased to sustain a high density of positive to negative affect. It would be analogous to the difficulty of producing experimental neuroses in some of the simple animals used in laboratory experimentation. They could not sufficiently connect and elaborate "traumatic" conditioning to become "neurotic."

By the same logic, an *exclusive* reliance on particular, scene-derivative positive affect would not sustain a stable equilibrium of high positive over negative affect, since it would inevitably confront the individual with underrepresented scripts in her personality. Such an individual would be like a lover who disregards too much and too long her other scripts of affluence, such as her parents, her children, her career, her friends, her health, her zest for food, for music, for travel, for nature, even for her daily routines, pallid though they seem in the midst of her obsession. The maintenance of a stable high positive affect over negative affect might *include* both pure affect scripts and scene-derivative affect scripts, but must also include systematic interscript, scripts of affluence, so that the scope and depth of the varieties of reward are guaranteed against either excessive diffusion and unconnectedness or against excessive concentration and alienation from the remainder of the inner and outer world.

From the viewpoint of strategy, the individual must neither attempt to minimize negative affect nor to maximize positive affect nor satisfice, but rather attempt to optimize positive affect to achieve the optimal stable equilibrium. The distance between the ideal and the actual must not be so great as to demoralize, nor so small as to trivialize.

Some balance must also be achieved between the several basic functions of perceiving, thinking, remembering, feeling, and acting, lest serious underdevelopment jeopardize the more magnified specialized functions that necessarily require all functions as auxiliaries at the very least.

Every differential magnification of scripted affluence is capable, if unbalanced, of jeopardizing the system of affluence scripts. Unless excitement affluence is balanced by some compensatory relaxation of enjoyment (as in the suburbs or wilderness, against overstimulation from the city) the individual is in jeopardy of being drained. Unless enjoyment affluence is balanced by some compensatory risk and excitement (as in the tendency to introduce gambling into predominantly stable, enjoyment societies) the individual will become restive and bored in her excessive enjoyment. Similar constraints appear with respect to affluence scripts located in different time frames. There cannot be fixation on the past, present, or future, or on brief durations, middle durations, or long durations without some compensatory balance lest the system of scripts of affluence be at risk.

Excessive breadth or depth of interest must be balanced by compensation at the least, though both might be optimized if neither is maximized.

Since scripts of affluence must be optimized rather than maximized, the *exclusive* magnification of scripts of affluence is invulnerable to serious disruption by what might have been easily absorbed except for *too little* exposure to, and immunization against, negative affect. The classic case is Buddha, the overly affluent prince, completely traumatized by his first exposure to the illness and suffering of an old man he happened to encounter by chance. The maintenance of affluence demands the capacity to understand and absorb negative affect when it *is* encountered. One cannot afford excessive specialization even of rewarding affluence without some capacity for the compensation of and absorption of the confrontation with the inevitable suffering by the self and by others. Indeed what I have called the "rewarding" program of the socialization of affect (Tomkins, 1963a, b) requires that the child be exposed to quantities and varieties of negative affect in sufficiently graded doses that she can learn both to confront them and to discover how she may find her way back from such bruising encounters.

Specialization of affluence is the rule, but it is ever vulnerable to disregard of neglected and underrepresented specialization unless there is provision for *some* compensatory magnification, even though it continues to be a minor script. The other alternative consistent with a stable equilibrium of high positive over negative affect is a more even, optimized balance between plural scripts of affluence.

There are numerous varieties of affluence scripts, and a stable high ratio of positive affect requires *many* such scripts. These include *repetition* scripts in which the individual seeks to reexperience either what was once rewarding or what has (sometimes years later) *become* rewarding. Such scenes, e.g., the attempt to revisit the past (which may indeed have been and is still remembered as having been painful), may become deeply rewarding as a possible reexperience from the vantage point of adulthood. These may in fact disappoint but nonetheless be compelling as a unique scene that one must recover in its particularity. One may discover, with Wolfe, that one cannot go home again, but nonetheless cherish the experience. It represents the perennial fascination of human beings with "origins."

These scripts are somewhat different from *repetition with exploration* scripts. The young man who wishes to see the young woman he has just met, once again, and then again, wishes to repeat for the exploration of more of the same. Any budding interest requires for magnification, further acquaintance and exploration. When such exploration has run its course, such scripts enter what I have called the valley of perceptual skill, in which the once beloved is daily *recognized* but without affect. Any affluence script of repetition with exploration is vulnerable to such attenuation if it is not magnified by continuing, further exploration in repetition, or by further shared enjoyment or celebration, or anticipation or by participation.

There are also *repetition with improvement* affluence scripts in which the major aim is to increase one's skill not to a plateau, but to continually redefined peaks, common among professional athletes and performing artists. Such improvement scripts include affluence commitment species in which the individual is excited by and enjoys the development of her talents and her skills of discrimination, and of generalization, whether as a connoisseur or gourmet or gourmand or as a critic, as a mathematician, composer, conductor, or linguist. In many such cases, the individual early on is excited by inherited talents for special kinds of achievement and becomes committed to development on a purely positive affect basis. This is to be distinguished from commitment scripts of limitation remediation, in which the individual feels she must remedy a scene that is punishing as a felt lack, or loss, evil, or false or ugly.

There are also affluence *production* scripts in which one attempts to produce, again and again, a rewarding scene. A comedian or actor's major script may consist in the successful evocation of audience response to the scene *she* has *produced*.

There are also affluence *creation* scripts that aim at the creation of a product and/or a response toward that product by the other and/or by the self. It is the uniqueness of the product, and of the response to it, that is criterial in such scripts. This is notably involved in the sensitivity to priority in artistic and scientific creation or discovery.

There are also affluence *responsiveness* scripts in which the aim is not to seek rewarding experiences, but rather to be open *to* them, should they occur or reoccur. These sometimes occur poignantly among the elderly who feel they have cheated themselves of what they might have found exciting or enjoyable in their youth and attempt a first, never experienced childhood.

These shade imperceptibly into *responsiveness quest* scripts in which the individual travels or frequents places where she believes she is more likely to be the target of others who will evoke deep positive responses in herself that she is incapable of either seeking directly or of initiating. Art, especially drama, is sought by many as one form of a responsiveness quest for a "good cry," as well as for excitement or enjoyment. Some will even seek the possibility of an attack for the enjoyment and excitement of the release of suppressed rage, distress, terror, or shame. These may be considered affluence scripts *if* the excitement or enjoyment is the primary aim, and the released negative affects are the instrumental vehicle for such rewards. Just as puritanical scripts seek to punish for pleasure, sadomasochistic scripts may seek pleasure from punishment.

There are also *positive celebratory* affluence scripts, in which there may be rituals for birth, recovery, progress, or victory or for anniversaries of beginnings or memorable scenes, or for rehearsals, as with old friends, or for revisiting cherished places or people, or comment on some admirable characteristic or behavior by the self or other or by a dyad or groups. Next are *instrumental-aesthetic affluence* scripts. These address the enrichment of the purely instrumental with varying admixtures of the aesthetic, beginning with singing at work, socializing at work, embellishing one's work, taking pride in it, savoring and celebrating it. Next are *positive anticipatory* affluence scripts in which the individual neither celebrates nor rehearses, but scripts future-oriented scenes of great reward that offer the *bonus* of positive affect in the present, in a manner similar to the bonus of good scenes remembered.

Next are *cross-referenced interscripted* affluence scripts, which order relationships between scripts advantageously. Thus, a career may be scripted as a way of supporting a family, hobby, travel, self-development, and contribution to citizenship, while the family may be scripted as a way of training and preparing for future careers, citizens, hobbies, or personality development.

There are, finally, also *aggregation* affluence scripts in which multiple sources of positive affect are conjoined in new scripts such as the choice of a mate, friend, career, or residence. When the individual has achieved a stable positive over negative affect equilibrium she is capable of increasing her demandingness so that her choice of a mate, friend, career, or place to live is based upon the *conjoint* several features of scenes she finds most deeply rewarding. Thus, such a choice will not represent a partitioning of values but an aggregation approaching a summum bonum in which she aggregates not only what kind of a person she will marry, what kind of a friend she will cultivate, what kind of a career she will pursue, what kind of a place she will choose to live in, but insists that these most wanted choices themselves be aggregated, so that she lives with her mate in a place they cherish, surrounded by mutual friends they cherish, pursuing shared or complementary careers together in a family and friend business or profession.

In the middle ages, the convergence on the building of great Christian cathedrals often represented the aggregation of the deepest motives and best energies of all members of a community in a celebratory, sacred, aesthetic, and educational enterprise.

When the ratio of positive over negative affect is great there are not only an abundance of types of rewarding scenes, but there is a general strategy of optimizing costs, benefits, and probabilities so that such affluence is not only achieved, but maintained at a stable equilibrium. Disadvantageous shifts in costs, benefits, or probabilities are countered by scripted shifts in tactics to maintain the optimizing strategy against both overweening demands and against unavoidable disappointments.

Next are the cost-benefit risk scripts of *limitation remediation*. These address those aspects of the human condition perceived to be imperfect, to which some enduring long-term response *must* be made and which it is believed *can* be remedied, with varying degrees of success, risk, effort, costs, and benefits. These scripts involve an optimizing strategy; though compared with scripts of affluence the positive benefits won involve much more absorption of negative affect as a necessary risk and cost of benefits. They are relatively clear in distance and direction, with little conflict or plurivalence. They bifurcate scenes into good and bad scenes and know which are good and which are evil and that one must strive for one at the same time one strives against the other. Limitation remediation scripts range from scripts of *commitment* to *acceptance,* to *conformity,* to *opportunism,* to *hope,* to *resignation.*

Commitment scripts involve the courage and endurance to invest and bind the person to long-term activity and to magnify positive affect in such activity by absorbing and neutralizing the various negative costs of such committed activity. Commitment may be altruistic or narcissistic or both. These scripts may be economic, political, artistic, religious, scientific, familial, or self-improving. Although these scripts of remediation vary radically in the apparent quantity of remediation over risks and costs and in their pretensions to making the world closer to the heart's desire, nonetheless when the individual's ratio of positive to negative affect is advantageous, though never so much as in scripts of affluence, even the resignation involved in willing, e.g., the obligatory state of slavery, which one may have inherited, and which one accepts because it is a choice of living against dying, may nonetheless provide the rewards of hope (e.g., in a Christian heaven), of evoking some positive affect for being a "good" slave, of a rewarding family life, of sharing a common fate with other slaves. Further, even the most miserable wage slavery of the very poor, as described by Lewis (1961) in *The Children of Sanchez,* reveals that the culture of poverty may co-exist with some psychological affluence in the opportunistic remediation of severe limitation. Thus, Jesus Sanchez regards very hard work for very little money as much better than being without money or being given welfare. He is quite prepared to give up play and games and his "childhood" in preparation for the severities of life he anticipates from seeing how hard his own father works. Though he has had little education he sees some opportunities for learning in the course of discharging his duties as a employee. He wishes to be like his father who also had no one to help him. Like his father he is not given to showing affection to his own children, since they too must be prepared for the same hard work. He likes his work, and he likes his boss (who "permits" him to work overtime on holidays). His reasons for liking his work are multiple. First, he must if he is to eat and to support his family. Second, he is neither passive nor controlled. Third, he is not abandoned when he has money. Nor is he spoiled. Like his father he exhibits his endurance and perseverance through his work. Next, it provides him with such education as he has ever had, and develops his skills in buying. Also, it satisfies his wish to be with many different kinds of people and to work for an admired father surrogate. Next, it enables generativity in providing him with money so that he can build a house, which he can leave as his inheritance to his children. Finally, as he describes it, it is his "medicine," making him forget his "troubles." This "poor man" is psychologically rewarded by his forced labor through which he remedies an inheritance which he has accepted but determined to remedy within the limits of possibility as he perceives them.

Historically many of the major religions have scripted limitation remediation via sacrifice (Hebraic), confession (Christian), resignation (Hindu), and cessation of desire (Buddhism). All of these enjoin acceptance, in varying ways, of the negative affects inherent in human existence. They are quite different than the secular ideals of the Enlightenment in subordinating pride in human effort to the cosmic and the divine power and perfection. Nonetheless, such limitation remediation scripts have provided, and continue to provide, hope, solace, and community for those who believe.

A more active set of limitation remediation scripts was propounded in the prescription of cultivation and integration of good heartedness and discipline by Confucius. In contrast, such complexity was rejected by Taoism in its classic prescription of the *simple way* of living in contact with and in accordance with nature.

There are a great variety of remediation scripts that vary significantly in their proposed balance of rewards, and benefits versus costs, versus risks, but all are alike in promising some reward over suffering.

Next are scripts of *contamination,* chief among which are the *nuclear scripts,* which are conjointly believed necessary to solve but are nonetheless insoluble. They exemplify the conjunction of greed and cowardice because of equally dense positive and negative affect. They utilize a self-defeating double strategy of *both* minimizing negative affect and of maximizing positive affect, and so do neither. Contamination takes the form of deep conflict, or turbulent multiple conflict and plurivalence, such that the individual suffers ambiguity and disorientation, as well as conflict, frustration, and threat. However she also enjoys scenes of the deepest excitement and enjoyment whenever she achieves a victory in her life-long struggles to resolve her conflicts, by purification or by integration, to resolve her plurivalences by simplication or by unification, to resolve her alienation by recovery of the promised land.

But though she runs, she cannot hide for long, though she may win battles she loses the war, though she may see the promised land she may never live in it. Her great benefits are paid for with great suffering and at great risk, which she has no choice but to accept for the benefits she can neither permanently possess nor renounce.

Although the formation of a nuclear script requires and maintains a less than optimal ratio of positive to negative affect, nonetheless variations in this ratio favor variations in the ratios of defensive, counteractive, and reparative nuclear subscripts. The more positive affect, the more the reparative subscript is magnified. The more negative affect, the more the defensive subscript is magnified, with the counteractive subscript magnification occupying an intermediate position.

Less punishing are *culture conflicted* scripts, in which an individual is at the same time possessed by one cultural inheritance while tempted by another alternative. Such is the case in Third World modernizing cultures and in the centuries old love-hate relations between the Judeo and Christian cultures, and between the Moslem, Christian, and Hebraic civilizations. Each appears at once divine and satanic to the other and so can neither live with or without each other. Although such conflicts and tensions have been deeply creative for all parties, the perennial warfare of such culture conflict has also radically magnified self-love and self-disgust as well as other love and disgust of the other. While such conflict is not quite as severe as nuclear conflict, it is not too different in its tragic destiny. The price of bonding by ideology is as severe as the benefits it endows.

The greater the ratio of positive to negative affect in the individual, as in the society, the more such severe conflict may be attenuated if not completely reduced.

Next are scripts of *toxicity,* which address scenes of sufficient negative affect density and threat that they must be opposed, or excluded, attenuated, escaped or avoided, or confronted or defeated, but which by virtue of their density and the disadvantage of a stable ratio of negative over positive affect limit the ability of the individual to permanently rid herself of experienced threat or of experienced negative affect. This is the mirror image of scripts of affluence. The equilibrium is equally stable, but self-validating and self-fulfilling of costs over benefits, of risks over security and affluence, of the greatest distance between actuality and the individual's ideals. She must struggle excessively for the most meager benefits achieved at excessive costs. She is neither ambivalent or plurivalent, but rather frustrated, threatened, and defeated. Her general strategy is neither an optimizing one, nor one of minimizing negative affect, nor of maximizing positive affect, but rather of *satisficing* by reducing suffering as much as she can. This suffering includes much distress, rage, terror, shame, guilt, disgust, and dismell. For *reductions* in any of these negative affects she must be uncertain, but pay excessive prices in effort to remain alive. She is one of the many millions of refugees who have suffered exile from a land that in idealization has become a remote and barely promised land.

She is also one of those who would wish to be exiled, but are imprisoned and abused either in their homes (as in child abuse) or in their homeland (as political prisoners who are tortured). They have only two options: to avenge themselves by reversing and recasting future scenes, so that it is they who abuse and torture the other (in murder) or a surrogate (e.g., a helpless animal). Secondly, even such victims seek and find refuge within their prison, as in a loved pet who reciprocates the desperate love of the victim or in a beloved sibling who is equally victimized. But these can never quite neutralize the overwhelming mass of intimidation and humiliation inherent in scripts of toxicity.

We turn now to a more detailed account of some of the major types of scripts.

IDEOLOGICAL SCRIPTS

Ideological scripts attempt to provide general orientation of the place of human beings in the cosmos and in the society in which they live, an account of their central values, guidance for their realization, sanctions for their fulfillment, their violation, and their justification, and celebration of how life should be lived from here to eternity. Though ideology begins in cosmology and religion, it ends in social criticism. Although ideology reaches for coherence and consensus, shared ideologies, as in religious or political sects, are at the same time fractionated and partitioned into conflict and polarity.

Ideological scripts are those we inherit by virtue of being a member of a civilization, a nation, a religion, a gender, an age, an institution, a class, a region, a family, a profession, or school. They represent the various faiths by which human beings live and, alas, die. They are the chief agents of bonding and of differentiation and division.

They are the most important single class of scripts because of their conjoint scope, abstractness and specificity, stability and volatility, past, present, and future orientation, shared and exclusive features, spatial as well as temporal references, guidance as well as rewarding and punishing sanctions, actuality and possibility concerns, and above all because they endow fact with value and affect. It deals not with truth per se but with the domain of the "real." As such, it is a matter of faith, without which human beings appear unable to live. It is the location of actuality and possibility in a world of affect and value. These scripts are at once self-validating and self-fulfilling. They are lived out as if true and good against others as false and bad, though just how tolerant they may be of competitors is generally included in the ideological script.

Twenty years ago (Tomkins, 1963a, b, 1965), I presented a theory of the structure of ideology in Western thought and a theory of the relationship between ideology and personality. I traced a recurrent polarity between the humanistic and normative orientations, between left and right, in fields as diverse as theology, metaphysics, the foundations of mathematics, the theory of aesthetics, political theory, epistemology, theory of perception, theory of value, theory of childrearing, theory of psychotherapy, and the theories of personality and personality testing.

This polarity appeared first in Greek philosophy between Protagoras, affirming that "man is the measure," and Plato, affirming the priority of the realm of essence. This polarity represents an idealization, positive idealization in the humanistic ideology and negative idealization in the normative ideology. Human beings in western civilization have tended toward self-celebration, positive or negative.

I further assumed that an individual resonates to any organized ideology because of an underlying ideoaffective posture (or script as I would now call it), which is a set of feelings and ideas about feelings that is more *loosely* organized than any highly organized ideology. An example from my Polarity scale would be the items "It is disgusting to see an adult cry" versus "It is distressing to see an adult cry." I further assumed that the script or ideoaffective posture was the resultant of systematic differences in the socialization of affects, in which affects were more punitively socialized on the right and more rewardingly socialized on the left. I outlined a systematic program of differential socialization of each of the nine primary affects that together produced an ideoaffective posture that inclined the individual to resonate differentially to ideology.

The postulated relationships between personality and ideology have proved reasonably robust over several years of systematic research (Tomkins, 1975, 1982) in which quite different methods were employed on samples of subjects varying broadly in age, educational status, intelligence, and sex, as well as normality and pathology. The consistent finding is that the ideological humanist is positively disposed towards human beings, in his displayed affect, in his perceptions, and in his cognitions. The ideological normative is negatively disposed towards human beings in his displayed affect, in his perceptions, and in his cognitions.

We first standardized (Tomkins & McCarter, 1964) a series of posed affect photographs in accordance with my theory of the nine primary innate affects. These produced an average intercorrelation of 0.86 between intended judgments and the obtained judgments. Many of these same photographs were later used by Ekman (1972) to demonstrate a worldwide, pancultural consensus in the recognition of affect from posed photographs, thus reconfirming with more sophisticated methods what Darwin (1965) had demonstrated a century before. Using these photographs, we selected one face showing the different affects for presentation in a stereoscope. The subject was presented, in each trial, with one affect on the right eye and another affect on the left eye, in conflict with each other. Each affect was pitted in turn against every other affect, e.g., the sad face of the subject presented to one eye, while the other eye saw a happy face. When the brain is thus confronted with two incompatible faces, the response is either a suppression of one face, a fusion of both faces, or a rivalry and alternation between the two faces. We predicted and confirmed that the left-oriented subjects would unconsciously select a dominance of the smiling face over all other affects (correlations 0.42, $N = 247$). We predicted and confirmed that right wing subjects would unconsciously produce a dominance of the contemptuous face (correlation of 0.60). The ideological orientation had been tested by use of my Polarity scale.

Next in a series of studies of 500 subjects, we compared the humanistic and normative positions with the scores on the Tomkins–Horn Picture Arrangement Test. This is a broad spectrum projective type personality test that had been standardized (Tomkins & Miner, 1956) on a representative sample (1,500) of the United States population. This was designed to be computer scored with separate norms for age, intelligence, education, sex, and a variety of demographic characteristics. The results again confirmed the same predictions we had made for stereoscopic resolution. The humanistic ideology is significantly related to general sociophilia, whereas the normative ideology is significantly related to sociophobia in which there is avoidance of physical contact between men, an expectation of general aggression from others, and, finally, an elevated social restlessness, which maximizes the number of changes from social to nonsocial situations.

Finally, Vasquez (1975) predicted and confirmed differential facial affective responses in left- and right-wing subjects. The videotaped subjects were previously selected on the basis of their Polarity scale scores. The questions here tested concerned the use of the face, whether conscious or unconscious, whether voluntary or involuntary, as a communication of affect. Again we predicted that humanists would smile more than normative subjects. It was confirmed that humanist subjects actually smiled more frequently while talking with an experimenter than did normative subjects. There was no such difference, however, when subjects were alone, displaying affect spontaneously. Our prediction was based, not only on the previously confirmed dominance of the smiling face in the resolution of stereoscopic conflict and on the dominance of general sociophilia over sociophobia in the Picture Arrangement Test, but also on the grounds both that they had experienced the smile of enjoyment more frequently during their socialization and because they have internalized the ideoaffective posture that one should attempt to increase positive affect for the other as well as for the self. The learned smile does not, of course, always mean that the individual *feels* happy. As often as not, it is a consequence of a wish to communicate to the other that one wishes him to feel smiled upon and to evoke the smile from the other. It is often that which extinguishes the fires of distress, hate, and shame.

We also predicted that humanists would frequently respond with shame and that normatives would respond less frequently with shame but more frequently with disgust and contempt. Our rationale was that shame represents an impunitive response to what is interpreted as an interruption to communion (e.g., in shyness) and that it will ultimately be replaced by full communication. In contrast, contempt and disgust are responses to a bad other, and the termination of intimacy with such a one is assumed to be permanent unless that other changes significantly. These hypotheses were confirmed for shame and disgust but not for contempt. The humanist subjects do respond more frequently with shame if there is any perceived barrier to intimacy. The normative subjects not only smile less frequently, but display disgust on their face more frequently to the other who is tested and found wanting.

Thus, whether we put the question to the brain faced unconsciously with conflicting perceptual information or to the fully conscious subject asked to decide in what order to place three different scenes to make sense of them, or whether unbeknownst to the subject we take moving pictures of his complex and ever changing facial displays, the individual continues to respond as though he lives in one world, consistent in behavior, cognition, perception, and affect. It is, however, one world that is systematically different if he views it from the left or from the right.

I have demonstrated (Tomkins, 1965) a deep coherence between the differential magnification of specific affects and quite remote ideological derivatives. Thus, if you believe it is distressing to see an adult cry rather than disgusting to see an adult cry, you also believe human beings are basically good rather than evil, that numbers were created rather than discovered, that the mind is like a lamp rather than a mirror, that when life is disappointing it leaves a bad taste in the mouth rather than leaving a bad smell, that the promotion of social welfare by government is more important than the maintenance of law and order, and that play is important for all human beings rather than childish. This polarity did not exist before social specialization and stratification. If one is primarily a herbivore, one has no need either of massive energy output nor of ferocity nor of cunning. Thus, the Semang, who according to Sanday (1981, p. 19) have a "plant oriented mentality," wander through their forest "lightfooted, singing and wreathed with flowers" searching the treetops for game or honey. Women gather wild plant food, which is the dietary staple. Men occasionally hunt small game, but not large game, nor do they engage in any kind of warfare, but are more involved with their families and childrearing. Everyone joins in harvesting fruit. They place a high value on freedom of movement and disdain the sedentary life of agriculture. The dieties are male and female. There is sexual differentiation without stratification. According to Sanday (1981, p. 21), "The earth mother is perhaps closer to human affairs and the sky father more distant. He makes the thunder and she helps the people to appease him. She is the nurturant figure and he the commanding figure." Under such benign physical and cultural conditions, there is both a zest for life and no stratification either between the affects or between the sexes. Both the excitement of mobility and the enjoyment of cyclical seasonal harvest are valued, as are men *and* women.

I would suggest that this polarity is a sublimated derivative of social stratification and exploitation. The left represented then as now the oppressed and exploited against their warrior oppressors.

Over time this debate shifted to classes, which protested their inferior status, who looked to expropriate the expropriators, aristocrats against kings, bourgeoisie against landed gentry, proletariat against bourgeoisie, peasants against all.

The most important ideological transformations in civilization occurred when small game hunting became large game hunting and nomadic and when gathering become settled agriculture. In one, origins and deities became masculine, skyward transcendant, aggressive, possessive, intolerant, competing with men, taking sides in convenants with elected men against their enemies, punishing their favored men whenever they contested for divine power. In the other, origins and deities became immanent earth or sea mothers, indulgent if sometimes capricious, a plenum that contracts and expands slowly (rather than quickly and destructively), more fixed than mobile, more conservative than radical and discontinuously creative, more cyclical than linear. In one, men dominate the society. In the other, women dominate. One represents a magnification of excitement, the other a magnification of enjoyment. The ideological magnification of excitement versus enjoyment did not occur because the sexes differed in their preferences, but rather because two very different ways of acquiring food became more and more differentiated. When the relatively undifferentiated hunter gatherers split into predatory big game hunters and sedentary agriculturalists, differentiation ultimately became increasingly specialized and finally stratified into warrior nomads who subjugated peasant agriculturalists, in the formation of states, empires, and civilizations.

According to Rustow (1980, p. 29), "where conquering drivers or mounted nomads ran into a population of sedentary plow-peasants, they installed themselves as the ruling stratum and thenceforth lived on the labor, dues, and services of the subjugated." The conquerors "now needed only to devote themselves to ruling, to fighting, and to the knightly way of life" in castles as "petrified horse" and the horse as "an itinerant castle." It was further elaborated as part of religious ideology "as in heaven also on earth"—as Genghis Khan said "One God in heaven, one Ruler on earth." Nomads were sometimes transformed into conquerors by religious enthusiasm. Thus, the Bedouins of Arabia had for centuries led a circumscribed existence until they were electrified into domination and conquest as a religious duty of Holy War by Muhammad about 650 A.D. They set the patriarchy of the stock breeders in the place of the matriarchy of the plow peasants. The settled peoples characteristically lamented the barbaric crudeness and rapacious aggressiveness of the nomads who rejected the culture of the settlers as degenerate and seductive, as well as overly invested in arduous physical labor.

As Tacitus (1901) had said of the German invaders, "they think it base and spiritless to earn by sweat what they might purchase with blood."

This invidious comparision was much magnified by the appearance of the war chariot and the horse. The rider appeared on the stage of history as a new breed of man, terrifying in his intoxication with speed and his ability to effect concentrated mass formations in concert with his fellow horsemen. Their superiority over the panicked settled peasantry was enormous and irresistible.

It was the intensification of violence and warfare, first against big game animals and then against human beings, that ultimately produced the now universal bifurcation, polarity, and stratification of the innate affects into excitement, surprise, anger, disgust, and dismell versus enjoyment, distress, shame, and fear. This polarity in families of affects not only appeared in cosmology and the nature of the gods but also in the relationship between the sexes and finally in secular ideological conflict.

The major dynamic of ideological differentiation and stratification arises from perceived scarcity and the reliance upon violence to reduce such scarcity to allocate scarce resources disproportionately to the victors in adversarial contests. Nor is this a uniquely human phenomenon. Many animals begin stratification in contests between males for exclusive *possession* of females. The paradox in this is that the prize of the contest, the female, is diminished to a position of lower status.

Sanday (1981) in her survey of 150 societies found balanced authority and power between the sexes in the absence of forces perceived to threaten social survival. Invidious stratification of the sexes appears to begin in environments perceived to be unfavorable (e.g., famine) and responded to by masculine violence. There appears to be a close link between using enemy *others* violently and stratification *within* beginning with gender stratification and then spreading to age and class stratification.

Consider what must happen when the world turns more negative than positive. First, feeling as such is confused with the predominant, unwanted negative affects. To the extent that anger and violence appear to offer the favored solution to a world turned bad many other consequences follow. The first is that of the believed benefits of slavery from warfare. One can thereby convert enemies to means to one's own happiness, as well as rob the other of whatever territory, property, or food he may possess. Second, anger is increased because the innate determinant of anger is a considerable increase in neural firing that is prompted by a variety of nonoptimal scenes of the now problematic world. Third, the conjunction of superior masculine strength and superior life-bearing feminine capabilities predispose the male to violence and death and the female against it. If the die is cast toward violence, then excitement and risk-taking must be elevated against the more pacific relaxation of enjoyment and communion. Fourth, surprise must be elevated against fear. Fear is a deadly affect for successful warfare, being the most serious enemy within. It is assigned to the enemies to be defeated. One should try to terrorize one's enemy. Fifth, anger must be elevated above distress. Distress must be born manfully. A man must not weep, but rather make his enemy cry out in surrender. Sixth, the warrior must above all be proud, elevating disgust, dismell, and contempt (the fusion of anger and dismell) above the humble hanging of the head in shame. Shame is what the proud warrior should inflict on his enemy. He as warrior should rather die than surrender in shame.

Notice that we have now partitioned the full spectrum of the innate affects into two and that these sets are now invidiously stratified. The successful man warrior is excited, ready for surprise, angry and proud, contemptuous and fearless. The loser has given up and is relaxed in dubious enjoyment, crying in distress, terrified and humble and ashamed. It is a very small step to assign these demeaned affects to women inasmuch as they are readily defeated by men in physical combat. It is also a small step to regard children as little slaves and little women, and to regard lower classes in the same way. Boy children then must prove themselves to become men in rites de passage. A variety of trials involve the mastery of the masculine over the feminine affects. I am suggesting that social stratification rests upon the affect stratification inherent in adversarial contests.

Women and lower status individuals are then pictured as loving, timid, distressed, shy, and humble. An effeminate man is a loser, but even warriors capable of seizing and possessing women necessarily remain deeply ambivalent about mothers and mother surrogates who are loving and tender rather than risk-taking, capable of distressed empathy rather than hostile, modest and shy rather than judgmental, distancing in disgust, dismell, and contempt, timid and fearful rather than competitive and dangerous. The very powerful magnification of the warrior affects guarantees that the feminine affects will become as alien as they are seductive. A masculine female becomes as repellent as an effeminate male.

Large-scale societies are necessarily stratified to the extent that they require government from centralized authority. The origin of both state and government appears to have been primarily adversarial in recorded history. Most large societies began either in subjugation or much less frequently in confederation against the threat of it. The resultant stratification, though responsible for "high culture" and "civilization," has exacted severe prices from the exploited populations ranging from the terror of mass killings, through severe privation and distress, through the shame of caste and class derogation, the reduction of autonomy and freedom of expression via imprisonment, to the reduction of opportunity for self-development via reduction of social mobility, and the acceptance of the exploiters as "superior" and of the exploited as "lower."

Stratification has inevitably generated a polarity of ideologies in defense of itself and in protest against itself. The defensive ideologies vary as a function of the nature of the society they defend, and so change as these societies are changed via ideological challenge. These are the normative, right-wing ideologies. Locked into polarized conflict with them are humanistic, left-wing ideologies, which also change as societies change. They inevitably address three somewhat independent, somewhat interdependent problematic social conditions. First of all, they emphasize the intolerable *costs* in one or another negative affect of the prevailing ideology. There is too much violence, too much terror, too much distress, too much shame, too much disgust or dismell. Second, they place the blame for the problematic on the established normative authority, which must then change itself or be changed by those who suffer. The ideological polarity arises because the normative ideology places the blame for the problematic squarely upon those who suffer and complain. It is thus the welfare "cheats" who are to blame for their own problems. Third, it inevitably represents not only the protests of those defeated in adversarial contests and who wish to win but in varying degrees the feminine affects diminished by the adversarial stratification. The left is constituted in varying ratios of outraged masculinity and suppressed femininity, the militants and the flower children. The right is much less complex, apologist as it is of primarily masculine, adversarial stratification, buttressed by "tradition"—"If it isn't broken, don't fix it."

Since different societies vary in their degree of stratification, in the costliness of exploitation, in the type of cost, in their degree of modulation and mixture of the masculine–feminine principles, the normative humanistic polarity is *both* universal and idiosyncratic for each society and historical moment.

Hertz (1973) and later Needham (1973) have shown that this polarity has appeared in many preliterate societies. The left and the right appeared to be a distinction about a family of analogs with a very large number of members. Left was widely believed to be related to right, as woman is to man, as profane is to sacred, as impetuous is to reflective, as dark is to light, as death is to life, as sin is to virtue, as falsity is to truth, as hell is to heaven, as the sky is to the underworld.

Every society and every civilization confronts somewhat distinctive sets of problems with a family of shared assumptions that is a larger family than the polarized differences in projected solutions to these shared problems. Variation and contest is around the major central tendency. Civilizations and their ideologies are at once orthogonal to each other in their central values and similar to each other in the range of polarized alternative solutions to these central problems. Thus, in early China, from the eighth to the third centuries B.C., there was increasing social anarchy with the collapse of the Chou Dynasty. Whole populations were put to death in mass executions. The problem forced upon Confucius and others was, how can such violent human beings live together? The major responses were, first, the classical right-wing position of the legalists or Realists. Han Fei Tzu's answer was massive and certain use of law and force. Human beings are inherently evil but they can be contained by a large militia and effective police force. Second was the classic left-wing response of Mohism. Mo Tzu proposed love, not force. Five hundred years before Christ, Mo Tzu argued "But whence did these calamities arise? They arise out of want of mutual love . . . It is to be altered by way of universal love and mutual aid." Confucious rejected both love and force, defending what appears to be the classic middle-of-the-road position. Both

Jen, the source of good heartedness in the person, and li, order, are needed for individuals to live together in harmony. Harmony is the primary aim for both the individual and the society. Only via great respect and love, filial piety in the family, can inner greatness and outer greatness be achieved. The good life is a hard-won achievement that results from the cultivation of the tradition that had existed in China's past, in the period of Grand Harmony.

There was another middle-of-the-road position in Taoism. Taoism, like Confucianism and Mohism and Realism, was for harmony and against strife, but it was *also* against Confucianism and its emphasis on regulation and tradition. It was for Nature and the easy way. The ideal life is the simple life, not the cultivated life. There is harmony and perfection in nature. Both man and society must be in tune with Nature.

Here we have then left, right, and two alternative versions of the center. It was not only a concern with social rather than individual problems, but also a concern with the finite and the immanence of this world and not with the transcendence of the infinite and otherworldliness.

Finally, it is a concern with the maintenance of tranquility, enjoyment, and stability, not with the guarantee of excitement, risk, competition, growth, and progress.

The Chinese conjoined the affect of enjoyment with its investment of sameness, particularly, and tradition in contrast to the Western investment in excitement, abstraction, transformation, and change. They loved the here and now and particularly the land that they inherited from their ancestors who had loved it before them. Their science was applied to satisfy present needs rather than pursuing a remote, never-to-be attained final truth. Their worship of learning stressed the mastery of particular texts. Their gods were their ancestors, not remote and out of space and time. Their interpersonal relations stressed the importance of affection and piety for their parents, their mates, and their children rather than the quest for the perfect romantic love and lover. Similarly, their political life included rebellions, but no revolutions in the Western sense. They would kick the rascals out, but expect no utopia as a result.

But all of these ideologies shared the same basic central problem of how to restore harmony to a society that had been torn asunder by violence and great disorder. This is quite a different problem than that which confronted Buddha in India. His was the sudden confrontation with the *individual* suffering the ravages of disease, old age, and death. And so China resisted the intrusion of the deeply introversive Buddhism until it had been tailored to meet the Chinese concern with social problems. India was not torn by violence. It was a much more stable caste society, which paid an excessive price in individual suffering as Buddha discovered when he first confronted the ravages of disease, old age, and death. It was also a much more introversive culture than China as well as more feminine than China. A favored solution to this complex was an introversive asceticism in which distress was to be reduced not by violence, but by renunciation of desire and individuality and fusion with Nirvana. One hundred years after Buddha's death, "Buddhism" divided into a left- and right-wing schism of Theravada versus Mahayanna, each defending a polarized interpretation. For one sect, Buddha had been a "kind and compassionate" man. For the other Buddha had been a "disciplined" man.

In radical contrast, the focus in the United States is on individualism, egalitarianism, freedom, the pursuit of money in a capitalistic competitive economy coupled with the transcendental Christian good works for those who fall behind, and the Christian sense of sin for both winners and losers, and the endless hot pursuit of the infinite and the transcendental in science, politics, love, and religion. The left–right polarity now centers on the relative importance of big business versus big government, the relative importance of the environment versus the need for economic growth, the relative importance of nuclear energy versus "natural" energy sources, the relative importance of military power versus peace, the relative importance of caring for the sick, the aged, the poor, versus self-help or turning the responsibility over to business, presumably more "efficient" than government.

But a left-wing American is more like a right-wing American than either is to any member of Confucian China. A Protestant is more like a Catholic than either are similar to a Hindu. A Marxist is more like a capitalist than either are to a hunter-gatherer. Polarities occur within extended families of ideologies, which characteristically are more orthogonal than polarized. The polarity appears to function as a universal *moderator* of widely differing ideologies. It is the variations *within* ideologies that are best described by the polarity.

COMMITMENT SCRIPTS

Commitment scripts are a species of *limitation* scripts, which address those aspects of the human condition perceived to be imperfect to which some enduring long-term response must be made. Limitation scripts are based on an assessment of what is desirable and undesirable, the ratio of positive to negative affect, and what and how much it would be desirable and possible to change for the better. Limitation scripts range from scripts of commitment, to acceptance, to opportunism, to hope, and to scripts of resignation.

The limitation script may elect to *accept* and *conform* to socially inherited limitations (e.g., class or ethnic), or individually inherited limitation (e.g., psychological or physical) and try to profit as much as is possible within these limitations, as in the English Victorian script described by the philosopher Bradley as "my station and its duties." It may elect a *resignation* script, as in slavery, when resistance would have been perceived as guaranteeing death.

Limitation might prompt a script of *opportunism* in the case of a peasantry that perceives itself to be exploited and intimidated, but capable of exploiting its limited freedom in the interstices of a feudal society via effective cunning. The trickster exemplifies such an opportunistic script. A later born child who is governed by primogeniture, actual or psychological, often elects an opportunistic script.

A limitation script need not represent resignation or acceptance alone. It may combine these with a script of *hope,* the great engine of the religions of the oppressed, from the days of the early Christians in Rome through the plantations in the United States South. The opiate of Christianity offered not only the promise of a life hereafter, but a counter culture in the here and now. Limitation shared becomes limitation attenuated under such circumstances. The lottery is yet another antidote for limitation to be overcome via hope.

If ideology reflects the orientation and faith that supports a way of life, commitment scripts represent the courage and endurance to invest and bind the person to long-term activity and to magnify positive affect in such activity by absorbing and neutralizing the various negative affect costs of such committed activity.

Although all limitation scripts are based on an assessment of the overall ratio of positive to negative affect, commitment scripts are distinctive in their bias toward positive affect. They originate in a favorable ratio of positive over negative affect and aim at increasing that advantage.

Both sources and aims of commitment are varied and complex combinations of components. Consider three distinct committed career choices each of which shares a passion for nature. Eugene O'Neill chose to live at the ocean's edge, in solitude, as he expressed himself in the plays he wrote. Compare such a commitment script with that of a lumberjack who also insists on working close to nature, but in the company of others, and in exercising the large muscles. Contrast both with an archaeologist who is enchanted with the rediscovery of the past, with others, in very special and remote nature sites, so that both time and space are remote.

Since commitments are heavily biased toward positive affects, and since individuals vary radically in their preferred locus of positive affect, commitments will reflect a wide spectrum of differential preferences for types and density of people (or solitude), for types of function drives (cognitive, affective, perceptual, verbal, memory, or motoric), for time past, present, or future, for types of place (calm, wild, remote, claustral, open, sea, mountain, urban, surburban, or village), for types of values (economic, political, religious, theoretic, scientific, aesthetic, or military).

Although every individual experiences a broad spectrum of scenes that either excite or provide enjoyment or that distress, anger, shame, disgust, or frighten, very few can result in commitment scripts, since these bind the person to substantial investments of affect, energy, and activity over long periods of time. The individual is thereby much more constrained in the number of her possible commitments than in the number of her interests and other types of scripts. Such demandingness of commitment scripts generates interscript scripts designed to deal with competing commitments (e.g., between work and family) as well as possible conflicts between commitments and other types of scripts (e.g., noncommitted hobbies as in some aesthetic scripts or noncommitted instrumental scripts, as in the necessary but nonetheless routine earning of money).

Although commitment scripts are exceptionally robust, they are nonetheless vulnerable to a variety of transformations. They may be eroded by successful completion of their aim or by excessive failure to make progress toward that aim, by the overload of neglected demands competitive with the major commitment, or by the conjunction of the routinization of that commitment exposing the individual to seduction by underdeveloped potentialities of her personality, as in the case of the middle-age neurosis described by Jung. Competing commitments may require changes in priority under radical changes of circumstance. Thus, a woman whose child required long-term hospitalization elected to subordinate her career to the nurturance of her child at considerable cost to that career, but with a compensatory deepening of her commitment to her child.

In a study of a representative sample of the population of the United States (Tomkins, 1962), I found that there was an inverse relationship between the interest in work and the interest in interpersonal interaction, such that the interest in work peaked between the ages of eighteen to thirty and diminished steadily thereafter as the sociophilia increased to the age of seventy-five.

Transformation of priorities among commitments are not necessarily unplanned reactions. Thus, commitment to family and to work may be partitioned by the individual to be dominant at different phases of the lifecycle. Such partitioning may be socioculturally specified, as in the Indian assignment of the first half of life to attending to the mundane, so that the second half of life may be committed to the cultivation of the spiritual.

SOME ORIGINS OF COMMITMENT SCRIPTS

Let us now examine more closely some of the varied sources of commitment scripts. Commitment may arise from violations of ideology, as in the case of those abolitionists of the United States who felt that both Christianity and democracy were intolerably violated by the institution of slavery. It may arise conjointly from ideology and a nuclear script, as in the case of Marx, who as a late adolescent was repelled by the "bourgeois" demand of his beloved liberal father that he give up his humanistic studies, settle down, and support his wife to be. Thenceforth, Marx committed himself to the liberation of all the exploited wage slaves, himself included, finding in Engels a surrogate father who not only worshipped him, but would also continue to support him.

It may arise out of the exercise of any talent whose reward is much greater than the costs of developing it. It may arise out of the fascination of a youngster at the deep commitment of a revered model to a particular kind of activity. Thus, Alfred Gwynne Vanderbilt became committed to the breeding and racing of horses when he was seduced by seeing the great excitement and enjoyment on the face of his father on the occasion of a horse he had bred winning the Belmont stake race.

It may arise out of respect and affection for a model who emits dense positive affect for the behavior of his or her child, as in the case of Hubert Humphrey who overheard his father boasting to his friends how pleased he was that his son was doing such a good job as his assistant in the store.

It may arise out of deep mutuality in excitement and enjoyment of game playing or any activity in which the child pleases the parents, e.g., by imitation. I have found this critical in the development of some entertainers and some writers (notably Chekhov).

It may arise from critically punishing scenes at the hands of otherwise loving parents, as in the case of Steichen, whose commitment to photographing "the family of man" appears to have originated when he had expressed an ethnic slur in the presence of his mother. She then closed her store, took him upstairs, and lectured him sternly that never again did she want to hear him express any kind of prejudice against any member of the human race.

It may arise out of deference to a parent who aspires to a status, vicariously, through a child and who is able to evoke in that child the commitment to satisfy those aspirations.

It may arise out of the loving overprotection of a child by a parent who displays intense concern for the child on the occasion of illness or distress, engendering a commitment to reciprocate and to recapture intimacy via helping others.

It may arise out of identification with a parent who is deeply committed to a helping or service profession, who does *not* either help or become intimate with members of his own family. I found such a constellation among some abolitionists in the United States whose parents were either nurses, priests, or politicians.

It may arise out of a wish to undo the humiliation of a beloved parent, as in the case of a Black politician who vowed he would devote his life to opening the barriers to full social and political participation against Blacks after witnessing the humiliation enforced on his father by exclusion from membership in a racist club.

It may arise out of the conjoint wish to undo and prevent and punish those responsible for the loss of life of a child, as in the case of the leader of an antigun lobby whose son was shot and killed and the case of the leader of a movement against drunken drivers after her daughter had been killed by a drunken driver. Such individuals commit themselves not only to revenge and prevention but, as they formulate it, to give "meaning" to the otherwise unassimilable random violence that robbed them.

Each specific type of commitment script has both idiosyncratic and general determinants, courses and consequences. We will now present some of these more general features.

First, there is required a massive density of experienced positive affect somewhere in the history of the individual if he is to be both excited into resonance by a positive vision of the possible and able and willing to endure the negative affect costs that will inevitably be encountered in the pursuit of any serious time-extended commitment. It may also (but need not) require a capacity for either outrage and/or for empathic suffering for those to whom one commits oneself.

The beginning of any commitment script requires that some *actual* scene be magnified by the construction of further possible scenes. This scene is but a beginning of a much extended family of possibilities.

Second, possibilities must be explored in a variety of alternative scenes *like* the beginning scene and these support magnification of the initial scenes. Thus, the abolitionist Phillips was sent by his Boston Brahmin parents on a trip to Europe in the hope of distracting their son from his interest in Black slaves. What he "discovered" was that there were all kinds of exploited oppressed people all over the world, increasing his resonance to the general idea of the salvation of others.

Third, there is required a *decision* to take risk on behalf of the commitment. This may involve a radical renunciation of the past way of life. In the case of Phillips, he had to renounce the conventional practice of law in Boston *and* most of his Boston Brahmin friends in favor of the men who were Black.

Fourth, as a consequence of the risk that has been taken, there is usually some punishment and suffering. In Phillips' case, it was alienation from white upperclass Boston society.

Fifth, as a consequence of absorption of such negative affect, resonance to the initial commitment is deepened. In the case of Phillips, this took the form of increased identification with the oppressed and increased hostility toward the oppressor.

Sixth, as a consequence of increasing magnification of commitment, there is an increased willingness and ability to venture more risk and absorb more punishment.

Seventh, there is a shift from strategy to tactics whenever the venturing of effort and risk and the absorption of negative affect reaches a stage of perceived no-return in commitment. This ordinarily occurs *after* a series of second thoughts and flirtations with the possibility of giving up the commitment as either unwise or too costly.

Even so, any commitment remains vulnerable to erosion at any stage. For one abolitionist, the conjunction of poor health and defeat as a political candidate for the presidency of the United States burned him out. After the Emancipation Proclamation, many abolitionists regarded their mission as completed and spent their later years in public appearances, enjoying being lionized in contrast to their former vilification. Others, such as Phillips, continued, arguing that the battle was just beginning.

What were some of the determinants of such commitment scripts? In the case of the abolitionists in the United States, I found (Tomkins, 1965), first, that all were deeply Christian. Three of four had had conversion experiences. For them, Christianity required that they save others if they would save themselves. In all four families, moral and Christian zeal for the salvation of their children was combined with great affection for their children.

Second, these parents had also shown a pervasive concern with public service as minister, nurse, mayor, and political activity.

Third, all appeared to have been physically active and extroverted as children. They had abundant energy, which they translated into vigorous play and into fighting with their peers, which was to be important later in their dangerous face-to-face confrontations before large groups, not infrequently intent on killing them.

Fourth, all were exposed to, influenced by, and modeled themselves after the great orators of their day. So, as Perry Miller (1961) noted, one of the salient features of the Puritans' reformation was the substitution of the sermon for the mass. All four men were early exposed to the magic of the great orators of the day, both Christian and political.

Fifth, all of them were physically courageous. They had all experienced and mastered the art of fighting with their peers, so that they had a zest for combat rather than a dread of it. Different types of commitment, however, call for different types of courage. For some it is shame courage, the capacity to be mocked, excluded, and isolated. For others it is distress courage, to endure endless suffering in the face of great labor and exertion. For others, it is guilt courage, to endure the guilt at the violence that one must inflict on others. For others, it is disgust courage, to endure the endless confrontation with the imperfect, the degrading, and the ugly. For others, it is that amalgam of courage required to support a strong and confident self against the multiple sources of doubt from within and from without. This occurred in the case of Freud when he envisioned himself an intellectual Robinson Crusoe, whose innovative ideas would one day be rediscovered by another adventurer.

AFFECT MANAGEMENT SCRIPTS: SEDATIVE, PREADDICTIVE, AND ADDICTIVE

The following typology of affect management scripts was generated to deal with the problems of substance dependency, particularly the dependency on cigarettes. My interest in these phenomena grew out of my conviction that dependency on cigarettes mimicked addictive dependency in the absence of a biochemical base. This suggested the possibility that psychological addiction was masked in drug addiction by the presence of biochemical addictive tolerance. If this were so, it would illuminate the puzzling phenomenon of ready resumption of addictive dependency after years of abstinence. It would also illuminate addictive phenomena that were clearly psychological in nature, such as in compulsive gambling, eating, and risk-taking.

An empirical program of research was undertaken in cooperation with the Clearinghouse for Smoking Information of the United States Public Health Service, then under the direction of Horn (Horn & Waingrow, 1966). A stratified sample of the United States of 15,000 was tested to determine the fit between my models of affect dependency and the factor structure of that sample. The factor structure obtained was a very close fit between these models and the test responses of that large stratified sample.

With the aid of Ikard (Ikard & Tomkins, 1973), I pursued a series of experimental studies on these models in which predictions concerning the differential responsiveness of sedative, preaddictive, and addictive smokers (using scales designed to distinguish these types) were in no case disconfirmed. These models were further tested in large-scale therapeutic programs in cooperation with the Public Health department of the City of New York, with the cooperation of Donald Frederickson.

Although these models were developed to understand substance dependency, I have since applied them to related types of management of negative affect.

Affect management scripts aim not at affect control, nor at the salience of affect as target, but at the reduction of negative affect.

A sedative script is one that addresses any problematic scene primarily as though the first order of business was to attenuate or to reduce entirely the negative affect which that scene has evoked. It is an escape script rather than an avoidance script, and what it aims to escape is not the problematic source of negative affect in the scene, nor does it seek the instrumental solution to the problematic source. Sedative scripts differentiate negative affects from their source and from remedial instrumental action. Such partitioning of scene, affect, and action is then followed by an increased salience of affect to which the rest of the scene becomes ground, to affect as figure. It is the reduction of this affect that is then scripted as the primary target.

By virtue of the general feature of modularity, an *instrumental sedative* script may combine both types of scripts, using a sedative to help the self deal more effectively with a problematic scene. The sedative script may in fact enable the individual once sedated to resume dealing with the source of the negative affect and to enable more effective remediation without such instrumental intentions in the sedative script itself. Further, the attempted sedation may or may not be successful. The cigarette may enable an individual made fearful to be less fearful, or entirely calm. Quite independent of its effectiveness as a sedative of the negative affect, the cigarette may enable the individual to be more effective in dealing with the problematic scene or not. Thus, she may be helped just a little to be less fearful, but this small affect difference may make all the difference in dealing with the scene. Or, she might become entirely free of fear via the cigarette and yet give up on solving the problem of the scene itself or try and fail, despite having become much less fearful because of the cigarette.

A cigarette is but one of many types of sedative act. One may attempt self-sedation via alcohol, drugs, eating, aggression, sex, travel, driving, walking, running, watching TV, conversation, reading, introversion, music, or a favored place.

There are a number of conditions necessary for the formation of a sedative script. Sedative scripts can occur only under a limited range of the ratio of density of positive to negative affect. One will have no need to generate sedative scripts if that ratio is greatly biased toward positive affect, because then the individual suffers too little negative affect to become salient enough to prompt strategies for negative affect remediation. Further, the basic optimism derivative of such positive affect bias usually makes attempted coping with problematic scenes both salient and effective. Nor do sedative scripts ordinarily occur when the ratio of positive to negative affect is extremely biased toward negative affect. Under these conditions sedative scripts are characteristically transformed into addictive scripts.

Further, in addition to a specific range of positive to negative affect density, negative affect must be differentiated from its source and become salient as problematic. Then, some act must have effectively reduced negative affect, independent of changing the perceived source of that affect. Next, the sedative act must be given priority over instrumental acts designed to deal with the source of the negative affect, moving from last, to middle, to first resort in any problematic scene. Next, the sedative act must be resorted to over an increasing variety of different negative affect scenes, with some degree of perceived effectiveness, whatever the type, intensity, or duration of the negative affect. Then, the relationship between the sedative act and the negative affect must become that of a unique one–many type, in which one and only one act will sedate any of an indefinite number of negative affects, rather than a many-relationship, in which there would be alternative ways of sedating any negative affect.

When these conditions have been met, the individual comes to believe in the *possibility* of reducing negative affect, rather than experiencing herself as a totally helpless victim, or as one who can do no more than celebrate her own misery. Further, she now believes in the *desirability* of reducing her own negative affect rather than be constrained by ideological norms against comforting herself. Further, she now favors the *self* as agent of sedation, rather than passively hoping for help from others to reduce her suffering. Finally, sedative scripts must then compete with a variety of other scripts that are in varying degrees incompatible with sedation.

Thus, an approaching automobile, apparently out of control, rarely prompts attempted sedation. The individual rather devotes full attention to driving her own automobile to avoid the threatened danger rather than to attempt to sedate her fear. There are also many scenes in which affect is so tightly bound to its source (as a species of affect worthy, affect salience scripts) that the individual cannot imagine sedating herself, e.g., upon first hearing of the death of a loved one. In such a case, one might seek to comfort oneself by seeking the company of someone else who also mourns. The total scene is too preemptive to be dealt with by affect sedation alone.

There are many types of scripts that attempt to deal with negative affect as one aim among many but which exclude sedation as such. Thus, a *commitment* script would absorb negative affect as a necessary price. A *doable* script would prompt the individual to turn to something easy enough to accomplish. A *celebratory* script would magnify and communicate the negative affect and the scenes connected with it. An *opportunistic* script would back off the problematic scene for another day that might be more opportune. A *resignation* script would prompt submission to overwhelming pressure. A *systematic* script would prompt transformation of the script in terms of reintegration of a complex matrix of scene consequences. An *affect control* script would address negative affect as a problem for suppression, hiding its expression, preventing its communication, inhibiting action, or suppressing awareness of negative affect. A *review* script would address negative affect as a sign of a radical change of status in the self and in other. A *toxicity* script would view the scene as intolerably threatening and prompt a mobilization of all resources in a war against threat. A *power* script would prompt an increase in skill to cope with this and any other problematic scene. An *insurance* script would prompt the insurance of a small amount of effort to limit very large possible negative affect losses (e.g., be courteous to all people). A *gambling* script would prompt the investment of a small amount of effort to win psychic affluence that would attenuate all negative affect (e.g., a lottery ticket or a courting of the rich and powerful). A *prudential* script would prompt the moderation of risk to avoid future negative affect. A *boldness* script would prompt risking a great deal for the benefits that would minimize negative affect (in contrast to gambling, in which little is risked, for the same aim). A *nuclear* script would prompt defense, counteraction, and reparation as strategies for dealing with troubling negative affect.

Sedative scripts are conditional scripts. They are quite different in this respect from addictive scripts. They are used *only* to sedate experienced negative affect, and therefore vary in frequency and duration of activation, dependent on the experienced frequency and duration of negative affect. As a consequence, the frequency of sedative acts is dependent not only on source affect, but also on the relative effectiveness of the scripted sedative, be it smoking a cigarette, a claustrophilic introversive response, or a claustrophobic extroversive response as in a flight to being with others. If such attempted sedation is effective, the sedative response is terminated and its general frequency reduced. If, however, the sedative act is relatively ineffective, it will be repeated and the general frequency of sedative responses will increase. Paradoxically, sedative acts increase as a conjoint function of the density of source affect and of the *ineffectiveness* of the sedative affect. Sedative smokers who smoke as frequently as addictive smokers (but who are nonetheless *not* addicted) are individuals whose overall density of negative affect is high and for whom the attempted sedation is relatively ineffective. To some extent such an individual suffers a phenomenon similar to biochemically based drug habituation. He needs more and more cigarettes as they become less effective as sedatives. Indeed, most sedative scripts suffer the difficulty that their capacity for reducing and attenuating negative affect is limited and diminishes as the density of negative affect increases.

Despite the fact that the sedative act is a response to negative affect and not to the problematic nature of the scene, it is nonetheless true that individuals are troubled by a set of scenes that are idiosyncratic for each individual.

We can, therefore, determine the characteristic loci of negative affect by noting the types of scenes in which the individual resorts to sedation. Thus, some smokers are surprised to learn that although they smoke only when they are alone, that some smoke only when they are surrounded by others, that some smoke only in the bosom of their family, whereas others smoke only when working at their business, whereas many smoke under all circumstances. Because of the specific conditionality of the sedative script and the unconditionality of the addictive script, one can reliably differentially diagnose these scripts by asking whether the individual smokes (or invokes other sedative acts) when she is on vacation. The addictive smoker is surprised by the question, responding immediately that she does. The sedative smoker may also be surprised by the question, but also by the answer which is evoked. She often discovers, for the first time, that she does *not* smoke at all at such times. This illustrates an important feature of many scripts, that the "rules" may be so overlearned and skilled, via compression, that their presence becomes visible even to the individual herself only by their effects.

PREADDICTIVE SCRIPTS

We turn now to another type of negative affect management. This is the preaddictive script, so labeled because it represents a critical step in the transformation of sedative to addictive dependency. In this case, sedation has been magnified by a substantial increment of urgency and required as a *necessary* condition to remain in the scene, and/or to *act* in it. Thus, there are preaddictive smoking scripts such that an individual believes he *cannot* answer the phone or he cannot meet others, or be alone, without the comforting cigarette *before* he enters the more threatening scene. At the sound of the telephone, therefore, he *must* find a cigarette. This increased urgency, and its moving forward in time, is the hallmark of part of the difference between sedation and what will later be transformed into the *unconditional urgency* of the addictive script.

But there is much more than an increase in urgency. In sedation, there is an activation rule for whenever any negative affect is experienced. The enactment rule is that a cigarette is a unique and necessary method of escape. The closure rule is that smoking terminates when negative affect terminates. In preaddiction, negative affect is now tightly linked with a specific scene that is anticipated will evoke more negative affect that will be tolerable unless *avoided* by a sedative. Its activation rule is to escape from present trouble when the anticipated increase of that affect can be avoided by sedation. At the beginning then it has been transformed from sedation into an *instrumental escape and avoidance sedation* script. It is no longer simply a response to any negative affect but to a specific problematic scene that promises unique punishment unless uniquely sedated in advance. It is a doable escape avoidance script, because it attempts to escape present negative affect and avoid more. It is instrumental because sedation is no longer its exclusive aim. Its major aim is to make it possible to tolerate a specific scene that is tightly linked with punishing affect. Its closure rule is the termination of that scene, not simply the termination of negative affect.

In the mother–child relationship, sedative scripts may require the presence of the mother or a knowledge that she is near or readily available whenever the child feels distressed, afraid, angry, or tired, but *not* otherwise. Such a child may be able to play endlessly without access to or wish for maternal comforting so long as all goes well.

In the parent–child relationship pre–addictive scripts, there is an increment of urgency about the *necessity* of the mother's presence, but it is now required *before* he can begin to do anything that is in any way problematic, such as meeting a stranger. Preaddictive scripts do not arise without a prior sedative script.

While a child might run in panic to his mother for comfort in the absence of prior sedative dependence, it is unlikely it will be thenceforth scripted as preaddictive on the basis of one single scene. For this to occur there must have been frequent prior experiences of sedation, effective or partly effective. Then, what is *added* is an increment of urgency about a restricted set of scenes within the larger family of less urgent dependency scenes. This proved to be clearly the case in the histories of smokers, since preaddictive scripts were never found without sedative scripts, though there were many cases of sedative without preaddictive scripts.

If the preaddictive script generalizes to more than one type of scene, it will characteristically be transformed into an *habitual skilled as-if* script in which the combined compression of the rules and avoidant action at a distance enables the individual to act as if there were danger, but without fear, and with skilled but minimal awareness of what must be done to deal with that scene. An everyday example is the pedestrian crossing a busy intersection with skilled action as if afraid of the potential danger, but without fear.

There *is* a restricted set of preaddictive smoking scripts in the absence of sedative scripts, which I discovered accidentally. In some of our attempts to help smokers give up their dependence, we encountered a very surprising and *new* disability among positive affect smokers. These are smokers who use the cigarette to *enhance* otherwise already rewarding scenes. They do not smoke to *become* happy or happier, but to *retain* or *enhance* their positive affect. Such smokers characteristically have a low frequency of smoking, e.g., with morning or evening coffee. Ordinarily it is just such dependency that is most readily renounced if the individual is convinced it is in his/her best interests to do so. To our surprise we found some positive affect smokers became preaddictive smokers when we requested them to give up smoking. Now they suddenly found a deep reluctance to give up just those one or two cigarettes that they had most enjoyed. These they *now* felt they *must* have. This proved to be a transient phenomenon, as well as a relatively rare occurrence among all positive affect smokers, but it did teach us that the *intention to renounce* has the consequence of increasing negative affect in a very specific way. It was upon this basis I counseled the American Cancer Society (as a member of their tobacco committee) against too vigorous a media campaign in favor of renunciation lest they convert the majority of smokers (who were sedative smokers) into preaddictive or addictive smokers. As we will presently see it is the *ineffective* attempt to renounce that is one of the ways in which sedative scripts are transformed to addictive scripts.

ADDICTIVE SCRIPTS

An addictive script is one in which a sedative has been transformed into an end in itself such that the individual is perpetually vigilant toward the absence or presence of the distinctive feature whose absence is punishing and whose presence briefly provides relief, but whose continuing presence becomes sufficiently skilled that it provides minimal awareness and affect (as in the case of preaddictive habitual skilled as-if scripts).

Let us illustrate this by cigarette addiction. First, there is a highly developed monitoring skill that informs the individual *that* she has a cigarette in her mouth. This is based on a phantom cigarette, a special case of the phantom limb and phantom body. Phantom limbs becomes conscious only after massive *discontinuous* change in the contours of the body (e.g., after amputation of a limb). They do not occur if such change has been gradual and continuous (as in the absorption of the limb in leprosy). Further, they do not appear before the age of five. It appears to require substantial perceptual learning, which can be unlearned if the changes are slow and gradual but not in the event of such rapid changes as occur through surgery. What appears as a "phantom" after surgery exposes what I believe is the normal general case, that we learn to construct images that require minimal information to trigger their continuing internal construction and neural transmission. *Any* massive change in new information, however, changes the skilled monitoring into a difference detection mode. Examples are the compulsive exploration of the "hole" in the mouth by the tongue after the extraction of a tooth, or the equally compelled awareness of the difference in interface between the body as a whole and the mattress of a new bed the first night one spends in an unfamiliar bed. This new information is quickly added to the family of body phantoms, so that the second night is monitored with increased skill and minimal awareness and affect.

The cigarette addict has learned the skill of knowing with minimal awareness when there is a cigarette in her mouth. The moment it is "missing," he has the skill to detect that absence and to centrate consciousness and affect on the "difference."

It sometimes happens to addicts that they will light up a cigarette when they have just momentarily put a still lit cigarette on a nearby ashtray. Acts may also be done with minimal affect and awareness, so that she does not know either that she has put one cigarette down or that she has immediately lit another.

To the extent that another cigarette is readily available, the addictive script continues in the skilled monitoring and skilled action mode. However, should a cigarette be unavailable, an immediate alert is sounded in what now becomes both *preemptive* and *urgent*. All else is, for the time of the alert, put on hold, and all resources are mobilized to find a cigarette. If, at this stage, one were to suggest to the addict that she "forget" about it or she were to suggest this to herself, she would discover that awareness and deprivation affect remain preemptive. She can "think" of nothing else. There are no viable alternatives. There is very limited capacity for delay.

Should her quest for the cigarette fail, deprivation affect grows in intensity, acceleration, and density, experienced as a deepening of a crisis growing more and more intolerable.

Next, there is a projection of expected further intensity, acceleration, and deprivation affect density, which itself generates panic at the future prospect, a self-validating scene. The addictive script is insistent on the intolerability of such scenes and the necessity for a *unique* act or distinctive scene feature that *alone* will reduce such massive deprivation affect.

Further, such projections are *in fact* universally confirmed. The cigarette finally found and put into the mouth *does* evoke intense enjoyment, relaxation, and relief. The addictive script is both self-validating and self-fulfilling. It demonstrates again and again the necessity to be ever alert to the possibility of being without some X, the punishment that is inevitable should that X not be recoverable, the increased rate of punishment the longer one is without that X, its irreplaceability, nondistractability, or nonsubstitutability, and finally how wonderful it is to have it again no matter how brief such enjoyment continues to be.

There are many cigarette addicts who will on just the occasion of recovery of the missing cigarette express extreme disgust at their dependence and vow to renounce their addiction. More often than not this proves to be a momentary revulsion.

There is an additional set of auxiliary scripts that may or may not be developed to fortify the addictive script. These are characteristically *not* themselves addictive scripts. One of them is an auxiliary hoarding script. After a particularly prolonged and harrowing crisis, say at 4 am on awakening in the middle of the night to discover one has smoked one's last cigarette in the house, an addict may resolve "never again." She thenceforth buys several cartons at a time to defend against the possibility of running out. But *this* act need not itself become addictive, though she may become preaddictive in checking the size of her hoard whenever she becomes particularly disturbed about something else.

There are two additional types of auxiliary scripts which do not occur with cigarette addiction but may with drug addictions. One is an external "hoard" script in which one develops multiple "connections" with dope pushers, lest one run out of fixes. This does not occur in cigarette hoarding because of the relative ease and reliability of the source. There is an additional auxiliary script that develops when the individual cannot afford her habit and then must do whatever she thinks necessary to either earn or steal the money to support her habit. This too is no part of the addictive script and is unnecessary to the extent either that the addict has the necessary money or the addictive substance is cheap or free.

Yet another auxiliary script that may be prompted by an addictive script is that of quality maintenance. To what extent is the addictive substance authentic, unadulterated, safe? Again, such concern may be massive but not necessarily addictive.

Let us consider the conditions necessary for the formation of such a script.

First, in contrast to a sedative script the ratio of the overall density of positive to negative affect must be heavily biased toward negative affect. Addicts are not happy people.

Next, addictive scripts require, as a precondition, a sedative script that has validated an act as a reliable means of attenuating or reducing negative affect. Further, however, it also requires an increase in the magnification of the need for and, in the demonstration, efficacy of the power of the sedative. The sedative act must become a one–many relationship, such that the *same* means is a means to an increasing *variety* of sedations as ends. The cigarette must make one feel better in many different types of scenes. Whether these scenes make one afraid, angry, distressed, ashamed, or disgusted, the cigarette must have prove to be equally capable of neutralizing such differently troubling scenes. To become addicted to seeking the mother's presence, she must have been comforting in many different bad scenes. Not only is a one–many magnification of sedation required, but the one sedation must *also* thereby have been magnified as the *unique* means to those many ends. When the chips were down and the individual most desperate she must have turned to her cigarette or to her mother as the only salvation, and that must have worked. This is a special case of the more general dynamic of the power script in which any means (whether for positive or negative affect) is transformed into an end in itself by being structured as both vital *and* scarce, as is the case with money and employment in an economic depression.

The next condition necessary for the formation of an addictive script is a transformation of the sedative script into an added preaddictive script so that the sedative act becomes under some conditions also *instrumental* for dealing with a variety of problematic scenes, over and above their negative affect. The experience of heightened urgency for the sedative in specific scenes provides a critical bridge to the more general addictive urgency. As more and more instrumental preaddictive scenes are added to more and more sedative scenes, the stage is set for the most radical and critical transformation. This is the shift from original negative affect as source to *sedative deprivation affect* as *new source affect*. One cannot become addicted until one has learned that to be without the sedative is much worse than any other negative affect that the sedative might reduce. It is similar in this respect to the power script of a miser who dreads the loss of money much more than he dreads the loss of what that money might buy.

It is a remarkably effective script paradoxically because it has *created* conjointly both a unique problem and a unique solution to that problem. But that problem arises from the conversion of a rational sedative script into a costly, illusory extrapolation of idealized bad *possibilities* that become both self-validating as well as self-fulfilling.

In the case of the child who develops an addictive dependency on the mother, it would be required that she had encountered a very disturbing scene that became much *more* disturbing by the dramatic unavailability of her comforting mother when it was most needed and, thenceforth, began to live with the disturbing knowledge of the *possible* repetition of unreducible, growing *deprivation* affect that became self-validating and self-fulfilling independent of any specific *source* affect. She has then taught herself that there is something much worse than being hurt, distressed, afraid, angry, or ashamed about anything, and that is to be unable to count on someone who would comfort her *whenever* she becomes acutely aware that the comforter is unavailable. She does *not* need her to comfort her about fear of school or whatever, but rather against fear of her not being available. With addiction there are few if any sources of misery that can compete with the panic of having run out of cigarettes. Such a script requires critical scenes of acute deprivation of the sedative otherwise intolerable until the sedative is found. Only then can the sedative be experienced as a sedative for its own absence rather than as simply instrumental to reducing other sources of affect.

It is a script whose activation rules are always in operation. Its enactment rules are engaged whenever the addictive act is interrupted. There are no closure rules, since whenever enactment ceases, activation rules begin again.

I have witnessed the beginning of addictive script formation that was possible to abort and to prevent its further magnification. This occurred with a child who had developed a strong sedative dependence on a pacifier that became stronger as a result of severe continuing pain from an infected ear. One day I saw her reach for this pacifier as her pain returned. It had somehow dropped out of sight. I witnessed a sudden new panic. "Where's my boppy?" (her word for her pacifier). After a few minutes we found it, but the child had been severely shaken and the pacifier had been radically magnified in its importance as an end in itself that *might* not be there. I therefore supplied her with a large number of pacifiers placed throughout the house to prevent the further magnification of the dread of running out. This proved effective, and, within a year, the sedative dependence itself disappeared when this child resumed her former predominantly positive affect orientation.

One may understand such a shift more readily in the case of pain sedatives. If one suffers severe pain that it is felt urgent to reduce whenever it becomes preemptive, one would, to become *psychologically* addicted (to an otherwise nonaddictive drug), have to have had a vivid demonstration of pain *without* the drug increasing radically the felt desirability of that drug and the felt panic or distress at its absence. One has then begun the critical transformation of dreading the absence of the sedative more than the original pain and negative affect source. It is as though aspirin, which was previously viewed as a means to reduce headaches, *now* became the *source* of the most severe headaches itself. This could not in fact happen, but something worse could. One could come to be vigilant and monitor for the presence of aspirin whether or not one had pain.

The addictive transformation must not only occur, but it must be further magnified by acting on it again and again, validating it by repeated cycles of deprivation and relief independent of its many original sources until there is a point of no-return to the sedative as simply instrumental so that one *must have* a cigarette no matter what else.

Such learning must also include an increasing *skill* in vigilant *monitoring* so that one knows at all times whether all is well *and* knows immediately whenever it is not, followed by radical increases in consciousness, affect, and action until all is well again.

Clearly the more alternative means one possesses to deal with negative affect scenes the less the probability of addictive script formation. The smaller the density of negative affect and the larger the density of positive affect, the less the probability of addictive script formation. Sedative scripts remain sedative for the majority of smokers and probably for the majority of human beings in general, because they are neither so disturbed nor so uniquely dependent on *one* sedative to become addictive. It must however not be forgotten that there are millions of Americans who are not only addicted but are addicted not only to cigarettes but also to drugs as well as to a variety of nuclear and nonnuclear scripts.

As an epilogue to these varieties of dependency scripts let us consider now their potential for change. By way of contrast we will include another type of script exhibited by a much smaller number of individuals who smoke cigarettes. These have a *positive affect savoring* script. They smoke not for sedative relief from negative affect, nor from addictive dependency, but to either enhance or maintain positive affect already experienced. Thus, they smoke at the end of a meal they have enjoyed, with a cup of coffee which they also enjoy, or to celebrate a special occasion. Characteristically, positive affect smokers smoke very few cigarettes daily. Some may smoke no more than a few per week. They are individuals with a very high ratio of density of positive affect over negative affect. They are at the other end of the scale compared with addicts. Paradoxically, the frequency of smoking appears to be inverse to the enjoyment experienced in smoking. Those who enjoy smoking least smoke all day long. Those who enjoy smoking most may smoke no more than a few cigarettes a day or week. Further, this paradox is paralleled by the ease with which smoking can be renounced and cessation maintained. Positive affect smokers are able to give up smoking most readily and to maintain this cessation in the face of medical evidence of its toxicity. The probable reasons for this are not obscure. These are individuals blessed with many sources of positive affect, and renunciation of smoking, though regretted, is not experienced as a severe loss, compared to the diminished health risks they weigh against the loss. They are readily persuaded by evidence, primarily, I would suggest, because rationality is fragile in the face of massive negative affect and flourishes most under positive affect.

The sedative smoker (and preaddictive smoker somewhat less so) is less able and willing to stop smoking, compared with the postive affect smoker, but more capable than the addict. Her ability to stop depends in large part on the variability of her experienced affect. When she is feeling very positive she is quite capable of renunciation, since she would not under these circumstances have smoked anyway. However, of all smokers, she is the most vulnerable to backsliding as soon as she again experiences the pressure of negative affect. She may have decided on her vacation to quit and maintained her resolve for a couple weeks. On return to a more stressful work environment, such resolve readily dissolves for the sedative smoker, the more so for the combined sedative and preaddictive. The sedative smoker will tell you she has quit smoking many times and that she will probably do so many times in the future.

In marked contrast, renunciation is most difficult for the addict, but *if* she is successful in quitting she is much more likely to maintain this resolve than the sedative smoker who has quit. The reasons most often given by addicts are, first, that they now have an investment in self-control in which they take pride. Second, they do not wish to reexperience the suffering of the cold turkey withdrawal again. In contrast, the sedative is likely to deceive herself into thinking she is capable of more self-control than she possesses, claiming that if she wished to she could give up smoking any time she wished. She tends to forget that quitting is but half the battle and that she has a history of inability to maintain her cessation. The addict who cannot muster the resolve to quit is much more likely to be ashamed of her failure of will, though she also has a tendency to deny the validity of the evidence of the toxicity of her smoking.

NUCLEAR SCRIPTS

If ideology is a faith in a systematic order in the world, and commitment is the courage and endurance to bind the self to an enhancement of a segment of that order, nuclear scripts speak to the conjunction of greed and cowardice in response to seduction, contamination, confusion, and intimidation. Nuclear scripts represent the tragic rather than the classic vision.

A nuclear scene is one or several scenes in which a very good scene turns very bad. A nuclear script is one which attempts to reverse the nuclear scene, to turn the very bad scene into the very good scene again. It succeeds only partially and temporarily, followed invariably by an apparent replay of the nuclear scene in which the good scene again turns bad.

Nuclear scripts arise from the unwillingness to renounce or mourn what has become irresistably seductive and the inability to recover what has been lost, to purify or integrate what has become intolerably contaminated or conflicted, and to simplify or to unify what has become hopelessly turbulent in complexity, ambiguity, and rate of change.

It is the seductiveness of the good scene that magnifies the intolerability of its loss and the intransigence of the relentless attempt at reversal of the bad to the good scene. It is the intimidation, contamination, or confusion of the bad scene that magnifies the hopelessness and ineffectiveness of that reversal. Thus, there is produced a conjunction of greed and cowardice. By greed I mean the inflation of positive affect seductiveness. By cowardice I mean the inflation of negative affect intimidation, contamination, or confusion.

The self victimizes itself into a tragic scene in which it longs most desperately for what it is too intimidated to pursue effectively. That part of the personality that has been captured by a nuclear script constitutes a seduction into a lifelong war that need never have been waged, against enemies (including the bad self) who were not as dangerous or villainous as they have become, for heavens that never were as good as imagined, nor would if attained be as good as they are assumed. Nuclear scripts are inherently involved in idealized *defenses* against idealized *threats* to idealized *paradises*.

They represent an entropic cancer in which negative affect increasingly neutralizes positive affect and does so by the varieties of mechanisms of magnification and growth, which are coopted by the nuclear script, which invades the lifespace of the more positive affect possibilities governed by other types of scripts. Growth and magnification are thereby excessively pressed into the service of psychological warfare on behalf of a beleaguered personality.

CONSTRUCTION OF NUCLEAR SCRIPTS

How could such improbable scripts have been constructed and, having been constructed, never relinquished? Briefly, several conjoint conditions both simultaneous and sequential had to have occurred. First, both good scenes and bad scenes had to be magnified through *repetition* and *aggregation* rather than repetition and attenuation. Second, such magnification must have become *reciprocally defined* rather than orthogonal. The good scene must have become more seductive by vidious contrast to the bad scene, made worse by its invidious contrast to the good scene. Reciprocal simultaneous contrast magnified both the good and bad scenes. Third, such reciprocal definition and magnification must have been *multidimensional,* thus further enhancing the magnification of both. Fourth, the *directionality* of *sequence* must have been *biased* from positive to negative, rather than in the opposite direction and rather than random. Fifth, such biased directionality must have magnified an intention to *reverse* that bias rather than modulate, accept it, or habituate to it. The nuclear script formation begins with this intention to reverse the magnified nuclear scene. Sixth, nuclear script magnification begins with the *reciprocal* definition of nuclear scene and script, since that script is defined as the rules by which the nuclear scene can be reversed. Seventh, the nuclear script is *multidimensional,* both in the varieties of dimensions of the nuclear scene to be remedied and in the varieties of strategies to be employed in reversing each dimension. Eighth, the nuclear script is *biased* in the *directionality* of its *sequences,* beginning with analogs of the bad scene that are reversed into *better* scenes as antianalogs, which invariably turn into replays and analogs of the bad nuclear scenes. Thus, a nuclear scene positive, negative sequence is transformed into a nuclear script negative, positive, negative sequence. Ninth, good and bad scenes are *bifurcated and intense* rather than continuous with gradations of degree. One is safe or in danger, victorious or defeated, loved or rejected. Strategies of the nuclear script are therefore judged entirely effective and ineffective. Tenth, nuclear scripts employ a *minimize* negative affect, *maximize* positive affect strategy rather than optimizing or satisficing strategies. Eleventh, nuclear scripts are further magnified by *biased uncontrolled lability* in which rapid uncontrolled shifts from positive to negative scenes, from antianalogs to analogs, occur more frequently than shifts in the negative positive direction. These latter are more controlled but slower and more arduous. Such lability is in contrast to scenes that are *stable,* and *polarized* or *segregated,* or *orthogonal,* or scenes that *change* but do so *slowly* with effort, or at a *controlled rate* as in any skilled performance. Twelfth, there is increasing *magnification advantage* over information advantage. In both cases, increasing quantities of information are controlled by compressed, smaller amounts of information, but in information advantage this is a relatively silent, skilled performance. In magnification advantage, the controlled information is affect magnified and conscious as figural rather than as ground. It is the difference between casual but skilled recognition of someone's presence as contrasted with the same recognition as intensely exciting or distressing.

Thirteenth, magnification is increased by *mutual support networks* in which succeeding scenes provide an increasingly interconnected network for each other as part of one system. These include increasing skill in analog and antianalog formation, increasing refinement of auxiliary "theories" that are nuclear script relevant, and increasingly refined "maps" for orientation in nuclear script space. Fourteenth, there is increasing stability of *nuclear script equilibrium* in contrast to erosion, attenuation, transformation by review, or modulation. Changes are assimilated and absorbed rather than transforming the script via accommodation.

NUCLEAR SCRIPT FORMATION

Let us now examine nuclear script formation in greater detail. What are the kinds of scenes that are likely to become nuclear and then generate nuclear scripts?

The origin of a nuclear scene and nuclear script is in a very good scene that turned into a very bad scene. The good scene is a *seduction* via excitement or enjoyment at others who provided either models, mirrors, stimulation, guidance, mutuality, support, comfort, and/or reassurance.

The bad scene is either an intimidation, a contamination, a confusion, or any combination of these that jeopardize the good scene. The bad scene is an intimidation whenever excessive violence or threat via anger, disgust, or dismell evokes excessive terror, shame, or distress. The bad scene is a contamination whenever excessive distress, anger, shame, disgust, or dismell is evoked by excessive overcontrol; or by indifference, distancing, or threat of withdrawal of love; or by character flaws of the other that contaminate the idealized image of the other as model, mirror, guide, provider of mutuality, support, or comfort; or by humiliation by the good other; or by excessive piety by that good other that evokes guilt, distress, or conflict; or via the death of the good other; or via any triangular rivalry. The bad scene is a confusion whenever there are both multiple affects from the good other and by the self in response, to create excessively turbulent scenes. Turbulence occurs above and beyond ambivalence and conflict, via negative plurivalence to and from the self and other. This may occur via any extreme lability of affect and action by the good other that evokes extreme lability of affect and action by the self; or via any inconsistencies (whether labile or not) of affect or action by the good other that evoke extreme inconsistencies of affect or action by the self; or via any combination of seduction and intimidation or contamination or confusion, since to be threatened or to be humiliated by the good other may be as confusing as it is intimidating or contaminating. No less confusing are serious character flaws perceived in the idealized good other. Turbulence and confusion are compounded whenever there are too many possible sources of blame for good scenes turned bad, and whenever one does not know whether it is the self or the other or some complex combination of both that is responsible for catastrophic problematic multiple good scenes turned bad in different ways. Thus, a young child suffering the divorce of a parent cannot be certain whether the good family has turned bad because of something or many things done or felt by the self, by a sibling, one or the other parent, or by every member of the family now suddenly in jeopardy. Similarly, the death of the good other may be as confusing as it is intimidating or contaminating. Any bad scene may be either intimidating and/or confusing and/or contaminating when it is sharply contrasted with the seductiveness of a good scene that precedes it.

There can be no greed without a seductive other. There can be no cowardice without an intimidating, contaminating, or confusing other. But neither can a seductive intimidating nuclear *scene* be converted into a nuclear *script* without massive, collusive reciprocal magnification.

If a nuclear scene occurs whenever there is a descent from heaven to hell, from magnified, dense positive affect to equally magnified, dense negative affect, it cannot occur in the absence of a nuclear script that represents a sustained magnified struggle to reverse the negative affect to positive affect and to ascend from hell to heaven. Heaven and hell are thereby locked in unholy wedlock until death do them part. What one elects to "do" about any scene is more than a response to a scene whose features are otherwise independent of those elected responses. The responses that follow any scene, whether they be immediate or delayed, constitute and *define,* as well as mirror the nature of a scene. Thus, a contemptuous remark is in part defined by whether the insulted one elects to begin a vendetta or to shrug it off as a momentary lapse of sensitivity.

A threat of violence is in part defined by whether one elects to hire a bodyguard or to assume it was a transient irritability unlikely to be repeated. The Watergate attempted burglary remained an inconsequential event so long as the nation preferred to "let sleeping dogs lie" given the alternative of the possibility of impeachment of a president. What one elects to do or not to do about any scene that is intense in affect in the scene itself, and in the projected consequences of how one further responds to that scene, is a complex function of the scene, the past, and the anticipated future scenes, and of their relative weighting with respect to costs and benefits. The "origin" of a nuclear script therefore is ambiguous. The nuclear script is a set of rules that define the "response" to the nuclear scene, but, in fact, those scripted responses define the scene as much as the scene "evokes" the responses. As the nuclear script encounters increasingly remote derivative scenes, over many years, and is progressively modified, the relationships between the ongoing nuclear script and its *multiple origins* become increasingly complex. A personality not only writes its own history in a nuclear script, but also constantly rewrites its history as well as its present and future. A nuclear script therefore is more properly regarded as a *connected set* or family of histories.

Some of these complexities are illustrated in Carlson's (1981) case study of the development of a nuclear script.

Nuclear scene and script are interdependent not only in their reciprocal *definition* of heaven and hell, but more importantly they are locked into *reciprocal magnification*. Many scripts become autonomous of their origins, but a nuclear scene as origin in heaven turned hell and a nuclear script as hell with terminal in heaven collude in not only keeping each other alive, but in providing the luxuriant soil for their reciprocal growth and magnification. Each *requires* the other to thrive. It is only the *repeated* intensely rewarding vision of heaven and the equally punishing replay of that heaven turned hell in unending, varied, but nonetheless inevitably recurrent sequences of scenes of delight and anguish that validates the nuclear script and prompts the lifelong pursuit of certain defeat amidst uncertain, partial, and temporary victories.

How such collusive reciprocal definition and magnification of nuclear scene by nuclear script may occur, we will now examine in the case of a creative sculptor. This was an individual whose life was at some risk in his first year. He suffered protracted hunger because of an inability to digest milk, to which he responded with violent projectile vomiting. His mother gave him to a wet nurse, for breast feeding, who described the infant's oral greed as "killing" her. This provided the earliest repeated model of a good scene, the pleasure of feeding, turned suddenly and unaccountably bad, shaking the whole body in frightening painful projectile vomiting. Because he was troubled with intestinal problems, he was given, on the advice of his mother's brother (an experimentally minded physician), high colonic enemas of argyrol. These were no less painful, nor less terrifying than the vomiting. Together they evoked a vivid sense of himself as a battlefield with concurrent explosions at both body orifices. Further, food and feces were fatally connected by his mother's insistence on giving him an enema to "clean" his body whenever he ate food that she feared might be bad for him. In this way, the good scene of oral pleasure was turned bad not only by vomiting but by intentional maternal invasion of his body by high colonic enemas. To this day he remembers the terror of the threat of the enema. But he was bound to his oppressor by the intense love she displayed, by her constant reassuring hovering attention, by her soothing bathing of him, by her constant feeding of him (after his first year's projectile vomiting had stopped), and, not least, by her remaining by his side when he went to bed, permitting him to hold her hand so that he fell asleep in her arms. If it was hell to be ripped apart at the mouth and anus, it was heaven to look at her, to be looked at, to be fed, to be bathed, and to be held in her arms.

If, too often, she appeared to wish to torture him, that only heightened those moments when she became his savior, and those moments became more continuous and sustained after his digestive problems diminished. The distinction between good food and good mother, and bad food and bad mother, bad vomiting and bad enema, was to become a permanent script in which he was to be forever vulnerable to the good turning bad as a nuclear scene. Even at this early date the sequences were at least two-dimensional. He was not simply the passive victim of his savior. He also knew that to be ravenously hungry and taking into his body meant that he would have to give up and give back what *he* had greedily sought and taken in, and that if he did not, it would be taken from him by force. Distress, pain, pleasure, and terror were tightly fused.

Taking in was then further contaminated by a severe whooping cough that left a residue of inhibited, shallow breathing discovered and disinhibited 30 years later in the course of psychotherapy.

When he was three years old, his precarious hold on life via his mother's eyes and hands was suddenly and violently shaken by the arrival of a baby girl. His mother's eyes and hands and whole being were now rivetted on that intruder and away from him. His own account of that scene is consistent with the account his mother gives.

For six months, he retreated to his own room and he spoke to no one. His mother reported he appeared angry. This primary initial response of defense by retreat is one of the universal first nuclear subscripts to the shock of the good nuclear scene turned bad. However, it must be insisted that this is nuclearity by reciprocal definition and magnification. Had Sculptor not been so sensitized by the prior reciprocal magnification of the good and bad mother, he might well have weathered the reduced attention from his mother.

If he could have modulated his anger and distress and shame, the scene would have not been nuclear and the script would not have become nuclear. It is the reciprocal density of positive and negative affect that is critical in the reciprocal magnification of paradise lost that must be escaped, fought, and recovered.

If his scripted *response* to this scene had not been to run away and hide and be mute, then that bad *scene* would not have been so intolerable. It was in *part* made more intolerable by his attempt to make it *less* so. In that very attempt he has characterized it as a scene that *must* be escaped. Second, the conversion of a scene to a nuclear scene via a nuclear scripted response is never totally or permanently successful, and so becomes a replay, an analog of the very scene the individual is trying to master. To run away and become mute is *not* to radically diminish his aloneness, but to exemplify it, no matter how much better it seems than continuing to passively suffer the scene of betrayal. A scene is made nuclear, and the scripted response to it nuclear when the response *must* be made *and* does not *effectively* deal with it. Nuclear scripts conjoin ineffectiveness with compulsion in contrast to the addictive script which is equally compelled but effective. The nuclear script response ultimately results in an analog for the intolerable nuclear scene, even when it is temporarily or partially effective. We will defer a discussion of Sculptor's other nuclear subscripts.

The nuclear script not only magnifies the nuclear scene by reciprocal definition but also by bifurcating the good and bad nuclear scenes into the starkest idealization and invidious contrast between the good scene and the good scene turned bad. Such a polarization excludes many degrees of freedom as possible alternative. Strategies for remediation are therefore similarly bifurcated and perceived to provide safety or danger, victory or defeat, reunion or exile. The self or the other is regarded as clean or dirty, conflicted or decisive, affluent or poor, confused or single minded. In the case of Sculptor, he is either hungry and greedy in eating, or vomiting or being robbed and invaded by enema. He is either in total possession of his mother or he has entirely lost her. He must therefore hold her hand tightly or withdraw, mute and hide in his room. There are no gradations in nuclear script space and this radically diminishes the possibilities of graded responses which might deal more effectively with the good scene turned bad.

Such bifurcation leads directly to action strategies that are equally radical.

With respect to their general strategies, nuclear scripts are typically two valued, requiring to minimize negative affect, and to maximize positive affect rather than optimizing or satisficing strategies. Greed requires a maximum of reward. Cowardice requires a minimum of punishment. Clearly a double maximum cannot be achieved, and the nuclear script consequently fails in *both* respects. It neither attains the prize nor escapes defeat. It is a game that must be played even though the player knows the dice are loaded against him.

There is a reciprocal relationship between the bifurcation of nuclear scenes and the minimizing negative and maximizing positive affect strategy. To the extent that Sculptor is confronted with either totally losing or keeping his beloved mother he is caught between greed and cowardice. He must have everything. He must lose nothing. He is necessarily forever suspended between heaven, which he can never reach, and hell, which he can never escape by pursuing a double minimizing-maximizing strategy.

Next, nuclear script formation is magnified by the *multidimensionality* and by *multiple ordering* the family of nuclear scenes and nuclear scripted responses to them. Because the change from a very good to a very bad scene is so momentous all the cognitive powers of the individual are inevitably brought to bear on it. The individual is totally engaged in trying to understand what has happened, why it has happened, what might have prevented it, how it might be prevented from happening again, how serious the consequences might be, how long such consequences might last, what he might do to mitigate these consequences, how much this is possible, whether this change means he will have to change his understanding of the other, or of himself, or of their relationship, how responsible he was for what happened, how responsible the other was, or both were, what he should do about it, and what are the consequences of every response, how can he discover what would be the optimal response, should he try to defend himself, to avenge himself, or to recover the good scene. These are but a sample of the multidimensional *possibilities* he now generates and with which he must come to terms by way of response. For every possible interpretation of what happened and what might further happen there are *many* possible remedies he is forced to entertain and to act on. The more biased and ineffective, or partially or temporarily effective these prove to be, the more other possibilities he is forced to try. Nor will such experimentation ever come to a complete halt in his lifetime of seeking a final solution to these his most urgent and central problems. In contrast to the increasing discrimination and enrichment of nonnuclear scripts by *convergent differentiation,* here *generalization* increases complexity in ever divergent nonconverging possibilities. It is like a strategy in a game of 20 questions in which possibilities are continually increased rather than decreased through differentiation and convergence.

TYPES OF NUCLEAR SUBSCRIPTS

Because of the multiple ordering of interpretation and responses to interpretation, it is not possible to enumerate all the theoretical possibilities in all nuclear scripts. We can nonetheless enumerate four of the more general types of nuclear subscripts ordinarily generated in any family of nuclear scripts. First are a set of positive and negative *celebratory* scripts. These describe, explain, and celebrate the nuclear scene that was once so wonderful and then turned so bad *and* the continuing family of scenes which have been repeated again and again and which cast a long shadow over the future as ever present possibilities. These celebratory scripts power continual monitoring of ongoing experience for *either* signs of good scenes (anti-analogs) or of bad scenes (analogs) or of possible sequences of good scenes that will become bad scenes. These celebratory scripts also then guide responses and celebrate their successes and failures, separately, as well as sequentially. Thus, the individual who has just won an apparent nuclear victory, by defeating his enemy, will react as an omnipotent hero. The same script may dictate the surrender to total ignominious defeat moments later, to be followed by the negative celebration of the sequence of how the mighty have fallen.

The second general type of nuclear subscripts are scripts of *defense.* These may take one of several forms of avoidance or escape in which the individual attempts primarily to minimize the negative affect of the nuclear scene, by, for example, running away from home, by becoming introverted, by being alone, by becoming mute. The negative affects usually involved in these scripts are terror, shame, or distress—the "feminine" affects.

The third general type of nuclear subscripts are *counteractive* scripts in which the individual attempts to reverse the sign of the affect in the scene by changing negative to positive affect, or by reversing the casting of the scene via recasting. In the latter case, the individual who had been terrorized would attempt to terrorize the other, or if humiliated would attempt to humiliate the other, or if distressed would attempt to distress the other, or if enraged would attempt to enrage the other, or if disoriented would attempt to disorient the other. The negative affects involved are usually the "masculine" affects of anger, disgust, and dismell. Recasting is however one type of counteraction. Thus, a loss may be counteracted by trying to understand how it happened or by action designed to give it "meaning" as in the case of the head of the gun lobby who elected to prevent the further use of guns after his son was killed. Counteraction may take the form of atonement for guilt, or increased skill to reduce shame, or toughening of the self better to endure distress. Counteraction may take the form of simplification of the lifestyle in the attempt to deal with the turbulence of the pluralistic nuclear script, to get away from the "rat race." Counteraction may take the form of hostile identification in which one attempts to make the other envy the self by surpassing the other.

Finally there are *reparative* scripts in which the individual attempts to reach the good scene, rather than to hide or to avenge himself. It is an attempt to recover excitement and enjoyment, not via relief, not via revenge, but directly. This may take one of several forms, either an attempted recovery of the preproblematic good scene before all the trouble started or a new scene projected into the future as a utopian scene which will *undo* all the problems created in part by *both* the nuclear scene and by the nuclear script. In some versions, the sinners must pay an appropriate price to be reinstated, and that sinner may be the self, the other, or both. Reparative scripts may be restricted to the level of phantasy and yearning, or may be expressed in political manifestos and political activity in favor of a future utopia, or in helping behavior in which one enacts an idealized good scene, "saving" both the self and the other.

Because the individual is continually being reexposed via analog formation to the contaminated nuclear scene, it appears to *him* (and to observers) that he is really trying to *recover* the good scene and to *minimize and escape the bad scene*. We are saying however that the nuclear scripts do *not* aim at recovering the original good scene but rather aim at recovering or producing an idealized good scene which has been magnified by contrast with an idealized contamination of the good scene, by double simultaneous contrast.

Consider how Sculptor generated these types of nuclear subscripts. In his celebratory scripts, he continually detected analogs of scenes of betrayal and antianalogs of lovers who were pure of heart and faithful until death did them part. He also found recurrent sequences of the apparently faithful turning treacherous. He was alternately attracted to the good beloved, repelled by the bad beloved, and crushed by the saint becoming a "whore."

He fled the betraying mother in a defensive set of nuclear subscripts which included mutism and hiding in his own room so that he would not have to look at his mothers' breast feeding his sibling rival. But he also attempted several counteractive strategies. He hit the sibling and made her cry. His counteractive attempts to assert his rights, to hurt his rival, to exhibit his own superior virtues failed to displace the other from center stage. Then he experimented with becoming his mother, walking around with an extended belly in simulation of his mother's pregnancy, evoking more laughter than joy. Then he attempted to become his own mother by feeding himself and overeating as he watched the mother lovingly feeding her new love.

Next he becomes increasingly curious about his extraordinary rival. What was it about such a toothless, hairless wonder that could turn that all wise, all loving mother's face away from his own, to that face? There is evidence of much more than curiosity and uncertainty. A year later he remembers an overwhelming excitement at the story of Genesis, of how God created the world out of "nothing" as he put it. Had his mother not earlier exhibited just such incredible creativity? Further, his mother often admiringly spoke of his sibling as perfectly "sculpted." Thus, I think were the foundations laid for a counteractive nuclear subscript of creativity as a sculptor, perfectly suited to emulate and compete with his mother as creator. His sculpture alas did not breathe life into his creation, but it was the best he could do.

Then, he attempted to be a better mother by feeding and caring for her child continuously, never once looking away and so never threatening her. At the same time he would hit his mother if she attempted to displace him in his counteractive script.

Finally, he would alternate between mutism, withdrawal and counteraction, and numerous direct and indirect *reparative* quests for resuming his interrupted communion with his mother. He would ask to be bathed because then he would be cared for. He would pretend to be sick because then he was immediately again his mother's beloved. He would ask to be fed by his mother. He would insist that his mother hold his hand as he went to sleep, guaranteeing at once her attention and the displacement of his rival. He attempted to do clever things to evoke her attention, and then repeated them endlessly to hold that attention, guaranteeing the ultimate loss of her attention.

None of these experiments was ever abandoned. I was able to trace their continuation and elaboration over many years. They constituted the basis for a lifelong family of partitioned nuclear subscripts.

It should be noted that the partitioning of the nuclear script into many varieties of celebratory, defensive, counteractive, and reparative subscripts introduces genuine novelties into the original nuclear scene responses. The individual never stops inventing new ways of celebrating, defending, counteracting and repairing both the original nuclear scene and succeeding *derivatives* over a lifetime. Thus, when an individual tries to escape the original nuclear bad scene, he might or might not have attempted that in the original nuclear scene and if he does in the derivative nuclear subscript successfully escape an experienced threat of the nuclear bad scene, this constitutes a genuine antianalog *victory* over *that* defeat. When that victory is attenuated or habituated and he begins to feel lonely again, this is characteristically experienced as a *double* defeat. It is in one case a defeat of the nuclear subscript of escape inasmuch as he may no longer feel "safe." In the second case, it is *also* a replay of the original nuclear scene, in that he experiences the attenuation of victory as equivalent to being alone again as he was in the nuclear scene. Finally, the sequence, possible threat of the nuclear scene, successful escape, attenuated escape is also an analog replay of the entire original nuclear good scene turned bad. In this whole sequence, the positive–negative nuclear scene hovers over the nuclear subscript threat, defense, victory, failure, as a double repetition of, positive turned negative, and negative turned positive turned negative. A dual sequence has been overcome in a triple sequence, but this *also* repeats the dual sequence as a *part* of the triple sequence. Every nuclear subscript success is also a specific failure *and* a repetition of the original nuclear scene failure. In one case his victorious escape has turned "weak," into loneliness. It has also turned back into the original loneliness he intended to escape. The paradox of such magnification of the original nuclear scene is that it is produced by the partial success and subsequent failure of the responses intended to weaken that original defeat.

At the same time that possibilities are multiplied by the generation of these four types of nuclear subscripts, further magnification of the nuclear script requires the learning of many new skills of analog formation of auxiliary theories and of generalized nuclear script space–time maps.

WAYS OF THINKING

In order to understand the *growth* and continuing magnification of the nuclear scripts, we must distinguish two different ways in which we think. One is by the principle of variants; the other is by the principle of analogs. A variant is a way of detecting change in something which in its core remains the same. Thus, if one's wife is wearing a new dress, one does not say to her, "You look very similar to my wife" but rather, "I like the new dress you're wearing." Scenes which are predominantly positive in affect tone thus become connected and grow through the classic principle of unity in diversity.

So, a symphony is written and appreciated as a set of variations on a theme. The enjoyment and excitement of such experience depends upon the awareness of both the sameness and the difference. So, an interest in any skill or in any friend can grow endlessly by increasing variation on an underlying core which does not change. It is of the essence of friendship to enjoy the rehearsal from time to time of a long shared past history.

Contrast this mode of reasoning with the principle of analog formation which, though it is used in dealing with positive affects too, is much more frequently and powerfully used in dealing with negative affect scenes. Let us first illustrate the nature of this mechanism on a neutral task. The art historian Gombrich (1960) demonstrated that if one asks that a series of contrasting words (e.g., "mouse" vs. "elephant") be categorized as to which one would properly be called a ping and which one a pong, then it is remarkable that over 90% of all subjects agree that a mouse is a ping and an elephant is a pong. This is an extraordinary consensus on an absurd task—without any communication or collusion among subjects. I repeated the experiment and studied it further and discovered that although most subjects agree that a mouse is a ping and an elephant is a pong, they do not, in fact, all use the identical thought processes in arriving at their conclusion. Thus, some subjects thought that since a ping seemed small, and a pong seemed large, then a mouse would be a ping since it is smaller than an elephant, however, other subjects thought that a ping sounded like a higher frequency sound and a pong sounded like a lower frequency sound—therefore, since a mouse has a squeaky voice and an elephant a low roar, a ping is a mouse and a pong is an elephant. Whichever reasons were used, however, the basic mode of thought was analogic and as often as not, somewhat unconscious. Many subjects said, "I don't know why, but a mouse just seems more like a ping to me and an elephant seems more like a pong." In fact, the individual was responding to imagined relationships between shared dimensions.

Such analogic constructions become the major mechanism whereby a negative affect scene is endlessly encountered and endlessly defeats the individual when the ratio of positive to negative affect becomes predominantly negative. Consider the following example of Sculptor. He is driving his automobile on a lovely spring day on a brand new just-opened interstate highway. He looks at the lush greenery all about him and at the shiny, white new highway. An unaccustomed peace and deep enjoyment seizes him. He feels at one with beautiful nature. There is no one else. He is apparently the first to enjoy this verdant and virginal scene. Then, as from nowhere, he sees to his disgust a truck barreling down the road, coming at him and entirely destroying the beauty of the setting. "What is that truck doing here?" he asks himself. He becomes deeply depressed. He can identify no apparent reason, but he senses that there is more to it—that his response is disproportionate to the occasion, but the depression is deep and enduring.

This scene was one of hundreds of analogs which he constructed and imported into scenes which would have quite different significances for individuals with different nuclear scripts. It is because he can neither re- nounce, forgive, nor possess his mother that he is destined to be victimized by endless analogs which repeat the same unsolved scene—seducing him to continually try to finally settle accounts with his hated rival and his beloved but faithless mother, and to restore the Garden of Eden before the fall.

He characteristically does not know why he feels as he does (as many do not know why a mouse seems like a ping and an elephant like a pong). He is victimized by his own high-powered ability to synthesize ever-new repeti- tions of the same scene without knowing that or how he is doing so.

This represents a major mechanism whereby disproportionate ratio of negative to positive affect can become stabilized.

Contrast the luxuriant growth potential of analogs compared with variants that stress the continuing sameness of the core, despite some changes, and thus increase differentiation rather than generalization. Variants do not lend themselves to the same rate of growth as analogs because the latter lend themselves to an increasing skill in abstract similarity detection between *different* scenes, and so generalize.

Nuclear subscripts are also supported by generalized nuclear space—time *"maps."* Just as one could not orient oneself in space without an abstract map of the location and distances in one's space of movement, so too in each of nuclear subscripts one requires and develops general maps of how different kinds of scenes may play in interpersonal space and time. Thus, Sculptor is acutely aware of scenes that threaten possible betrayal which he must avoid. He is no less aware of contrary scenes that promise the possibility of counter- active turning of the scene, to his advantage over hated rivals. Finally, he is forever alert to scenes that promise the possibility of true love, whether for him or for others.

But the nuclear subscripts require not only the information necessary to detect analogs and antianalogs, and the more abstract nuclear space–time maps for orientation, but they also require *mini-theories* to deal with the deeper dynamics underlying the space–time surfaces of scenes. These are particularly required to deal with counterintuitive scenes that appear on the surface to contradict the nuclear script.

As with any general theory of personality, so may an auxiliary theory of a nuclear script possess the characteristics of a scientific paradigm which enables the individual to extrapolate explanations for apparently remote and contradictory phenomena consistent with the paradigm.

Consider again the case of the sculptor who has suffered excessive humilia- tion over a lifetime, when he is confronted by unexpected praise. How may his nuclear script absorb and neutralize such evidence? First, the sincerity of the judge may be questioned. Second, "He praised only this work of mine because he knows that everything else I have done is trash." Third, "He may be sincere, but he is probably a fool." Fourth, "What I have done is a fluke, which I can never do again." Fifth, "He is trying to control me, holding out a carrot of praise. If I eat this, I am hooked and I will thenceforth have to work for his praise and to avoid his censure." Sixth, "He is exposing how hungry I am for praise and thus exposing my inferiority and my feelings of humiliation." Seventh, "He is seducing me into striving for something more, which I cannot possibly achieve." So may defeat be snatched from the jaws of victory by a nuclear script. Such a nuclear script can be produced only by a long history of failures to deal effectively with positive affect scenes turned negative.

Not only is there increasing generalization via analog formation and theory construction, but this is done more and more skillfully with increasing *magnification and informational advantage,* in the same fashion as a scientific theory decreases its assumptions as it increases its explanatory power.

The continuing proliferation of alternative nuclear subscripts not only occurs within and between such types of scripts as celebratory, defensive, counteractive and reparative, but also in generating *mixed* types of nuclear and nonnuclear scripts.

Nuclear scripts are capable of further magnification by invading and coopting other scripts and by being transformed into other types of scripts. Thus, in one case, a nuclear script may invade and coopt an addiction. In the other, a nuclear subscript may be transformed into an addictive nuclear subscript.

Consider the transformation of a nuclear subscript into an addictive form.

A script response which may not have been effective in dealing with a nuclear scene, but only partially so (e.g., introversive running away from nuclear scenes or analogs), may *become* addictive to the extent that not doing it becomes a new source affect to which the doing of it becomes a *new* sedative and the analogs of reexperience of (e.g., nonintroversion) are further magnified. In all other respects, the addictive nuclear response is similar to addictive responses. Absence makes it a source; effective sedation of deprivation requires continual response; there is magnification of absence (and absence potential) whenever one cannot respond by urgent restoration after monitoring and detecting "absence." Like money whose absence becomes (in addiction) worse than the absence of what it can buy, in addictive nuclearity the absence of introversion can become equal to and/or worse than the nuclear scene's humiliation. For the nuclear script to *become* addictive, it must have been effective for more than one nuclear scene analog, *and* have been critically blocked and its absence magnified, leading to magnified relief affect at running away to the (either) introversive (or extroversive) refuge. This is to be compared to a nonaddictive nuclear introversive script which sometimes works, sometimes does not, prompting the continuing generation of other nuclear scripts to deal with the same nuclear scene. This is readily misunderstood because introversion was *originally* a partially successful *means* to escaping and avoiding such nuclear scenes which continues to be necessary in the nuclear script in general. Therefore, the addictive nuclear introvert will necessarily continue battling betrayal, the sibling, the intrusive parent via introversion, and via many other scripts (e.g., travel, creativity, salvation, reading, sex, eating, gambling, music, etc.) some of which are *not* introversive. What is different is the special status of the script as generating its own negative affect (independent of its instrumental value). In other words, he wishes to be alone rather than *not* being alone (no matter how free of nuclear threats that presence of others might be, just as an addict smokes when "happy," e.g., on vacation). He cannot be "reassured" because defensive introversion has received an increment of affect beyond its instrumental value. Since the burden of the *entire* family of nuclear scenes and scripts remain, the addictive nuclear scene cannot become the major value, but rather adds an additional burden to an already heavy one, which is only partially lightened by the attempted addictive script response. It is in part because of its relative ineffectiveness and the consequent *pluralism* of multiple nuclear scripts that the addictive nuclear script remains one among many scripts rather than completely dominating the nuclear scripts. The nuclear script never puts all its eggs in one basket as in pure addiction.

A nuclear script may be transformed not only by becoming addictive but rather by invading and coopting an already existing addiction.

In any nonnuclear addiction, the response "works" either via habitual skilled continuing responses or via relief of panic following a quest for the missing act. This is because of its simplified end of reducing the absence of the addictive object and act. If and when such an addiction is captured by a nuclear script so that the addictive act (of smoking, eating, or drinking) becomes *instrumental* to dealing with either the nuclear scene or nuclear scripts, it loses its efficacy as a habitual skill *or* as dealing simply with the absence of the missing object, and is *overloaded* with attempted sedation of what is both very magnified and perceived to be essentially insoluble. This results in increasing the frequency and intensity of the attempted solution such that there is an addition of nuclear affect to what would otherwise either have been a habitual skilled act or a temporary addictive panic effectively reduced by the addictive act. Therefore, such a captured addiction will result in orgies of compulsive bottoming out in the hopeless attempt to sedate what cannot be sedated (as in eating more than one wants, in fighting till one is beaten into unconsciousness, in drinking into stupor, or in endless masturbation).

A nuclear script is more unrelenting in its demandingness, and so when it captures an addicted drinker he is much more likely to drink to unconsciousness than in the case of a nonnuclear addicted drinker. The same act will be more *relentlessly repeated* because it is aiming at more than reduction of addictive affect.

Such capture of an addiction by a nuclear script may be continual or intermittent (depending on the waxing and waning of threatening analogs) or preaddictive conditional, which requires the addictive act under very specific, fixed scenes.

In the first case *(continual),* the individual *superimposes* the nuclear burden on all the addictive responses reducing radically the effectiveness of the habitual skilled addictive response. In the second case *(intermittent),* a *massing* of nuclear scene analogs may seize upon the addictive act as vehicle for sadomasochistic desperation and oblivion. In the third case *(conditional),* it may be only when, e.g., positive longing for the reparative nuclear scene is magnified that eating or drinking may be coopted for a symbolic attempt to recover the lost good scene, leading to excessive eating or drinking, not in a sadomasochistic manner but in a symbolic reparative quest for oceanic fusion. Such behavior may be indistinguishable from sadomasochistic overloading to oblivion, despite radical differences in aim. Further, one may lead into the other, changing a perceived hope of oceanic fusion into massive analogs of nuclear desperation, or changing sadomasochistic nuclear addictive compulsions into positive longing for the good nuclear scene. These are possible because of the inherent connectedness of nuclear scenes and scripts.

The ever-growing family of nuclear scripts and subscripts guarantees a growing variety of challenges, successes (partial and temporary) and failures, as replays of the nuclear scene as well as new types of failures. This occurs in part because the possible relationships between all of these scripts create new problems, new barriers, new conflicts, and new ambiguities.

There continue to be a sufficient number of positive antianalogs to maintain the family of nuclear scripts and to preserve the bifurcation of good and bad scenes, the possibility of partial and temporary reversal, and the impossibility of total and enduring reversal.

Thus, he learns the overall lesson that his defensive scripts permit him to run but that he cannot hide. His counteractive scripts permit him to win battles, but not the war. His reparative scripts permit him to see the promised land, but not to live in it.

Although he may achieve deep victories, privileged sanctuaries, and oceanic communions and reunions these antianalogs remain tragically fragile for a variety of reasons.

First is insatiable greed. The deeper the reward the more he craves, the longer he hugs it to his bosom. He tries in every way to hoard the transient and secure its permanent possession. He envisions not only more, but better, and undermines his security, his victories, and his love by testing for possible flaws. He seeks continually to increase his power to repeat and to extend the good scenes attained. He is also acutely aware of the *incompleteness* of his good scenes just because they are partitioned. Thus, perfect security is *not* victory, nor reparation. Victory is not security, and it is not reparation. Reparation is his deepest wish, but it leaves unfulfilled his need for safety and his need to avenge his defeats.

Further, each general type of nuclear subscript is further partitioned, and so even reparation may leave unfulfilled another reparative script calling for the other to express regret and atonement for past sins, and for promises never again to sin.

The victory of revenge does not necessarily constitute a victory of demonstrated superiority over the other, and neither of these necessarily constitute a demonstration of identity with the other.

The victory of security against intrusion by introversive hiding is not necessarily a victory against imagined rejection or criticism by the other, nor necessarily a victory against overcontrol and engulfment by the other, nor necessarily a victory over the others' occasional indifference.

Finally, attained rewards are inevitably vulnerable to attenuation through habituation. The moment of perfect security, the moment of glory in victory, the moment of ecstatic rapture in communion will fade in intensity, and be transformed not to a regret, but to a major replay of the nuclear scene as analog invades antianalog. Thus, the departing guest characteristically plunges Sculptor into the deep depression of reexperienced abandonment, not simply as an analog of the good scene turned bad, but because the vivid sense of the other's rewarding presence ultimately becomes weaker and the absence of the image becomes a bad scene.

If Sculptor's rewards are fragile to analog formation, his several partitioned scripted attempts to reach such rewards are more fragile still. First, are serious conflicts inherent in his partitioned aims. He cannot at the same time woo the other, fight with the other, and hide from the other without defeating all of these aims, and plunging himself into new scenes as punishing as the nuclear scene these scenes attempted to reverse. He cannot exhibit his sculpture and hoard and hide it at the same time.

In the case of the nuclear script of Sculptor, production and hoarding of a beautiful artistic object is the major chosen and self-validating antidote to loss and emptiness. This individual not only becomes his own creative mother, creating both himself and a sibling who contaminated his exclusive possession of his mother, but also in recasting the scene, turns away from the mother, making *her* suffer loss as he had suffered loss at her hands. So long as he can create he does not need her. To the extent to which he seeks more than revenge and safety, he is prompted to seek a more idealized version of his original relationship in which he is still the beloved child. He can do this by exhibiting himself through his created objects. In the evocation of love and appreciation from an audience which bestows upon him the sense that he is valued passionately and exclusively, he would succeed in his long-deferred quest. But that script first of all violates the introversive hoarding script by surrendering his exclusive possession of the substitute mother, as though he were to share a security blanket whose great charm had been his exclusive control over it. To exhibit his sculpture is also to give it away and thus lose it. So also, Picasso held on to many of his paintings—Hemingway held on to many of his stories. Freud cherished his Robinson Crusoe island isolation because, as he expressed it, he did not have to publish and worry about priority.

But going public with the created internal hoard threatens another kind of reexposure to the nuclear scene, in the possibility that the exhibited product will evoke contempt or even worse, indifference, or interest that is too moderate, or, if intense, too transient. Should this happen he is entirely lost; since he has squandered his hoard, and it has proven to be valueless, so that now the tragedy of the original nuclear loss is deepened because of the *proven* inauthenticity of his ineffective and illusory pretensions to coping with the nuclear scene, by being as creative as his mother.

Because of his dread intuition of these possibilities, the life of the nuclear creative artist or scientist, most notably in the case of Leonardo da Vinci, is tortured by ambivalence and indecision about completion and exhibition of his most cherished products. The classic consequence is that completion and exhibition are at best partial, withholding both effort and products so that there is always a fall-back position if there appears too much risk.

Sculptor is further troubled by conflict inherent in the differentiation within each partitioned script. If he hides, *and* continually monitors his security, *and* further tests the adequacy of his refuge, he will be unable to enjoy the security he actually possesses.

If he fights with the other, tries to be just like him and also to defeat him and to make him envious of the self, these several simultaneous attempts cannot but diminish their effectiveness, and his whole-hearted commitment to them.

If he attempts to woo the other, but also to extort a confession of regret and a promise never again to offend, these conflict and overload the reparative script.

Finally, his partitioned scripts are vulnerable to the frequent unwillingness of others to play their assigned roles.

His hiding may be frustrated by intrusive others, by demanding others, by hostile others.

His counteraction may be frustrated by his adversaries, by invidious comparisons, by rejection, by indifference, by obsolescence of his products.

His reparation may be frustrated by rejection, by indifference, by lability of affect, by hostility, by criticisms and by rivalries.

All of these may in varying degrees be real or imagined as analogs.

REFERENCES

Bruner, J. (1968). *Processes of cognitive growth: Infancy.* Worcester: Clark University Press.

Carlson, R. (1981). Studies in script theory: I. Adult analogs of a childhood nuclear scene. *Journal of Personality and Social Psychology, 40,* 501–510.

Darwin, C. (1965). The expression of the emotions in man and animals. Chicago: University of Chicago Press.

Ekman, P., Friesen, W. V., & Ellsworth, P. (1972). *Emotion in the human face: Guidelines for research and an integration of findings.* New York: Pergamon.

Gombrich, E. H. J. (1960). *Art and illusion.* New York: Pantheon Press.

Hertz, R. (1973). The pre-eminence of the right hand: A study in religious polarity. In R. Needham (Ed.), *Right and left.* Chicago: University of Chicago Press.

Horn, D., & Waingrow, S. (1966, April). *Behavior and attitudes questionnaire.* Bethesda, MD: National Clearinghouse for Smoking and Health.

Ikard, F., & Tomkins, S. (1973). The experience of affect as a determinant of smoking behavior: A series of validity studies. *Journal of Abnormal Psychology, 81,* 172–181.

Lewis, O. (1961). *The children of Sanchez.* New York: Random House.

Miller, P. (1961). *The New England mind: The seventeenth century.* Boston: Beacon Press.

Needham, R. (1973). Right and left in Nyono Symbolic Classification. In R. Needham (Ed.), *Right and left.* Chicago: University of Chicago Press.

Rustow, A. (1980). *Freedom and domination.* Princeton: Princeton University Press.

Sanday, P. R. (1981). *Female power and male dominance.* Cambridge: Cambridge University Press.

Tacitus (1901). *Germania 14.4* (revised translation). London: Oxford.

Tomkins, S. S. (1962). *Affect, imagery, consciousness: Vol. I. The positive affects.* New York: Springer.

Tomkins, S. S. (1963a). *Affect, imagery, consciousness: Vol. II. The negative affects.* New York: Springer.

Tomkins, S. S. (1963b). The right and the left: A basic dimension of ideology and personality. In R. W. White (Ed.), *The study of lives.* New York: Atherton Press.

Tomkins, S. S. (1965). The psychology of commitment. Part I. The constructive role of violence and suffering for the individual and for his society. In S. S. Tomkins & C. Izard (Eds.), *Affect, cognition and personality.* New York: Springer.

Tomkins, S. S. (1975). The phantasy behind the face. *Journal of Personality Assessment, 39,* 550–562.

Tomkins, S. S. (1979). Script theory: Differential magnification of affects. In H. E. Howe, Jr. & R. A. Dienstbier (Eds.), *Nebraska Symposium on Motivation (Vol. 26)*. Lincoln: University of Nebraska Press.

Tomkins, S. S. (1981a). The quest for primary motives: Biography and autobiography of an idea. *Journal of Personality and Social Psychology, 41,* 306–329.

Tomkins, S. S. (1981b). The rise, fall and resurrection of the study of personality. *Journal of Mind and Behavior, 2,* 443–452.

Tomkins, S. S. (1982). Affect theory. In P. Ekman, W. V. Friesen, & P. Ellsworth (Eds.), *Emotion in the human face* (2nd ed.). Cambridge: Cambridge University Press.

Tomkins, S. S., & McCarter (1964). What and where are the primary affects? Some evidence for a theory. *Perceptual and motor skills, 18,* 119–158.

Tomkins, S. S., & Miner, J. B. (1956). *The Tomkins-Horn Picture Arrangement Test.* New York: Springer.

Vasquez, J. (1975). *The face and ideology.* Unpublished doctoral dissertation, Rutgers University, New Brunswick, New Jersey.

7

Personality and the Unification of Psychology and Modern Physics: A Systems Approach[1]

Gary E. Schwartz

According to Webster's unabridged dictionary, second edition, personality is first "the quality or fact of being a person" and second "the quality or fact of being a particular person; personal identity; individuality." Webster goes on to state that personality is the "habitual patterns and qualities of behavior of any individual as expressed by physical and mental activities and attitudes; distinctive individual qualities of a person, considered collectively."

These definitions of personality, published in the mid 1930s, capture well the fundamental orientation that guided the remarkable work of Murray and colleagues on personality in this same era at the Harvard Psychological Clinic (see Murray, 1938). It is interesting and, I propose, important to recognize that these definitions of personality also capture well the fundamental orientation that guided the remarkable work of von Bertalanffy and colleagues on systems theory in this same era at the University of Vienna and later in the United States and in Canada (see von Bertalanffy, 1948, 1968a, 1968b).

I propose that it is no mere accident of history that Murray's concept of personality and von Bertalanffy's concept of a system emerged at a similar time and with a similar thrust. The similarity is deeper than this. I propose

[1]Parts of this chapter were adopted from the author's Presidential Address to Division 38 (Health Psychology) of the American Psychological Association in 1984. The comments of Heinz Pagels, a physicist from the New York Academy of Sciences, and an anonymous physicist from Michigan State University who reviewed the chapter are gratefully acknowledged.

that the essence of the concept of personality and of the concept of a system are one and the same. Once this similarity is understood, a new synthesis becomes possible not only for personality theory, but for the field of psychology in general, as well as for integrating theories from modern physics with theories from modern personality psychology.

The idea that the essence of the concept of personality and the concept of systems are one and the same has direct relevance to the general theme of the present volume, namely the mechanisms through which personality processes emerge and are maintained through the course of social experience. According to systems theory, the organized functioning (i.e., personality) of a given system (e.g., a person) is determined by the *interaction* of the component subsystems (e.g., including cognition and emotion at higher levels, and biology and chemistry at lower levels) comprising the system with the suprasystem (e.g., social environment) of which the system is one part. As will become clear as the chapter unfolds (and will be summarized in Figure 7.1), a systems point of view requires that social experience be included literally as part of the definition of personality development.

This chapter is broken into three major sections. The first section carefully examines Webster's definition of personality in the context of systems theory, illustrates how personality theory can be viewed from the perspective of systems theory, and how systems theory can be viewed from the perspective of personality theory. It is here that the fundamental identity between the concept of personality and the concept of a system is made clear. To the extent that the concept of "identity" is fundamental to the concept of personality and that systems theory has a unique "identity" (compared to other theories), this section illustrates how systems theory can be applied to the concept of personality to help us understand "the system inherent in personality theory" and "the personality inherent in systems theory."

The second section applies the systems approach to personality and places personality in the context of the discipline of psychology and related biological and social sciences. It is here that I propose how personality theory, when viewed through the eyes of systems theory, can help remove the apparent disorder and disunity in psychology (Staats, 1983) by proposing a tridimensional structure for organizing the various specialities within psychology.

The third section takes this analysis one step further by showing how systems theory can be used to help apply theories from modern physics, particularly quantum physics, to personality theory. Drawing on predictions that follow from the Metasimilarity Hypothesis and Metaconnection Hypothesis, I propose that the seemingly unique "personalities" of quantum matter are actually apparent in the matter of human affairs. Four specific examples integrating modern physics with psychology are developed: (1) the Uncertainty Principle applied to the effects of self-attention and self-measurement on self-regulation, (2) the Complementarity Principle applied to the wave/particle (waveicle) theory of emotion/cognition (cogmotion), (3) General Relativity Theory applied to the General Relativity/General Relaxation Hypothesis, and (4) the $E = mc^2$ hypothesis applied to the theory that health is the potential to be well. Specific implications for research are highlighted, as well as applications relevant to physical and mental health. In the same way that modern physics is currently working toward a "Grand Unified Theory" (affectionately abbreviated GUTs by the physicists) to integrate the four established fundamental forces (fields) of nature, I propose that with the aid of systems theory and a deep concept of personality, modern psychology should have the guts (pun intended) to work toward unifying its own field (pun intended again) by working if not toward grand unification, at least toward modern integration.

Theoretically, if systems theory is completely general and integrative, then it should point the way to the essence, or gist, of the integration of psychology. This potential can be affectionately abbreviated as GIST (for General Integrative Systems Theory). As we will see, the GIST of personality and the GIST of psychology are ultimately one and the same.

PERSONALITY AND SYSTEMS THEORY

It is meaningless to talk about a system without talking about its "personality." And it is meaningless to talk about personality theory without talking about the system underlying its organization. This insight requires some explanation.

According to Webster, second edition, "personality" refers not only to the quality or fact of being a person, but also the quality or fact of being a particular person, and therefore having a personal identity and individuality. The terms "quality," "person," "identity," and "individuality" should be highlighted. Also according to Webster, personality refers to the habitual patterns and qualities of behavior of any individual as expressed by physical and mental activities and attitudes. These habitual patterns reflect distinctive individual qualities of a person, considered collectively. The terms "habitual," "patterns," "behavior," "physical," "mental," "activities," "attitudes," and "collective" should also be highlighted.

Webster's use of the terms "quality," "person," "identity," "individuality," "habitual," "patterns," "behavior," "physical," "mental," "activities," "attitudes," and "collective" are easily understood and straightforward when considered in the context of personality theory, and they are especially meaningful when considered in the context of Murray's comprehensive approach to personality. It turns out that these terms are also easily understood and straightforward when considered in the context of systems theory, and they are especially meaningful when considered in the context of von Bertalanffy's comprehensive approach to systems theory.

What is a system? In the glossary to Davidson's (1983) recent book reviewing the life and thought of von Bertalanffy, the term "system" is defined as "any entity maintained by the mutual interaction of its parts." A system, therefore, is an entity—a whole—that is composed of and is maintained by the mutual interaction of its parts. But what is an entity? What defines an entity? An entity has *qualities* that define its *individuality,* it has a *pattern* of qualities, and this pattern of qualities must be viewed *collectively.* It follows that we cannot speak of an entity without speaking of its pattern of qualities, which, when viewed collectively, defines its individuality. Describing a system as an entity begins to sound curiously like personality.

Systems theory goes further than this by proposing that the behavior of a system as a whole depends upon the mutual interaction of its parts. I underscore the concepts of *behavior* and *mutual interaction.* A system (entity) is not merely composed of parts. The parts must interact in some mutual manner for the identity of the system as a whole to be expressed. In other words, the *behavior* of a system that defines the system depends upon the *collective* parts interacting in a collective (mutual) manner. Describing a system in terms of its expressed behavior as a function of its collective interactions sounds curiously like personality.

I should point out at this point that systems theory was originally refered to as general systems theory. Systems theory was conceived of and developed into a general theory that could be applied to any scientific discipline and associated body of knowledge. Although von Bertalanffy was trained as a biologist, his mind functioned as a generalist. He searched for general principles that could be applied to all entities and, therefore, to all forms of organization regardless of the level of the entity (system) examined. This was no small feat, and it required substantial effort and courage. Von Bertalanffy had the guts to put forth a grand unifing theory that not only applied within the discipline of biology, but conceptually applied across all disciplines.

Systems theory is better described as being a meta theory or transdisciplinary theory rather than a theory per se. By definition a transdisciplinary theory must be general enough to apply to all entities, and yet be specific enough to make it possible to distinguish between different entities within and across disciplines. In the language of personality, such a theory would have to be general enough to apply to all persons (entities), and yet be specific enough to make it possible to distinguish between different persons (entities) within and across races, sexes, and cultures. The parallels between personality theory and systems theory continue.

Returning to Webster, personality is concerned with *habitual patterns* of *behavior* that are expressed in *physical* and *mental activities* and *attitudes.* The strong implication here is that personality refers to the organized information that defines a person. The habitual patterns of behavior express this organization. The organization is dynamic in the sense that the behavior will be expressed as the person interacts with his/her environment. Moreover, we infer physical and mental activities and attitudes from the behavior observed.

The parallel between personality and systems theory is particularly striking here. All entities (systems) behave. Here the term behavior is used in its most general sense—to refer to the observed functioning of an entity. From the perspective of systems theory, all science is actually the study of behavior for the purpose of understanding (by inference) underlying processes (organization). To the general systems scientist, all science is actually behavioral science. In the spirit of the present chapter, we could conclude that to the general systems scientist, all science is actually personality science (where the term "personality" is used in its general sense—e.g., that personality is the quality or fact of being an entity).

From the perspective of systems theory, a physicist studies the behavior of atoms, a chemist studies the behavior of molecules, a biologist studies the behavior of cells, tissues, and organs, a psychologist studies the behavior of individuals, a sociologist studies the behavior of groups, and so forth. The official journal of the Society for General Systems Research is aptly titled *Behavioral Sciences* and publishes articles from all disciplines that search for general principles that cut across the disciplines. To the extent that the behavior of the entity being studied is habitual, patterned, and can be identified as an organized collection of activities, the transdisciplinary, general systems meaning of the term personality can be said to apply.

Table 7.1 presents an organization of disciplines and interdisciplines derived from the systems concepts of parts, wholes, levels, hierarchies, and emergent properties. The term "emergent property" refers to the fact that when parts interact mutually and collectively, unique properties (behaviors) are observed (expressed) for the entity as a whole. In the language of personality, unique personalities arise from the unique combination of components that comprise a person. The idea that the components interact in a person as emergent properties is implied by, but not made explicit by, most personality theorists (Singer, 1984).

It can be seen in Table 7.1 that certain levels (such as mathematics, physics, chemistry, biology, psychology, and sociology) reflect *disciplines* of knowledge that follow directly from the level of the entity being studied (e.g., atoms combine to form molecules—the shift from physics to chemistry). It can also be seen in Table 7.1 that certain levels (such as theoretical physics, physical

Table 7.1 Levels of system organization and their associated academic disciplines.

Levels of system	Associated academic disciplines
Institutions	Political Science
	Political Sociology
Groups	Sociology
	Social Psychology
Organisms	Psychology, Ethology, Zoology
	Psychophysiology
Organs	Physiology (e.g., Neurology)
	Neuroendocrinology
Cells	Cellular Biology
	Biochemistry
Atoms	Physics
	Subatomic Physics
Abstract	Mathematics
	Philosophy

Indented disciplines reflect interdisciplines that interconnect levels. Levels above Institutions (e.g., National Systems, Global Systems, or Galactic Systems) and their associated disciplines and interdisciplines are not shown for the sake of brevity. Levels are organized from the micro to macro.

chemistry, biochemistry, psychobiology, and social psychology) reflect *interdisciplines* that follow directly from the need to connect one level with the next (e.g., the bridge between atom and molecules is physical chemistry). The distinction between discipline, interdiscipline, and profession should be kept in mind. From a systems perspective a profession such as medicine deals with problems that require techniques and knowledge from various disciplines and interdisciplines. The emergence of behavioral medicine reflects the recognition that medicine has the responsibility to integrate biological, psychological, and social variables in order to understand, treat, and prevent illnesses and promote health (Schwartz, 1982).

Returning to personality theory, Webster stated that personality refers to habitual patterns and qualities of behavior of any individual as expressed by physical and mental activities and attitudes. I underscore *physical* and *mental* activities and attitudes. Implicit in personality theory is the idea that personality is expressed at multiple levels within a person. From a systems perspective, it follows that the personality of a person should be expressed "biopsychosocially" (if one looks from the micro to the macro) or "sociopsychobiologically" (if one looks from the macro to the micro). Whereas the biopsychosocial approach tends to move from the parts to the whole, the sociopsychobiological approach tends to move from the whole to the parts. Note that from a systems point of view, the combination of these two approaches is required to fully understand the structure and function of personality.

It follows that theoretically, a healthy person is one whose parts function collectively, that is, the various components interact mutually in an organized, synchronized manner. Conflicts within and between various levels should lead to various degrees of dissociation and disorder within a person. To the extent that a person is an "entity," then he or she should function as an organized whole.

What then, is the "essence" of both personality theory and systems theory? The essence, I propose, is the concept of an organized whole. Every organized whole can be said to have a "personality" (using the term "personality" in a general sense) and be a "system." To have a personality is to be a system. To be a system is to have a personality. This concept can be trivialized, or it can be developed deeply. It may sound silly to talk, for example, about the personality of a rock. But beyond the silliness may lie an important truth. If a person behaved like a rock, the first thing we might conclude is that the person was stable, dependable, and strong. The person might also be described as quiet, heavy, nonresponsive, and boring. Theoretically, from a systems point of view, *it should be possible in principle to formulate a general set or pattern of personality dimensions describing classes of behavior that can be universally applied to all entities (systems).*

If we could derive a standardized set of dimensions, it would be possible to classify and compare all systems at all levels in terms of their habitual patterns of behavior, in other words, their "personalities." The result might sound silly, but this could be a blessing in disguise. Many concepts in modern physics are deliberately humorous. Recall the concept of GUTs. Or consider the idea that the universe began with a Big Bang and may eventually be followed by a Big Crunch. Sometimes humor helps to not only put things in perspective, but to stimulate creative theorizing and research.

To help keep the essence of general systems theory clearly in mind, I will sometimes use the letters GIST (for General Integrative Systems Theory) to refer in a humorous vein to the general case of which GUTs are special cases. The essence of systems thinking is to seek the heart (i.e., gist) of any matter (hence the meaning of GIST). I will return to the question of humor, personality, and modern physics in the last section of this chapter.

The important point to recognize here is that what sounds humorous on first hearing may signify an important concept worth thinking about. If systems theory can bring personality theory to mineralogy (a humorous example), maybe systems theory can bring personality to the discipline of psychology as a whole to help remove psychology's current chaotic state of disunity (a more serious example). It is to this challenge that we now turn.

PERSONALITY AND THE UNIFICATION OF PSYCHOLOGY: TOWARD A SYSTEMS SOLUTION

As we have already said, personality and systems theory are both concerned with organized wholes. As Staats (1983) indicates, the discipline of psychology is not functioning as an organized whole. According to Staats (1983), the current degree of disunity in psychology suggests that psychology is at a preparadigmatic stage in its evolution. What psychology needs is a paradigm that can serve not only to unify the discipline, but to stimulate new theory, findings, and applications through the unification process. Systems theory promises to provide such a paradigm (i.e., the GIST of psychology). Moreover, personality psychology becomes central to such an effort when we view personality from a systems perspective (i.e., the GIST of personality).

First, as Webster indicates, personality psychology is concerned with all habitual patterns of behavior that are expressed as physical and mental activities and attitudes. This implies, of course, that all of psychology should be relevant to personality theory and ultimately be included in it. This is a sweeping and grand (some might say grandiose) implication. I present this implication with appropriate trepidation and necessity. The trepidation is straightforward given the scope of the implication. However, the reason behind the necessity may seem less straightforward and should be explained. Simply put, the reason for the necessity follows directly from the hypothesis that systems theory is both a useful and valid paradigm for organizing information in all science. To accept the systems perspective is by necessity to accept the hypothesis that all disciplines of knowledge can be organized using systems theory. As I will illustrate below, systems theory does help to provide a framework for organizing all of psychology. What is particularly interesting is the role that systems theory gives to personality theory.

Figure 7.1 presents a tridimensional model for organizing the discipline of psychology. Following Table 7.1, the first dimension (the Y axis) organizes processes from the more micro levels (psychochemistry) to more macro levels (international psychology). This dimension follows directly from the concept of a system (the dimension of hierarchy of parts as levels). On the left side of the Y axis the basic science specialities are organized (referred to in general as "basic levels"), on the right side of the Y axis the applied science specialities are organized in a parallel fashion (referred to in general as "applied levels"). Not every possible speciality (basic or applied) is listed for reasons of visual clarity. The reader should be able to use systems theory to insert additional specialities (e.g., psychophysiology for basic; consulting psychology for applied) at their appropriate levels on the Y axis.

The second dimension (the X axis) organizes the moment to moment (more micro) temporal processes that cut across systemic (Y axis) levels, moving from the input (stimulus) through information processing (organ-

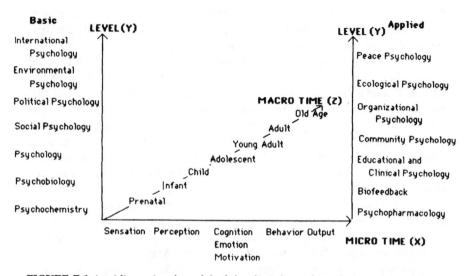

Basic

LEVEL(Y)

International
Psychology

Environmental
Psychology

Political Psychology

Social Psychology

Psychology

Psychobiology

Psychochemistry

MACRO TIME (Z)
Old Age
Adult
Young Adult
Adolescent
Child
Infant
Prenatal

LEVEL (Y) **Applied**

Peace Psychology

Ecological Psychology

Organizational
Psychology

Community Psychology

Educational and
Clinical Psychology

Biofeedback

Psychopharmacology

Sensation Perception Cognition Behavior Output
Emotion
Motivation

MICRO TIME (X)

FIGURE 7.1 A tridimensional model of the discipline of psychology derived from systems theory. Applied levels are shown in parallel with their basic level counterpart. The term "personality" is not shown because from a systems perspective, personality includes all three dimensions. See text for details.

ism) to the output (response) processes (i.e., the dimension of time). The relationship between cognition, emotion, and motivation are illustrated as a subdimension within the second dimension. The organization of this subdimension can be debated (and will be in the last section of this chapter). Again, not every possible content area is listed for reasons of visual clarity. The reader should be able to use systems theory to insert additional areas (psychophysics, memory, decision making, motor skills, and so forth) at their appropriate positions on the X axis.

The third dimension (the Z axis) organizes processes along a more macro dimension of time from prenatal through adulthood to old age. The scope of this dimension includes early child development and extends to geriatric psychology. Clearly, the psychology of conception, birth, and death apply to this dimension.

Note that conceptually, the concept of personality certainly includes both the X axis and Z axis temporal dimensions. Moreover, as defined by Webster, the concept of personality includes the Y axis levels of systems as well (i.e., physical and mental activities and attitudes). However, I will extend Webster's definition to include social activities and attitudes in order to be consistent with systems theory.

It follows that a unified theory of psychology as a discipline should also be a unified theory of personality. If the essence of personality theory and systems theory is the idea of organized wholes (i.e., the GIST of an organized whole) then as psychology moves toward becoming an organized whole, psychology will move more toward becoming a unified personality psychology and therefore a systems psychology.

Note that Figure 7.1 does not list specific content areas. However, the reader should be able to insert specific content areas within and across the various dimensions. This exercise is useful, because it helps point out that *every content area exists along each of the three major dimensions. No content area exists along only one dimension.* In this sense, the system proposed here for organizing psychology itself functions as an organized whole. It follows that when we describe this system for organizing psychology, we end up describing the personality of the discipline of psychology as a functioning system.

Also note that this diagram does not explicitly depict a dimension comparing different species (the evolutionary/comparative perspective). Implicit to the Z axis, however, is a more macro time frame that can be extended to reflect the evolutionary time scale. If age (of person) is replaced with age (of life on earth), the diagram becomes more comprehensive and encompasses an evolutionary scale. The issue of evolution will be returned to in the last section of the chapter.

From a systems perspective, it becomes clear why the study of human personality is so comprehensive, complex, and time consuming. Hopefully, the systems perspective described here captures the spirit of (and maybe the GIST of) Murray's pioneering work and presents it in a way that helps clarify his broad vision.

PERSONALITY PSYCHOLOGY, MODERN PHYSICS, AND HEALTH: WHY INCLUDE MODERN PHYSICS IN THIS CHAPTER?

Based on the discussion to this point, one might be tempted to conclude that systems theory provides a framework not only for integrating personality psychology within the discipline of psychology, but also for integrating all scientific disciplines (including psychology). Unfortunately, there is one glaring apparent exception to this sweeping generalization. The exception is found in modern physics.

Simply stated, concepts and findings in modern physics, particularly quantum physics, seem to challenge all attempts to unify science. The findings from quantum physics seem to be at odds with the rest of science (as well as common experience). However, I will propose that what seems to be at odds with the rest of science (as well as common experience) is more apparent than real. In fact, I will propose that systems theory actually contains within it a strategy for integrating fundamental concepts from modern physics with the rest of science. The implications of this strategy for personality psychology are sufficiently striking (and significant) to warrant serious consideration here. At the same time, the implications of this strategy for personality psychology are sufficiently unusual (and at times humorous) to warrant explanation before presenting the strategy.

It is appropriate for a number of reasons to present the systems strategy for integrating modern physics with psychology in this chapter. One reason is that Murray himself developed an interest in systems theory and became systems oriented (see Murray 1967, p. 75). He believed strongly in the importance of integrating key concepts from other disciplines (such as evolutionary biology and sociology) with the study of human personality. Also, Murray was not afraid to infer "invisible" or "unconscious" processes from observable behavior (which you will recall is a premise underlying the systems approach to science). In fact, Murray relished this challenge and developed instruments such as the TAT to do just this.

A second reason is that modern physics poses a serious challenge to systems theory. This challenge questions the essential assumptions underlying the whole theory. One could choose simply to ignore these apparent problems with systems theory. However, to ignore these problems would be deceptive and, moreover, would be contrary to Murray's spirit of openness to scientific controversy. As Murray describes in the third of his autobiographical essays (Murray, 1967), he was strongly influenced by reading the writings of (and eventually working with) Jung. Moreover, he had some dream experiences that led him to conclude that there was more to reality than met the eye, a reality waiting to be inferred through the careful study and interpretation of phenomena that could be experienced (e.g., dreams) as well as observed (e.g., projective responses to stimuli such as the TAT). One infers from reading Murray's autobiographical essays that he would welcome serious attempts to face the difficult and controversial challenge of integrating modern physics with psychology so long as it was done with the spirit of openness coupled with experimental evaluation.

The third reason is personal. About a month prior to giving the Murray Lecture upon which this chapter is based, I presented an Invited Address at the Eastern Psychological Assocation meetings (April, 1985). The title of my address was "Psychology, modern physics and health: A new challenge for health psychology." Following the lecture I ate lunch with David McClelland, the chairperson of the session. During lunch a distinguished woman came to our table. She started a conversation by offering some kind comments about the lecture. She then proceeded to tell us that she was currently teaching a seminar at the Harvard Medical School and that the students were pressing her for information about the potential applications of modern physics to psychology and medicine. She told us that she thought the students would be especially interested in the ideas presented in my lecture and asked me if I had prepared the lecture for publication. I, somewhat sheepishly, said "not yet."

I confessed to her that I found myself reluctant to put the modern physics/ psychology synthesis into print. I explained that I had previously given a lecture on these ideas as part of my Presidential Address to Division 38, Health Psychology in August of 1984. This lecture was only a few hours of work away from being ready to be submited for publication, and yet I waited.

At this point David McClelland asked me if I knew who this women was. I said no. Her name was Nina, and she happened to be Henry Murray's spouse. I then told her about the upcoming Henry Murray lectures and how I planned to give my lecture on personality theory and the unification of psychology from a systems perspective. She indicated that she thought her husband would be especially pleased to learn about my ideas integrating modern physics with psychology. I therefore decided to expand my Murray lecture to go beyond personality theory and the unification of psychology. I made the commitment to discuss the unification of science in general and to develop the implications of modern physics for personality and health using the systems strategy.

I therefore include the following ideas about modern physics and personality theory in the present chapter not only because these ideas are directly relevant to the application of systems theory to personality theory and the unification of psychology, but also because these ideas seem to be in the spirit of Henry Murray's approach to science.

MURRAY, HUMOR, AND MODERN PHYSICS: ON THE DISTINCTION BETWEEN INTERESTING AND AMUSING THEORIES IN SCIENCE

A distinctive quality of Murray's writings is that his writings reflect not only a sense of life and enjoyment, but a sense of wit and amusement as well. Consider, for example, the first three sentences of his third autobiographical essay, titled "The Case of Murr":

> It occurred to me that the easiest way for a veteran examiner of men to cope with this present assignment would be to hold the mirror up to the manifestations of his own nature pretty much as he would do in the case of any individual who volunteered as subject for exposure to the threatening and dubious procedures of assessment. This notion was particularly inviting at this moment since it offered me a chance to illustrate the applicability of some unfamiliar ideas to which I am nowadays attached, and since, by so doing, I might alleviate to some extent the tedium of a long parade of unexciting and unilluminated facts. Full of enthusiasm, I

embarked on the execution of this plan with the special purpose of representing and explaining the professional mentational history of my subject, whose pseudonym is Murr. (Murray, 1967, p. 52)

If these three sentences help set the stage for his third autobiographical essay, the last few sentences provide a fitting epilogue that serve to illustrate Murray's eloquence and amusement:

> I told you at the start of this case portrait that my functionally autonomous will, the conscious governor of my ego *system* [italics added] (the little self) had resolved to check the incontinence of the sanquine surplus from the larger Self and adhere to the corrective maxim. But it must have been apparent to you almost from the start that although I was managing to focus pretty well on the eccentricities of Murr, there was more functional autonomy in the Self than in the self: the legs of the portrait came out too long and lanky, the belly of childhood memories was too bloated, and I had hardly stretched above the eyebrows when I found myself simultaneously at both the ordained space limit and the time limit. Down came the blade of the editor's guillotine, and my last section, the forehead and crown of the portrait, which contained whatever retrospective bits of wit and wisdom Murr could muster, rolled into the basket with a thud. In short, I need not have taken a paragraph of the prologue to describe the sanquine surplus, because it was fated to make a disastrous spectacle of itself in the ensuing pages, and to leave Murr and myself, the viewed and the viewer, with one residual query. (Murray, 1967, pp. 75–76)

It could be argued that the "blade of the editor's guillotine" should have come down on the last section of the present chapter as well. Will the "ensuing pages" be a fitting "forehead and crown" to this chapter, or is it "fated to make a disastrous spectacle of itself"? You may wonder, what right does a psychologist/psychophysiologist have to discuss modern physics and relate it to psychology in particular and science in general?

A brief history is in order here. For as long as I can remember, I have had an interest in physics. This included building an electronics laboratory (of sorts) in the basement of my parents house as a child, participating in numerous science fairs in junior and senior high school, beginning my undergraduate education as an electrical engineer, and selecting psychophysiology for my research career. However, my interest in modern physics seemed destined to remain a hobby, since I saw no direct relevance of its concepts and findings to my research or clinical work.

All this changed when I read a book by Pagels, a physicist at Rockefeller University and the New York Academy of Sciences, titled *The Cosmic Code: Quantum Physics as the Language of Nature* (Pagels, 1982), in the summer of 1983. Pagels' idea that nature is a language or code to be decoded, and that modern physics is an attempt to decipher this code, provides a metaphor linking the goals of modern physics with those of psycholinguistics.

The Cosmic Code introduces the educated layperson to the history of the discovery of the key concepts and findings in modern physics. I suspect Murray would approve of this book. Not only is the book written with eloquence and wit, but it describes the personalities and the minds of the key figures who made the discoveries and places these persons in historical perspective. One could conclude that the book is as much about the psychology of modern physics as it is about modern physics itself.

It was the chapter on Einstein and General Relativity Theory (to be described shortly) that triggered my insight about how theories of modern physics could be translated into theories of modern psychology. It was this chapter that triggered the general relativity/general relaxation hypothesis (cited in Schwartz, 1984), and we began doing research to test the hypothesis in the fall of 1983. At that time I also had the good fortune to be on sabbatical and spent a significant portion of the time reading extensively in modern physics. I came to realize that systems theory provided a key for translating theories of modern physics into general theories that could be applied to any discipline.

I was about ready to begin sharing these ideas publicly with my colleagues. However, since I was not a card-carrying physicist, I was not about to share these ideas publicly without first putting the ideas to critical test by an appropriate physicist. I therefore made contact with Pagels to test the ideas on him (parenthetically, the editors of this volume had this chapter reviewed by a card-carrying physicist at Michigan State University for a second opinion).

I first asked Pagels if I understood correctly from reading his book how Einstein came to discover the concept of general relativity. He said "yes." I then asked him if by following the same logic as Einstein, did my predictions linking general relativity with general relaxation follow? He said "yes." I then finally asked him if he thought I should consider pursuing a new interdisciplinary speciality termed "quantum psychology" (or more generically, "behavioral biophysics") to develop and test the evolving list of concepts linking modern physics with psychology. After some pause, he said "Gary, I think your theory is quite amusing."

I said, "What! Here I am, trying to make a major personal decision affecting my future research in psychology and health, and your response, your advice, is simply 'I think your theory is amusing!'?" Pagels replied, "Gary, I think you do not understand what I mean by the term 'amusing.'"

Pagels went on to explain that there is a famous physicist at Princeton, Eugene Wigner, who is fond of saying that there are two kinds of theories in science, "Interesting Theories" and "Amusing Theories." According to Wigner, Interesting Theories, though often true, are often "forgotten," whereas

Amusing Theories, though often untrue, are "absolutely worth thinking about."

It is within this spirit that I wish to "amuse" you (both literally and figuratively) concerning a strategy for integrating modern physics with psychology, focusing on personality theory and health. The section consists of three parts. The first presents two fundamental assumptions underlying systems theory. Based on these fundamental assumptions, I show how systems theory can be used to uncover general hypotheses implicit in the concepts and findings of modern physics and how one can put these general hypotheses to empirical test in psychological research. The second presents four examples where concepts and findings in modern physics are integrated with modern psychology, focusing on personality theory and health. The third ends with an amusing analysis of the evolution of the concept of what we consider to be "impossible" in science, as viewed through the eyes of systems theory.

MODERN PHYSICS–MODERN PSYCHOLOGY CONNECTION: UNDERSTANDING THE GIST CODE

In order for systems theory to be completely general, the theory must consist of principles or laws that prove to be completely general. The collective set of these principles, in essence, must be univeral. These universal principles must enable scientists in any discipline to get to the gist of any system at any level (hence the letters "GIST"). It turns out that systems theory, so defined, is actually the easiest of all theories to disprove. All that is required is the discovery of one solid exception. As we will see, modern physics appears not only to be a solid exception, but it is a huge and peculiar one as well.

There are two fundamental assumptions underlying systems theory that I propose should be relabeled as hypotheses: They are (1) The Cross-Level Metasimilarity Hypothesis, and (2) The Between-Level Metaconnection Hypothesis.

The gist of the Cross-Level Metasimilarity Hypothesis is that in order for systems theory to be proven to be true, all systems at their core must share certain universal properties and must express the functioning of certain universal laws or principles. These metalaws or metaprinciples transcend specific disciplines (e.g., metaconcepts such as information and feedback are hypothesized to be universal and can be applied to areas as diverse as electronics and economics). These metaconcepts can be inferred to exist only to the extent that all systems across all levels are shown to manifest specific properties in common (i.e., they show metasimilarity). Metasimilarity has been discovered to occur across all levels except at the extreme macro level (the cosmic). At these extremes, seemingly peculiar things happen (e.g., phenomena are both wave-like and particle-like, time becomes relative, and things can happen synchronously across time and space).

From a personality point of view, one could say that nature seems to express two kinds of core personalities: (1) "normal" personalities expressed by systems at most levels, and (2) "peculiar" personalities expressed by systems at the extreme micro and macro levels. If the core behavior of systems at the extremes does not apply to the core behavior of systems at all the levels in between, and vice versa, then the Cross-Level Metasimilarity Hypothesis can be disproved.

The Cross-Level Metasimilarity Hypothesis, of course, refers to common similarity in observed functioning only. Common similarity in observed functioning may or may not reflect the operation of common underlying laws or principles. Metasimilarity refers to *observed similarity only*. It follows that Cross-Level Metasimilarity is a necessary, but not sufficient condition for systems theory to qualify as a universal theory (i.e., GIST). The strong version of systems theory is that both Metasimilarity and Metaconnection prove to be true: the weak version of systems theory is that Metasimilarity proves to be true, but Metaconnection does not.

The gist of the Between-Level Metaconnection Hypothesis is that in order for systems theory to be proven to be true, it must be demonstrable that all systems at all levels are directly or indirectly connected. Systems theory in its strongest form requires that all components of a system be interconnected. It follows that the behavior of each component (each subsystem) has some demonstrable effect on every other component (subsystems) in the system. The effect of one subsystem upon another may be extremely small and account for an extremely little portion of the variance of the behavior of the subsystem in question. But directly or indirectly, intersubsystem effects must be observable if the measurement is made with appropriate sensitivity and consistency and the data are collected and averaged over a long enough period of time.

This implies, of course, that processes (and hence laws) at the subatomic level must have some measurable effect on processes at the psychological level. Morever, the reverse should be true as well, i.e., that processes (and hence laws) at the psychological level must have some measurable effect on processes at the subatomic level. If one adopts the strong version of systems theory, one is forced to entertain the possibility that the effects of General Relativity, for example, should be measurable at the psychological level, not merely as a Metasimilarity across levels, but as a Metaconnection between levels as well. As will be discussed below, it is much more difficult to prove (or disprove) the modern physic/psychology Metaconnection Hypothesis than the Metasimilarity Hypothesis. Nonetheless, one is forced to hypothesize

Metaconnection if one wishes to view systems theory as a truly general, transdisciplinary theory.

Once these two assumptions implicit in systems theory are made explicit and stated as hypotheses (Metasimilarity and Metaconnection), a strategy emerges for integrating concepts and findings of modern physics with modern psychology. Only three steps are required to implement the creation of Metasimilarity Hypotheses and associated experiments.

Step 1: Select an apparent exception to systems theory in modern physics. For example, one could select the phenomenon that light exhibits both wave-like and particle-like properties.

Step 2: Consider the apparent exception to be a special case of a general principle, and restate the exception as a hypothesized new general principle. Using the wave-particle example, one would propose that phenomenon exist at all levels that show both wave-like and particle-like behavior.

Step 3: Look for examples in psychology that can be reinterpreted as reflecting the predictions of the new general principle and/or design new experiments to discover new phenomena predicted to exist based on the new general principle. As I will describe in more detail below, using the wave-particle example again, we can create a new theory of emotion and cognition (which I call the "Wave-Particle Theory of Feeling and Thought") and posit the existence of "Feelthoughts" just as physicists posit the existence of "Wavicles." Such a theory turns out to not only integrate seemingly disparate data in psychology, but also encourages new experimentation that can prove (or disprove) the Metasimilarity Hypothesis.

It should be recalled at this point that Metasimilarity between modern physics and psychology implies a common personality, a Metapersonality if you will, shared with the subatomic world and the world of animal and human behavior. Can our thoughts and feelings really share some fundamental properties with photons and electrons? Is there really a metapersonality linking feelthoughts and wavicles? The metapersonality is implied in Figure 7.1 if the X axis is extended downward to include the integration of psychology with physics. These are amusing thoughts.

The stategy for implementing the creation of Metaconnection Hypotheses and associated experiments follows the same pattern as the strategy described above for implementing the creation of Metasimilarity Hypotheses. Again, three steps are required. The major difference is the difficulty in uncovering and then understanding the assumptions made by physicists when they create their theories, especially since these assumptions are often implicit rather than explicit. The three steps for implementing Metaconnection Hypotheses are as follows:

Step 1: Select an apparent exception to systems theory in modern physics. For example, one could select the phenomenon that time becomes slower in stronger gravitational fields, relatively speaking. This step is identical to Step 1 for Metasimilarity.

Step 2: Analyze the assumptions made in the theory to explain the phenomenon, consider the assumptions to be special cases of general assumptions, and restate the assumptions as possible new general assumptions. Using the time-gravity example, one would examine Einstein's assumption that "time is what you measure with a clock," and as will be described in more detail below, restate this assumption as "A is what you measure with X."

Step 3: Select instances in psychology where the new general assumption can be applied and then look for examples in psychology that can be reinterpreted as reflecting predictions following the new theory and/or design new experiments to discover new phenomena predicted to exist based on the new theory. As I will describe in more detail below, using the time-gravity example again, we can create a new theory of relaxation (which I call the General Relativity/General Relaxation Hypothesis) and posit that by consciously increasing one's subjective experience of gravity, one's biological clocks and time perception will slow down in accord with predictions made by General Relativity Theory.

Metaconnection Hypotheses are more difficult to formulate and to prove than Metasimilarity Hypotheses. They are also more controversial and more far-reaching. Consider, for example, what would happen if it could be demonstrated through careful research that mind could directly connect with and alter time/mass relationships (e.g., by spending more time attending to gravity, one could literally live longer, relatively speaking!). These thoughts, as peculiar as they may seem, are required by the strong version of systems theory.

Metaconnection predictions often seem peculiar on first hearing, and they may well prove to be wrong. However, if we are to consider systems theory seriously, then these predictions are, as Wigner would say, "absolutely worth thinking about."

What follows next are four examples of Metasimilarity Hypotheses linking modern physics with psychology. Each example has direct implications for personality theory and health. The examples from modern physics move from relatively simple concepts to more complex concepts, from more well-known concepts to less well-known concepts, from more well-established concepts to less well-established concepts, and from less amusing concepts to more amusing concepts. I include one example from modern physics of a Metaconnection Hypothesis that we have begun testing in laboratory research.

EXAMPLE 1: HEISENBERG'S UNCERTAINTY PRINCIPLE AND THE SELF-ATTENTION/SELF-REGULATION HYPOTHESIS

A well-known principle in modern physics is Heisenberg's Uncertainty Principle (see Heisenberg, 1971). Heisenberg was concerned with the problem of measuring both the position and momentum of an electron. Very briefly, if one measures the position of an electron precisely, it is not possible to know the electron's momentum at the same time. Conversely, if one measures the momentum of an electron precisely, it is not possible to know the electron's position at the same time. There is built-in uncertainty in the very process of making measurements at the level of the electron.

The concept of uncertainty in measurement is not foreign to other disciplines, and Heisenberg's Uncertainty Principle has been loosely used in the past as a metaphor in biology and psychology. However, if we apply the three steps outlined above to transform Heisenberg's Uncertainty Principle from a discipline specific principle to a transdisciplinary principle, we might restate the principle as follows (Step 2): To measure is to alter to some degree, and to measure one quality of a system is to produce uncertainty in the simultaneous measurement of other qualities of the system.

How might this metaprinciple apply to psychology? Consider, for example, the phenomenon of behavioral self-monitoring. It is well known that the seemingly simple request of asking a subject to monitor his/her behavior often leads to changes in not only the behavior being measured, but other behaviors as well. Such self-monitoring effects are often explained as examples of self-attention and self-interpretation producing conscious and/or unconscious changes in the behavior monitored (e.g., Carver & Scheier, 1981). Moreover, viewing self-attention as the connection of self-generated feedback processes leads to specific predictions about effects of self-attention on self-regulation (Carver & Scheier, 1981). What has not been considered as yet is the possibility that the *pattern or organization* of these effects at the psychological level may parallel the *pattern or organization* of effects found to occur at the quantum level. Though the *mechanisms* may differ at the psychological level compared to the subatomic level, the *pattern organization* of the processes still show a fundamental similarity across the two levels.

The specific nature of these self-measurement effects may themselves help define the nature of individual personalities (since the way a given person attends should alter the self-measurement effects observed). If a person self-monitors in a nonthreatened (e.g., friendly) manner, the effects of the self-measurement may be quite different than if a person self-monitors in a threatened (e.g., unfriendly) manner. According to self-regulation theory, friendly self-measurement should encourage a negative-feedback, stabilization process, whereas unfriendly self-measurement should encourage a positive-feedback, disstabilization process. I have proposed that friendly self-attention from a systems point of view is health-promoting, connecting psychological, biological, and chemical levels along a hierarchically organized, common negative feedback process, whereas unfriendly self-attention is health-damaging at multiple levels (Schwartz, 1984).

To measure is to alter. This metaprinciple implies that to self-attend is to self-regulate. The extreme form of this metaprinciple is that any instruction given to a subject must produce a specific self-measurement effect. We have yet to chart the rules governing which responses evidence increased certainty and which responses simultaneously evidence increased uncertainty as a function of the type of instructions and tasks used. In a recent study conducted in our laboratory, when subjects were asked to simply attend to their breathing in a nonthreatening manner, this led to increased certainty in the behavior of breathing (e.g., respiration rate became less variable, more stable) coupled simultaneously with decreased certainty in the behavior of the heart (e.g., heart rate became more variable, less stable). Conversely, when subjects were asked to simply attend to their heart beats, this led to increased certainty in the behavior of the heart (e.g., heart rate became less variable, more stable) coupled simultaneously with decreased certainty in the behavior of breathing (e.g., respiration rate became more variable, less stable) (Schwartz & Rennert, 1982).

Do such psychophysiological self-measurement effects parallel predictions derived from Heisenberg's Uncertainty Principle? Or are such effects found to be parallel only when the measurement is made by "self" rather than by "others"? Note that at the subatomic level, the distinction between "self" and "other" breaks down, which is why the very act of measurement is so interactive (i.e., the measurement becomes part of the system since the processes of measurement are at the same level as the processes being measured). Hence, from a systems point of view the situation of human self-measurement (rather than other-measurement) more directly parallels the situation of quantum physics when measurements are taken at the subatomic level. Stated in this manner, the hypotheses become amenable to systematic investigation.

People vary to the degree that they feel "a part of" versus "apart from" other people, groups, situations, and so forth. Does this general personality variable influence the degree to which self- versus other-measurement affects parallel measurement effects observed at the subatomic level? One tends to think quite differently about the nature of measurement, self-monitoring, and personality when one becomes cognizant of the metasimilarity hypothesis.

EXAMPLE 2: THE COMPLEMENTARITY PRINCIPLE, THE WAVE-PARTICLE THEORY OF EMOTION AND COGNITION, AND PERSONALITY STYLES

The Uncertainty Principle, though interesting, is not particularly novel or controversial. More novel, and more controversial, is the search for metasimilarity involving the complementarity principle in modern physics. Very briefly, quantum physics tells us that light sometimes behaves as particle—localized in space—and at other times behaves as a wave—distributed over space. In the famous "single slit" experiment, light passing through the slit behaves like a particle, and its wave properties are essentially hidden. However, if the single slit is changed to a "double slit," the light passing though both slits now behave like a particle, and its wave properties are essentially hidden. How can something be both a wave (distributed) in space and a particle (localized in space), and have its expressed personality (so to speak) *change depending upon the measurement conditions* (Heisenberg type effect?)?

Physicists explain this seeming paradox by proposing the concept of a "wavicle." Light is viewed neither as being a wave or as being a particle per se. Rather, light is viewed as having both wave-like and particle-like properties that are expressed selectively in certain situations and not others.

We rarely consider seriously the idea that "wavicle" processes may apply to high levels, including biology and psychology. However, if we apply the three steps outlined above to transform the Complementarity Principle from a discipline-specific principle to a transdisciplinary principle, we might restate the principle as follows (Step 2): All systems have both wave-like and particle-like properties that are expressed to different degrees depending upon the measurement situation.

Before considering how this general principle might apply at the psychological level, let me briefly illustrate one important application at the biological level. There continues to be a major paradox and controversy in the neurosciences that is concerned with localization of brain function versus distribution of brain function. Very briefly, there is strong research support for both localization of brain function and distribution of brain function. The brain seems to act both as a kind of complex parallel processor system—localized brain model (e.g., Luria, 1973)—and as a kind of holographic system—distributed brain model (e.g., Pribram, 1971). Interestingly, data supporting localization versus distribution of brain function tend to depend upon the kind of experiment that is designed and the specific measures taken. This paradox in the neurosciences sounds curiously similar to the wave (distributed) versus particle (localized) paradox in modern physics outlined above. Is it possible that the brain as a whole system is more like a "wavicle" than it is a "wave" per se (distributed hologram) or a "particle" per se (localized processor), and that the brain's wave-like versus particle-like properties are expressed depending upon the nature of the measurement situation (a clear application of Example 1: Uncertainty Principle applied to Example 2: Complementarity Principle)? The brain may function more like, for lack of a better term, a Complementarity System. Maybe all systems are ultimately Complementarity Systems, and "Complementaritiness," so to speak, is a core aspect of a system's metapersonality.

The same sort of apparent paradox can be found in psychology. We tend to conceive of subjective experience (and associated physiology and social behavior) as consisting of two types. In everyday language, the words used are "feeling" and "thought." In professional language, the words used are "emotion" and "cognition." These two classes of experience are viewed as being independent though interactive. There is a long-standing debate that continues to the present concerning the relationship between emotion and cognition. Some investigators conceptualize cognition as existing independent of emotion and always preceeding it (e.g., Lazarus, 1984), whereas other investigators conceptualize emotion as existing independent of cognition and often preceeding it (Zajonc, 1980).

However, most theories of emotion and cognition tend to ignore two important points relevant to the complementaritiness question. First is that feelings and thoughts have different subjective qualities. Whereas thoughts are quite specific, and images, for example, can be localized in relative space (e.g., visual images may be experienced in the vicinity of one's eyes), feelings are more general, and emotions, for example, cannot be localized in relative space (e.g., happiness as a global feeling is not experienced in any particular place). Second is that the relative degree of emotion versus cognition observed in a given experiment tends to vary as a function of the nature of the experiment and the kinds of measures taken. Although this question has not received systematic investigation to date, it is certainly logically possible that the reason why experiments fail to replicate *patterns* of findings involving emotions and cognitions is that the experiments vary to the extent that subjects are requested to self-monitor their feelings versus their images.

Is it possible that what we presumably observe as emotion versus cognition are not really separate processes but rather are two different expressions of a whole process that we have yet to name and describe? Just as light is ultimately a whole process with seeming wave-like and particle-like properties, and the brain is ultimately a whole process with seeming wave-like and particle-like properties, is it possible that consciousness is ultimately a whole process with seeming wave-like (feeling?) and particle-like (thought?) properties? Is it possible that the whole can, for lack of a better term, be called "cogmotion" (for professional language) or "feelthought" (for everyday language)?

People vary in the extent to which they experience the contents of their consciousness as being "apart from" versus being "a part of" each other. Lane and Schwartz (1987) have developed a sociopsychobiological theory of emotional awareness that proposes that levels of emotional awareness basically parallel levels of cognitive development and that human development involves parallel structural transformations in brain functioning, emotional and cognitive functioning, and social functioning. As individuals become more highly developed, they become both more differentiated and more integrated. In plain language, they are more likely to experience differences in thoughts and feelings and yet simultaneously experience thoughts and feelings as two different aspects of their true subjective experience of events.

Is it possible that the very act of attending to one's images versus one's feelings alters one's subjective experience, physiological reactions, and behavior in a manner that parallels the effects of viewing light through a single slit versus double slit? Are some people more particle-like, so to speak, in general, whereas others are more wave-like, so to speak? Are such parallels merely sloppy metaphors, or do they reflect true metasimilarities in terms of predicted mathematical parameters and relationships? An amusing, researchable question.

The Complementarity Principle in modern physics, when viewed from the perspective of systems theory, offers an intriguing solution to another apparent controversy in personality psychology. Some personality theories focus on "types" (categories or classes) of normal or abnormal personalities, whereas other personality theories focus on "dimensions" (continuous variables or processes). For example, depending upon the particular theorist, extraversion is viewed either as a "type" or as a "dimension." However, is it possible that personality has both "wave-like" (i.e., dimensional) and "particle-like" (i.e., categorical) properties, depending upon how one measures a person and, therefore, interacts with a person?

What is needed is a term that captures both the wave-like/dimensional and particle-like/categorical qualities of personality. It turns out that such a term already exists in personality psychology. That term is "style." I propose that our difficulty in conceptualizing and measuring personality styles reflects the fact that embodied in the meaning of the term "style" are both structural (categorical) and functional (dimensional) qualities. Style may be to dimension and type as waveicle is to wave and particle. Style may be like cogmotion, if you understand what I feelthink.

EXAMPLE 3: THE GENERAL RELATIVITY/GENERAL RELAXATION HYPOTHESIS

By now the Metasimilarity Hypothesis strategy should be relatively straight-forward, and one should be prepared to predict that the resulting new hypotheses will be novel if not peculiar (though the new hypotheses at the psychological level should be no more novel and pecular than the original hypotheses expressed at the subatomic level). It is now appropriate to go beyond the creation of a Metasimilarity Hypothesis and formulate a Meta-connection Hypothesis as well. The example involves the concept of general relativity.

As I mentioned above, it was the book written by Pagels, *The Cosmic Code,* that provided the key for unlocking the door separating modern physics from modern psychology. Pagel's analysis is not as thorough as other books written for the lay public (e.g., Kahan, 1983) or the introductory student (e.g., Narlikar, 1982) on Einstein's theory of general relativity. In fact, Einstein himself wrote a book for the general public about his theory that is quite informative and complete (Einstein, 1961). What is unique about Pagels' book is that it provides a historical perspective and social context for understanding the personality and logic that led physicists such as Einstein to think as they did.

What becomes clear upon reading Pagels' book (although Pagel does not make this particular point per se) is that modern psychologists and modern physicists are ultimately in the same theoretical boat. That is, we both make *inferences* about *underlying* processes from *observable* phenomena (i.e., behavior), and these observable phenomona are often *quite distant* from presumed processes of interest. There are many layers of inference in modern psychologist's studies of subjective and cognitive processes just as there are many layers of inference in modern physicist's studies of subatomic processes.

To understand the connection between Einstein's theory of general relativity and modern psychology, it is essential to understand some of the key assumptions made by Einstein that enabled him to make the remarkable predictions that he did (Step 2). According to Pagels (1982) Einstein made two simple yet brilliant assumptions that employed the identical underlying logical process. One assumption was that *space is what is measured with a measuring rod.* If we take this assumption literally (most of us do not do this, but Einstein proposed that we do precisely this), it follows that *if a rod appears to be smaller (or larger), then we should conclude that space itself is smaller (or larger), relatively speaking.* Note that Einstein proposed that we not conclude that the *rod* was smaller (or larger) (or that the rod merely *appeared* smaller or larger), but that *space* itself had become smaller (or larger), relatively speaking (since space is what is measured by a rod!).

A related assumption has to do with time. According to Pagels, Einstein made the assumption that *time is what is measured with a clock*. If we take this assumption literally (again, most of us do not do this, but Einstein proposed that we do precisely this), it follows that *if a clock appears to be going slower (or faster), then we should conclude that time itself is going slower (or faster), relatively speaking*. Again note that Einstein proposed we not conclude that the *clock* was going slower (or faster) (or that the clock merely *appeared* to be going slower or faster), but that *time* itself had slowed (or become faster), relatively speaking (since time is what is measured by a clock).

Armed with these two amusing assumptions, and by making one more (that the speed of light is constant), it was possible for Einstein to derive his general theory of relativity that revolutionized modern physics and modern society at large. Space does not permit me to present the essence of the derivation here, nor does space permit me to present the spectrum of new and unusual predictions made by the theory and the kinds of data obtained in support of the theory (see Pagels, 1982, for an introduction to this material). However, one particular prediction regarding the relationship between time and gravity is central to my formation of the General Relativity/General Relaxation Hypothesis, and we will consider this prediction and its ramifications in some depth.

Einstein predicted that the stronger the gravitational field, the slower would be the passage of time. Various experiments using atomic clocks as well as "biological" clocks (e.g., rates of cell division) have documented that if the gravitational field is decreased (e.g., in orbit around the earth) clocks are measured to run faster relative to clocks on the earth's surface. Pagels made a humorous though serious comment in passing that *theoretically,* a person living on a mountain top outside of Denver should age a little bit faster than a person living at sea level (assuming all other things being equal, which of course they are not) (Pagels, 1982).

I had recently returned from a trip to Denver, and I was struck by the fact that I felt no particular decrement in the gravitational field in the Colorado mountains relative to Connecticut coast (which is to be expected, since the difference in field strength is tiny indeed). However, I knew it was possible to *amplify* my *experience* of the effects of gravity simply by *focusing my attention on feelings of heaviness and connectedness.* Images of bodily heaviness, connectedness, and "centeredness" are commonly used in a wide variety of relaxation techniques, including autogenic training, hypnosis, and meditation (Woolfolk and Lehrer, 1984). I wondered, if we *experience* gravity as being stronger, relatively speaking, should the time/gravity predictions of Einstein apply (i.e., should biological clocks slow down, should time perception slow down, and, therefore, should the aging process slow down?).

Normally one would reject such thinking as mere fancy. However, so too would one normally reject Einstein's thinking as mere fancy. What Einstein did that was different from mere fancy was that he made specific assumptions, which *if* true, and I underscore *if,* would logically lead to the formation of certain predictions that could be confirmed by research. Conversely, if the specific assumptions turned out to be false, then the predictions that logically followed from the assumptions could be proven to be false through research.

The General Relativity/General Relaxation Hypothesis directly follows when the logical process that Einstein applied to the rod and the clock is applied to the brain. The general principle (Step 2) derived from Einstein's analysis is basically this: If A is a direct measure of X, and A changes, then X has changed. If rods can be said to measure space, and clocks can be said to measure time, then it logically follows that *brains can be said to measure energy fields* (Schwartz, 1984).

The brain can be thought of as a *field-amplifying system.* With the aid of sense organs, the brain *detects* miniscule levels of energy in selected frequency bands, and *transforms* and *amplifies* these energy fields into signals that the brain can interpret and act upon. It has been documented that photoreceptive cells in the eye can detect single photons of light, and chemoreceptive cells in the nose can detect electromagnetic properties of single molecules. The brain amplifies these tiny electromagnetic waves into much larger waves that are expressed, for example, as brain waves recorded from the surface of the skull.

It has also been shown that when subjects control their attention and therefore alter their conscious experience, their brain waves change accordingly. Psychophysiological research on sensory augmentation and reduction, both as a state that can be self-regulated and as a personality trait that is more enduring (Buchsbaum, 1976), supports the hypothesis that the brain can be thought of as acting like a field-strength amplifier.

The concept of the brain as a field-strength amplifier is not new, though it can be debated. What is new is the application of the Einstein's logic to this concept. By following the identical logic described above for rods and clocks, which becomes Step 2 for creating Metaconnection Hypotheses, a new assumption is made: *amplified field strength is what is measured with a brain.* If we took this assumption literally (most of us would not do this, but Step 2 proposes that we should do precisely this) it follows that *if a field (such as gravity) is experienced to be weaker (or stronger), and the brain is a field-strength amplifer, then we should conclude that the field itself (such as gravity) is weaker (or stronger), relatively speaking.* Note that Step 2 says that we should not conclude that the *brain's detection of gravity* is weaker (or stronger) (or that the gravity merely *appears* to be weaker or stronger), but that the *gravitational field* itself had become weaker (or stronger), relatively speaking (since fields are what are measured by the brain).

If for the moment we accept this assumption, the General Relativity/ General Relativity Hypothesis logically unfolds:

1. If a person is instructed to focus his or her attention on feelings of heaviness (or other manifestations of the gravitation field), and the person experiences the gravity as being stronger, then the gravitational field will in effect be stronger for this person, relatively speaking (following Schwartz's assumption).

2. If the gravitational field is stronger for the person, relatively speaking, then the person's biological clocks will appear to slow down accordingly (following Einstein's predictions of general relativity).

3. If the biological clocks have slowed down, relatively speaking, and time is what a clock measures (following Einstein's assumption), then the person will perceive time more slowly and the person will age more slowly, relatively speaking (following Einstein's predictions of general relativity).

Once stated in this fashion, it becomes possible to conduct laboratory research to test the hypotheses in a rigorous fashion. To date, we have conducted five experiments that test the basic predictions, and all generate data consistent with the predictions. Due to space limitations, only the first two studies (Schwartz & Gotchberg, 1986) will be discussed briefly.

In the first study, physiological responses (heart rate, systolic and diastolic blood pressure, respiration rate, and facial and forearm muscle tension) were recorded from 26 Yale University students during various imagery conditions. A 5 × 2 within-subject design was used. The major comparisons were attention to feelings of heaviness (feeling heavy and sunk in the chair) versus feelings of lightness (feeling light and floating on a cloud). The control comparisons were attention to a somatic process (sensing the inspiration and expiration of breathing), attention to a cognitive process (saying the word "rom"—a classic mantra—silently to oneself), and simple resting. Half the trials were done with eyes open, the other half with eyes closed. Each subject received a different order of the 10 trials (five imagery by two eyes open/eyes closed). Subjects were told that *all* trials were pleasant and relaxing, and this instruction was repeated for each trial. Subjects rated feelings of heaviness, imagery vividness, and various emotions after each trial.

The major prediction was that the biological clocks would be slowest during the heaviness trials and fastest during the lightness trials. The physiological data were combined using a modified range correction procedure. Percentages of range were computed for each physiological parameter individually. The derived percent of range scores were then combined to produce an average physiological score. Higher scores reflect overall increases in neural firing (i.e., faster biological clocks), relatively speaking. As can be seen in Figure 7.2, collapsing across the eyes open/eyes closed condition, the average scores are lower in the heaviness condition and somewhat higher in the lightness condition, compared to rest. In general, the

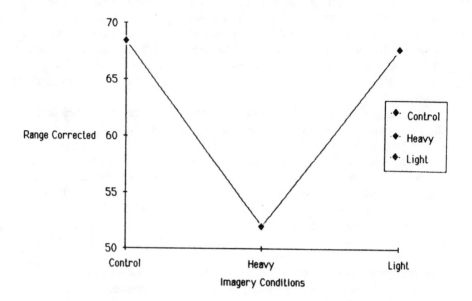

FIGURE 7.2 Mean range corrected physiological activity for 26 subjects comparing heaviness and lightness imagery with baseline.

average scores were lower in eyes closed compared to eyes open, collapsing across imagery conditions. As will be discussed shortly, attention to breathing also led to lower average physiological scores when compared to attention to the mantra "rom," but this effect is different in *pattern* from the combined findings for attention to heaviness.

If attention to heaviness is associated with relative decreases in overall biological clocks, is this accompanied by a corresponding slowing in perceived subjective time as would be predicted by the General Relativity/ General Relaxation Hypothesis? To address this question, 20 new subjects were run using the 5 × 2 within-subject design developed in Study 1. A time perception task was employed in which subjects were asked to estimate a fixed elapsed time. Briefly, subjects were given an electronic stop watch with the digital readout covered. On cue from the experimenter, subjects were asked to press the button, count silently to themselves for 60 seconds, and then release the button. The experimenter recorded the actual times elapsed. The prediction was that although subjects would *experience* each unit of time as being one minute, the *actual* time elapsed per trial would vary, relatively speaking, as a function predicted by the theory. The averaged times elapsed, collapsing across eyes open/eyes closed, for the heaviness, lightness, and rest trials are shown in Figure 7.3. Clearly, across all trials, subjects in this

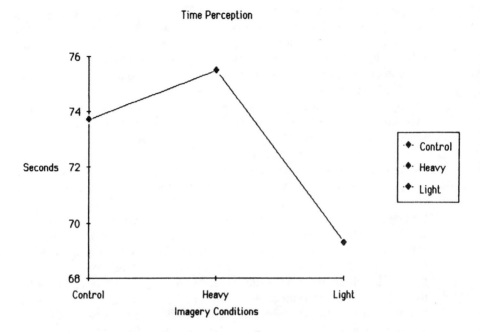

FIGURE 7.3 Mean time estimation (in seconds) for 20 subjects comparing heavy-ness and lightness imagery trials with baseline trials. Each trial was 60 seconds in duration.

experiment overestimated a 60-second period. However, it can also be seen that relatively speaking, subjects estimated 60 seconds as being somewhat longer when they were focusing their attention on feeling increased gravity (heaviness), compared to the rest or lightness trials. It is important to mention that, collapsing across the imagery trials, subjects estimated 60 seconds as being somewhat longer when their eyes were closed then when their eyes were open (which parallels the physiological findings in the first experiment). However, unlike in the first study where physiological decreases occurred both in heaviness trials and breathing trials, in the second study the corresponding time perception changes occurred in the heaviness trials and not in the breathing trials. A more complete description of the data combining the two studies would be as follows: (1) attention to breathing leads to decreases primarily in respiration rate and heart rate accompanied by little change in time perception, (2) attention to heaviness leads to decreases in all physiological processes recorded and corresponding changes in time perception.

Taken together, these two studies suggest that increases in awareness of gravity are accompanied by the slowing of biological and subjective clocks. These findings, though consistent with the Metaconnection Hypothesis, do not prove the Metaconnection Hypothesis. This is because specific physiological and/or psychological processes could explain these findings necessarily involving direct connections to the physical level. Likely candidates include cybernetic self-regulation mechanisms (e.g., attention to heaviness may involve attention to multiple somatic processes, evoking a self-attention negative feedback stabilization process discussed previously in the context of Example 1, the Schwartz and Rennert experiment) and learned cognitive mechanisms (e.g., images of movement associated with gravity and corresponding effects on physiology and time perception).

It is essential to understand, however, that the existence of biological and psychological mechanisms does not rule out the potential existence of physical mechanisms as well. In fact, to be complete, we would have to consider Newtonian as well as Einsteinian predictions to test the Metaconnection Hypothesis completely. More important to appreciate here is that even if the Metaconnection Hypothesis were disconfirmed, the Metasimilarity Hypothesis could simultaneously be confirmed. That is, the *organization or pattern* of findings at the biological and psychological levels may nevertheless *parallel* the findings found at the subatomic level. To confirm or disconfirm the strong (i.e., Metaconnection) version of systems theory in this instance, future experiments will have to be conducted where the psychology (i.e., attention to gravity) and the physics (i.e., the external strength of the gravitational field) were manipulated. This could be done, for example, by doing comparison studies on earth and on a space shuttle orbiting around the earth. Also, future experiments are required to test other predictions related to general relativity (e.g., relationships of mass to gravity) to determine how broadly the parallels hold (both in MetaSimilarity and in MetaConnection).

I believe that it is reasonable to hypothesize that biological and psychological processes may follow predictions emanating from the theory of general relativity, even though the mechanisms may operate at the biological and psychological levels (Metasimilarity). More improbable is the hypothesis that actual connections are made between the modern physics and psychophysiological levels. However, it must be remembered that in order for general systems to be true it is required that some sort of connections be made between all levels (Metaconnections). It is indeed a challenge to design research to test the Metaconnection Hypothesis, and as in modern physics, it probably will take many years of creative experimental design to prove or disprove the theory definitively.

There are numerous implications of the General Relativity/General Relaxation Hypothesis. It is possible that awareness of gravity has self-regulatory and even homeostatic consequences of import for personality and health. For example, one wonders why it is that organisms, including humans, lie down when they do not feel well. Is this merely to conserve energy, or does this spontaneously lead people to be more aware of and, therefore, be more connected with gravity as predicted by the theory? Do people who pay attention more to the process of lying down heal more effectively? If subjects were trained to amplify their awareness of gravity at key points in the healing process, would this facilitate healing? What about sleep, particularly stage 4 (nonREM sleep)? This is the period where physiological processes are most regular and slow, and one suspects that time passes slowly during this period. Contrast this with REM periods, where physiological processes are quite active and disregulated, and time in dreams often goes very fast. Is there some amount of attention to gravity that is healthy?

It is claimed in the ancient literature that being "centered" is good for one's health and contributes to one's longevity. Most of us dismiss such beliefs as being mere fancy and unscientific. However, it is possible that there may be a grain of truth to these ancient beliefs that in the light of modern science will turn out to contain some wisdom. Do dance therapy, movement therapy, and athletic training in general promote health in part because they all lead people to become more connected with gravity? What about the possible lack of awareness of gravity in Type A individuals? The list of potential implications can become quite large. Fortunately, the implications all follow directly from the theory, all can be tested, and all can be proved or disproved.

The personality researcher should immediately think about such concepts as absorption and openness to experience (Costa & McCrae, 1978) on the one hand, and repression and defensiveness (Weinberger, Schwartz, & Davidson, 1979) on the other, as being related to Example 3. The link between personality and health may in part relate to the General Relativity/General Relaxation Hypothesis, either in terms of Metasimilarity per se or with the addition of Metaconnection as well.

EXAMPLE 4: HEALTH IS TO WELLNESS AS ENERGY IS THE MATTER

Gravity, like personality, is something we all take for granted, and rarely do we question the logic underlying our inference about its existence. However, our belief in gravity, like personality, is ultimately an inference. In fact, Einstein pointed out in his Special Theory of Gravity that it is impossible to distinguish between the existence of a *force* (energy) *pulling* one object toward another and the existence of *objects* (matter) accelerating, *pushing* one object against another. It follows that gravity is never measured directly. Rather, the *behavior* of objects interacting with each other is measured, and the concept of a force is created (inferred) to explain the *organization or pattern* in the observed behavior. The same can be said for personality.

Modern physics has been concerned with the relationship between energy and matter. Einstein's famous equation "$E = mc^2$" indicates that energy can be converted into matter, and vice versa, as a function of the speed of light (c) squared (^{2}). However, physicists go one step further when they define energy as the "potential to do work." Implicit here is the making of a general systems concept and another potentially important Metasimilarity.

Implicit in the concepts of energy and matter are the distinctions between "potential" and "expressed." There is "potential" energy stored in matter. Matter, by definition, is known to the extent that certain properties are "expressed." However, not all of the "potential" properties (e.g., potential energy) are "expressed" in matter in its normal state (i.e., its trait behavior at a given temperature). In fact, the way modern physics uncovers the potential energy in matter is to "stress" the matter with bursts of high energy or particles expressing high energy. Matter is bombarded with high energy matter, and new potential properties (behaviors) of the matter are revealed.

This phenomenon (Step 1) can be readily translated into a general principle (Step 2) in the following manner: All systems contain "potential" properties (behaviors) that are "expressed" only under specific circumstances. It therefore follows that at any given moment in time, what we measure are "expressed" properties that partially, but not completely, reflect underlying "potential" properties.

Of what relevance are such concepts to personality and health? First of all, the distinguishing between potential and expressed clarifies what Murray and his colleagues attempted to do with instruments such as the TAT. They sought to uncover and reveal certain core "potential" properties of a person by presenting people with stimuli that had the potential to release such organized "energy." The person/situation interaction model in personality research can be seen as a special case of the potential/expressed distinction. In other words, situations can be thought of as necessary conditions to reveal inherent potentials (and limitations) in persons.

It follows that we share more metaproperties with atomic and subatomic particles than we realize. In a sense, the potential within atoms is hidden from direct view just as the potential within people is hidden from direct view. The way we uncover either is by arranging the situation properly and taking the proper measurements (recognizing that to measure is to alter, and the properties measured can be both local and distributed—Examples 1 and 2 above).

Space precludes a more detailed development of this basic idea. The reader may wish to ponder how the concept of the unconscious would be reformulated as a function of the distinction between potential and expressed. For example, what is normally unconscious in one state can become conscious in another state. This implies that the *potential* for consciousness is situationally—state—determined in terms of its *expression* (it follows that preconscious may be a better term than unconscious). The reader may also wish to ponder which personality traits are really *inferences* about *potential* behaviors versus *descriptions* about normally *expressed* behaviors.

The distinction between potential and expressed has fundamental implications for models of health, including the healthy personality. I have proposed that there is a fundamental distinction between health and wellness, and that the health/wellness distinction parallels the potential/expressed distinction (Schwartz, 1984). Briefly, it follows from the above analysis that any given moment in time, what one measures in a person is the person's current state of wellness. The therapist catalogs the current signs and symptoms and describes the current status of a patient as diagnoses. However, as is well documented in the literature, the *current expressed state* of wellness does not (and should not) directly or completely predict the person's *potential to cope* with future stressors (be they biological, psychological, or social pathogens; Matarrazzo, 1984). To reveal the potential to cope or heal—i.e., health—it is necessary to expose the person to appropriate stimuli—e.g., stressors—and measure response to and recovery from such stimulation. This "challenge" model has been used successfully in research on Type A behavior and health.

What I am proposing is that whereas the concept of wellness is an expressed concept and can be measured directly, the concept of health is an inferred concept (of underlying potential) and can only be measured indirectly. If health is the potential to be well, just as energy, so to speak is the potential to "be" matter (i.e., create and maintain matter), then some important implications emerge. For example, it is possible to create a 2×2 table of health $\times$ wellness, as is shown in Table 7.2.

Table 7.2 Combinations of health and wellness from a systems perspective, drawing on the distinction between potential (health) and expressed (wellness).

		Wellness	
		Poor	Good
Health	Poor	Sick at moment/healing poorly	Well at moment/poor resistance
	Good	Sick at moment/healing well	Well at moment/good resistance

Note that a person may be sick at a given moment yet be in good health (e.g., healing well), or a person may be well at a given moment yet be in poor health (e.g., have poor potential to resist pathogens). See text for details.

We normally assume (1) if a person appears well, then the person is healthy, and (2) if a person appears to be unwell, then the person is unhealthy. However, these combinations reflect only two corners of the 2 × 2 table. Two other combinations are theoretically possible: (3) A person may appear to be well at the moment, but actually be in poor health. In other words, although such a person may "check out to be just fine," when faced with certain stressors in the future (be they biological, psychological, and/or social), this person may readily become ill (i.e., unwell) and heal poorly. In other words, although the person was measured to be well at a given moment in time, his/her potential to remain well (i.e., health) was apparently low. (4) A person may appear to be ill (unwell) at the moment, yet actually be in good health. In other words, although such a person may currently be fighting off a disease, the person may be doing so successfully, and moreover, when faced with certain stressors in the future (be they biological, psychological, and/or social), this person may remain well or heal quickly if he/she becomes ill. In other words, although the person was measured to be unwell at a given moment in time, his/her potential to remain well (i.e., health) was apparently high.

The long standing myth linking energy and health may prove to be more than mere fancy. The process of drawing a Metasimilarity between health/wellness and energy/matter is relatively straight forward and has the potential to clarify and advance our understanding of personality, health, and the relationship between personality and health. Maybe we need to go beyond the concept of the "normal" personality (i.e., the "well" personality) and the concept of the "healthy" personality (i.e., the "hardy" personality; Kobassa, Maddi, & Kahn, 1982) as well.

The process of drawing a Metaconnection between health/wellness and energy/matter is also straightforward, but much more amusing. Following the same steps that led to the formation of the General Relativity/General Relaxation Hypothesis, it is possible to derive a Metaconnection Hypothesis about healing that, for example, encourages the search for potential energy field effects that could mediate the clinical effects reported to occur for a modern version of the "laying on of hands" termed "therapeutic touch" (Borelli & Heidt, 1981). Researchers in this field (most of whom are research-trained nurses) claim that the purported healing effects occur above and beyond traditional personality and attitudinal variables (though according to systems theory, any modern physics effects—if they exist at all—should interact with the psychological variables).

Parenthetically, the concept of a "healthy" personality, in systems terms, applies conceptually as well to the "hydrogen" personality as it does to the "human" personality. The concept of energy bridges all levels when the logic underlying the creation of the concept in the first place is made explicit. The potential for a synthesis between modern physics and psychology seems to become more meaningful when the concept of potential itself becomes more self-evident.

ON THE CHANGING NATURE OF WHAT IS IMPOSSIBLE IN SCIENCE

This chapter has attempted to show how systems theory can serve as a metatheoretical framework, a general way of thinking, that has the potential to (1) clarify the core concept of personality by pointing out how the concept of personality and the concept of system are fundamentally similar, (2) create a structure to help unify psychology as a discipline, and reveal the core position that personality psychology should take within the organized structure, and (3) integrate modern physics with psychology, in the process, broadening and deepening our understanding of mechanisms of personality, health, and the relationship between personality and health.

Whereas some of the implications derived from systems theory seem straightforward (e.g., recall the three fundamentional dimensions for arranging core components of psychology), others seem quite peculiar (e.g., recall the concept of "feelthought"), and some may seem frankly impossible (e.g., recall how attention to gravity may directly alter one's biological clocks in a manner paralleling general relativity). Why end a potentially reasonable chapter with a seemingly unreasonable, though logical, set of conclusions?

My answer involves more than just a sense of scientific responsibility. My answer also involves a historical observation. In 1964, when I was an undergraduate psychology student at Cornell University, the textbooks (and professors) stated unequivocally that operant conditioning of autonomic responses was impossible. It was at that time generally assumed that psychophysiological self-regulation was impossible. However, only two years later I conducted my honors thesis documenting that operant conditioning of autonomic responses was possible, and the major studies of Miller, Kimmel, and Shapiro and colleagues were beginning to appear in print (reviewed in Schwartz & Beatty, 1977).

Furthermore, by 1974, only 10 years later, it had become generally accepted that psychophysiological self-regulation was possible. However, the next lowest level, chemistry, was considered off limits in terms of self-regulation. Although it had become accepted as a serious possibility that the mind could selectively regulate physiological processes, chemical processes were considered too far removed and complex to be controlled selectively by mind.

Nonetheless, by 1984, another 10 years later, it was becoming clear that science was evolving from the more macro to the more micro in terms of self-regulation. First of all, psychophysiological self-regulation had now become an accepted fact, and applications to the treatment of specific psychophysiological disorders were well established. In the span of only 20 years, the concept of psychophysiological self-regulation had gone from being unequivocally impossible in 1964, to becoming seriously possible in 1974, to becoming an established fact in 1984. Moreover, by 1984, psychochemical self-regulation had gone from being impossible to quite possible. The emerging new field of psychoimmunology (Ader, 1981) illustrates this evolving trend. Note that while psychological self-regulation of processes at the chemical level is now considered a serious possibility, most scientists believe today that the next lowest level, psychological self-regulation at the physical level, is quite impossible. It is hard enough for us to hypothesize, let alone imagine, specific mechanisms whereby the mind, operating through the central nervous system, can regulate highly specific and localized chemical reactions. To extend these hypotheses to physical processes strains our current theories, which only further encourages our incredulity.

However, one wonders whether an evolutionary pattern is unfolding in science, especially when viewed through the eyes of systems theory. Certainly, measurement techniques in all disciplines are continuing to become ever more sensitive, selective, and accurate. Moreover, developments in computer hardware and software are making it possible to detect ever more complex relationships in increasingly large sets of data through advanced multivariate and pattern recognition techniques.

One wonders what the state of science will be in 1994. Following the trends outlined above, will we come to view psychochemical self-regulation as an accepted fact, and will applications to the diagnosis and treatment of specific disorders have become established? And will we then, armed with advanced NMR (nuclear magnetic resonance) systems, neuromagnetometers, and other micro biophysical measurement techiqnues yet to be discovered, begin to hypothesize that psychological/physical self-regulation (e.g., the General Relativity/General Relaxation Hypothesis) is actually possible (what we might term "behavioral biophysics")?

One wonders how our concepts of self, and hence our personality theories, will change to the extent that these evolutionary patterns in science continue. In what ways will personality psychology and psychology in general change if modern physics actually becomes part of personality theory? How will our theories of the mechanisms by which personality processes emerge and are maintained through the course of social experience reflect this evolving "social behavioral biophysical" synthesis?

These are amusing thoughts, and as such, they deserve our serious consideration.

REFERENCES

Ader, R. (Ed.). (1981). *Psychoneuroimmunology.* New York: Academic Press.

Borelli, M. D., & Heidt, P. (Eds.). (1981). *Therapeutic touch.* New York: Springer.

Buchsbaum, M. (1976). Self-regulation of stimulus intensity: Augmenting/reducing and the average evoked response. In G. E. Schwartz & D. Shapiro (Eds.), *Consciousness and self-regulation* (pp. 101-136). New York: Plenum.

Carver, C. S., & Scheier, M. F. (1981). *Attention and self-regulation: A control-theory approach to human behavior.* New York: Springer-Verlag.

Costa, P., & McCrae, R. (1978). Objective personality assessment. In M. Storandt, I. Siegler, & M. Elias (Eds.). *Clinical psychology of aging* (pp. 119-143). New York: Plenum.

Davidson, M. (1983). *Uncommon sense.* Boston: Houghton Mifflin Co.

Einstein, A. (1961). *Relativity, the special and the general theory.* New York: Bonanza Books.

Heisenberg, W. (1971). *Physics and beyond.* New York: Harper & Row.

Kahan, G. (1983). $E = mc^2$ *picture book of relativity.* Blue Ridge Summit, PA: Tab Books.

Kobassa, S. C., Maddi, S. R., & Kahn, S. (1982). Hardiness & health: A perspective study. *Journal of Personality and Social Psychology, 42,* 168–177.

Lane, R. D., & Schwartz, G. E. (1987) Levels of emotional awareness: A cognitive-developmental theory and its application to psychopathology. *American Journal of Psychiatry, 144,* 133–143.

Lazarus, R. S. (1984). On the primacy of cognition. *American Psychologist, 39,* 124–129.

Luria, A. R. (1973). *The working brain.* New York: Basic Books.

Matarazzo, J. D. (1984). Behavioral immunogens and pathogens in health and illness. In B. L. Hammonds and C. J. Scheirer (Eds.), *Psychology and health, The Master Lecture Series, Volume 3* (pp. 9–43). Washington, DC: American Psychological Association.

Murray, H. A. (1938). *Explorations in personality.* New York: Oxford.

Murray, H. A. (1967). The case of Murr. In E. G. Boring & G. Lindzey (Eds.). *A History of psychology in autobiography.* (pp. 283–310). New York: Appleton-Century-Crofts.

Narlikar, J. V. (1982). *The lighter side of gravity.* San Francisco: W. H. Freedman & Co.

Pagels, H. R. (1982). *The cosmic code.* New York: Simon & Schuster.

Pribram, K. H. (1971). *Languages of the brain.* Englewood Cliffs, NJ: Prentice Hall.

Schwartz, G. E. (1982). Disregulation theory and disease: Applications to the repression/cerebral disconnection/cardiovascular disorder hypothesis. In J. Matarazzo, N. Miller, & S. Weiss (Eds.), *Special Issue on Behavioral Medicine, International Review of Applied Psychology, 32,* 95–118.

Schwartz, G. E. (1984). Psychobiology of health: A new synthesis. In B. L. Hammonds & C. J. Scheier (Eds.) *Psychology and Health, The Master Lecture Series, Volume 3* (pp. 149–193). Washington, DC: American Psychological Association.

Schwartz, G. E., & Beatty, J. (Eds.) (1977). *Biofeedback: Theory and research.* New York: Academic Press.

Schwartz, G. E., & Gotchberg, J. (1986). *Physiological and time perception changes during heavy and light imagery.* Manuscript in preparation.

Schwartz, G. E., & Rennert, K. (1982) *Effects of attention and sensory feedback on automatic self-regulation of heart rate versus respiration.* Unpublished manuscript.

Singer, J. L. (1984). The private personality. *Personality and Social Psychology Bulletin, 10,* 17–30.

Staats, A. W. (1983). *Psychology's crisis of disunity.* New York: Praeger.

von Bertalanffy, L. (1948). *Theoretisch biologie* (1932, 1942). Ann Arbor, MI: J. W. Edward.

von Bertalanffy, L. (1968a). *General systems theory.* New York: Braziller.

von Bertalanffy, L. (1968b). *Organismic psychology and systems theory.* Worchester, MA: Clark University Press.

Weinberger, D. A., Schwartz, G. E., & Davidson, R. J. (1979) Low anxious, high anxious and repressive coping styles: Psychometric patterns and behavioral and physiological responses to stress. *Journal of Abnormal Psychology, 88,* 369–380.

Woolfolk, R. L., & Lehrer, P. M. (Eds.) (1984). *Principles and practice of stress management.* New York: Guilford Press.

Zajonc, R. B. (1980). Feeling and thinking: Preferences need no interferences. *American Psychologist, 35,* 151–175.

Index

Abstract attitude, 116
Active organism, 5–7
Activity, 16–17
  defined, 28
  in primates, 16–17
  and temperament, 28
Affect, 128
Aggressiveness, 38; *see also* dominance
Amplification, 149–150
Analog formation, 208–209, 213
Asthmatics, 137
Attachment
  and mother's behavior, 29–30
  primate, 18, 29–31
  and single births, 25–26

Behavior genetics
  challenges to personality theory, 57–60
  designs assessing family effects, 56–57
Bellow, Saul, 107
Biological clocks, 234, 243, 251

Cellular biology, 222
Character structure, 90–91
Cognition, 108, 110, 128, 237–238
Cognitive structure, 127
Cognitive style, 129
Commitment scripts, types of, 179–180
Complementarity principle, 219
Consciousness, 107, 139

Darwin, C., 71, 79, 215
Daydreams, 111, 116, 123
  guilty-dysphoric, 125
  hostile-aggressive, 125

Day residue, 133
Defensiveness, 136
Depression, 125
Dominance
  and aggression, 32–33
  in humans and primates, 34–35, 38–39
  in primates, 19, 22–23, 32

Einstein, A., 230, 234, 240–243, 247, 248
Electronic pager, 123
Emotions, 8, 148–216
  density of, 158
  negative, 27
  in primates, 17–18, 26–27
  ratio of positive/negative, 158–159, 163, 166, 175, 186, 198, 208
Environmental influences
  press, 59
  role of in development, 63–75
Evolution, 13, 44–46
  and life span in primates, 25–26
  and personality differences, 49
  theory, 52, 62–63

Family
  differential effects on children, 72
  effects on behavior, 53–57, 61
Fantasy, 106, 111, 121, 124, 126
Field dependence, 129
Fitness, 84
Freud, S. 79, 82–83, 97, 107
Future orientation, 128

Gardner, Allan & Beatrice, 13, 36
General relaxation hypothesis, 240, 246, 250

Genotype-environment interactions, 62–75
  active type, 66–68, 71
  evocative type, 66–68
  and maturational sequences, 66
  passive type, 66–68, 71
Gesell, A. & Ilg, F. L., 63
Goldstein, K., 116
Gravity, 241, 246, 247, 251

Hardiness, 138, 250
Head, H., 116
Heisenberg, W., 235–237
Huizinga, J. 79
Humor, 223
Hypertensive disease, 136
Hypnosis, 110, 125, 127, 241

Identity, 88, 218
  negotiation of, 88–90, 92, 98
Ideology and polarity, 170–179
Idiographic data, 121
Imagery, 128, 135, 139, 244–245
Images, 109, 137
Individual differences, 50
  and group differences, 52–53
Individuality, 50–53, 54–56
  and genetic influences on development, 66
Information advantage, 151–152, 210
Interior monologue, 107, 131, 139
Introversion-extraversion, 110, 127, 129, 239
IPAR, 80–81

Joyce, James, 107
Juvenile period, 31–33
  power relationships, 17, 32–33
  social bonds and, 31

Klinger, E., 116–117, 124, 133

McClelland, D. C., 12, 51
McDougall, W., 3, 12, 79
Magnification, 149–153, 158, 163, 173, 197–198, 201, 203, 207, 210
Magnification advantage, 151–152
Maslow, A. H., 3, 12
Mathematics, 222
Mead, G. H., 79
Meditation, 241

Memories, 109
Metaconnection hypothesis, 231
Metaphors, 134
Metasimilarity, 218, 231
Modern physics, 218, 228, 252
Mourning, animal, 19–20
Murphy, G., 3, 12
Murray, H. A., xii, 1, 10, 12, 36, 50–52, 147, 217, 227, 228, 248

Negative affects, 108
Nightmares, 108
Nuclear scripts, 204–207

Object relations, 131–132
Occupations, 64
Operant conditioning, 251
Operant thought, 116

Pagels, H. B., 240–241
Parental confrontations, 118
Parenting, 52, 56–57, 70
Parsimony, law of, 52
Peremptory thought, 116
Personality
  abnormal, 239
  assessment, 93–96
  biological bases, 3, 5, 6, 8, 83, 88, 148–150
  chimpanzees, 14–16
  as cognitive processes, 9
  development of, 1, 2, 3, 6–8, 11, 63–75, 87–90, 207–215
  differences, 49–50
  and evolution, 3–5, 83
  factor structure, 81, 85
  genetic components of, 17, 57–59, 60–61
  genetic variability, 57–62
  and health, 11
  human, 36–44
  perspectives on, 1–12
  private, 106
  public, 106
  resemblances among sibs, 72–74
  and social interaction, 79
  and social rules, 79–104
  stability of traits over development, 34
  styles, 237, 239
  taxonomy of, 96

theory and behavior genetics, 57–60
traits, 33–36
Physiological
functions, 136
reactions, 128
Piaget, 63
Preconscious, 107
Primates
characteristics shared with highly social mammals, 19–23
characteristics shared with most mammals, 16–18
communication and imitation in, 24–25
curiosity in 23–24
gender differences in, 18–19
personality traits, 33–36
Psychoimmunology, 252
Psychotherapy, 131, 135

Quantum physics, 226, 235
Questionnaires, 127, 138

Reality, 106, 126
Relativity theory, 219, 233, 240, 250
REM sleep, 124, 133, 247
Repressors, 127, 136
Respondent thought, 117
Role structure, 90–91

Scenes, 130, 131, 148, 149
Scripts
affect management, 185–196
commitment, 179–184
general features, 153–158
ideological, 170–179
nuclear, 196–215
personal, 107, 124, 127, 130–132, 137, 139
types of, 159–169
Script theory, 10, 147–216
Secondary process, 107, 116
Sedative scripts, 187–188
Self, 108, 130, 252

complexity, 129
esteem, 109
regulation, 219, 251
Self-presentation, 6, 90–104
Sex differences, 61
Siblings
changing similarity among, 70–74
confluence model of I. Q. and, 55
environmental variation among, 70–74
similarities and differences, 53–54, 58–60
statistical measures of similarity, 53–54
Signal detection, 111, 113–114
Sociability, 19–31
Social identity, 10, 92
Socialization, 39–40
Status
in primates, 23
and social organization, 23
Stimulus independent thought, 112–115
Stream of consciousness, 107, 109
Stress, 120
Symbolism, 135
Systems theory, 218–220

Task-irrelevant thought, 114
Temperament, 15, 26–29, 45–46
in infant primates, 30–31
Thought sampling, 117
Traits, 34–42
Transference, 131

Uncertainty principle, 219, 236
Unconscious, 107, 124, 127, 131, 138, 227, 248

Vigilance task, 112, 116
Von Bertalanffy, 217, 220

"Wavicles," 233, 237
Webster, 219, 221–222
Wellness, 247
Wigner, 230, 234